JUST A LITTLE

LYNCHING

NOW AND THEN

True Crime Tales
From 1930s
Northern California

ALAN J. MCMURRY

ISBN 978-0-9768321-5-7

Originally self-published in 1988 by Alan J. McMurry.

New material on pages 15 and 46-47 © Living Gold Press.

Maps by Jill Livingston, © Living Gold Press.

Cover design by Kathryn Golden Maloof, © Living Gold Press.

Front cover photo by Kathryn Golden Maloof.

Back cover photo: Entering Yreka on Highway 99 (Siskiyou County Museum).

Interior layout by Living Gold Press.

LIVING GOLD PRESS

PO Box 2
Klamath River,
CA 96050

www.LivingGoldPress.com

My father, Alan McMurry (affectionately known as "A.J. with the cigar"), was a historian, orator, and local public servant of the highest order. This book is a testament to the care with which he approached his research of historical facts and his conclusions about the lessons we all must learn from the acts of our ancestors. It's also a darn good read that paints a colorful picture of the excitement and tension of these horrific events. My thanks to Living Gold Press for bringing forth this second printing embellished with photos and other lore to round out the stories even more. A.J. loved Yreka and Siskiyou County. I am very proud of his legacy and strive to carry it forward.

Lisa McMurry Nixon
(serving as Siskiyou County Supervisor,
District 4, 2017-2020)

YREKA  JOURNAL

Devoted to the
Interests of
Siskiyou County

Established in 1853

VOL. LXXXIII   YREKA, SISKIYOU COUNTY, CALIFORNIA, THURSDAY, SEPTEMBER 19, 1935   No. 8

SLAYER EVADES NOOSE!

The Yreka Journal

SHASTA—CASCADE WONDERLAND
IN THE HEART OF THE — SISKIYOU COUNTY — PEOPLE
A COUNTY PAPER FOR

Steve Kent and Lester Quigley Both Murdered By Desperate Criminal

Plane Joins Yreka Hunt for 2 Killers

POSSIBILITY OF CAPTURE LESSENS AS BRITE BOYS ENTRENCH IN WILDERNESS

Expectation Of Gun Battle Before Nightfall Stirs Yreka Residents

Contents

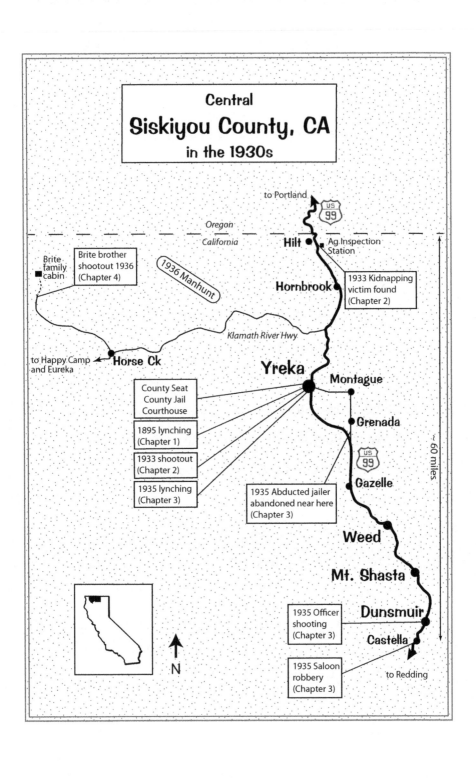

Central
Siskiyou County, CA
in the 1930s

to Portland

US 99

Oregon
California

Hilt

Ag Inspection Station

Brite family cabin

Brite brother shootout 1936 (Chapter 4)

1936 Manhunt

Hornbrook

1933 Kidnapping victim found (Chapter 2)

Klamath River Hwy

to Happy Camp and Eureka

Horse Ck

Yreka

Montague

County Seat
County Jail
Courthouse

1895 lynching (Chapter 1)

1933 shootout (Chapter 2)

1935 lynching (Chapter 3)

Grenada

US 99

1935 Abducted jailer abandoned near here (Chapter 3)

Gazelle

~ 60 miles

Weed

Mt. Shasta

1935 Officer shooting (Chapter 3)

Dunsmuir

Castella

1935 Saloon robbery (Chapter 3)

to Redding

N

1

The Prelude:
Strung Up by a Mob, 1895

By 1895 the Gold Rush town of Yreka seemed to be finally settling into the quiet prosperous rural western community envisioned by the civic leaders. All was well in Yreka.

That is, until one o'clock in the morning of August 26th, 1895....

When gold was discovered on the Yreka Flats in 1851, the government of the State of California had only been in existence for approximately six months. Like the law "west of the Pecos," there was very little of it north of Sacramento.

One of the first acts of the young state government was to designate and name its counties. At the time, they knew little about the far northern reaches of the territory. The gold strikes had been made that year in what was to become Shasta County and Trinity County. The legislators knew that they had people in that area. Accordingly they just took everything in the state north of Butte County, sliced it vertically with the western third designated as Trinity County and the eastern two thirds as Shasta County.

After the Yreka discoveries and the rush to this far northern area, the state carved out Siskiyou County in 1852. Yreka was designated as the County Seat.

From the very first year of its existence, Yreka along with its governmental superior, Siskiyou County, had seen the need for law and order. The first manifestation of this had been the formation of the vigilante committee for which gold discoverer Abraham Thompson served as the first constable. As the organization of the community matured, it continued in its effort to maintain law and order. After the county government was formed, the responsibility of law and order was assumed by it. The system, from then on, was slowly converted into one of a more legal and traditional nature; better organized and more stable, especially after the incorporation of Yreka in

1857. But it must be stressed that Siskiyou County, and Yreka in particular, was a "far away place with a strange sounding name." The niceties of formal government were in place but it was fundamentally structured and operated with a great degree of independence. This was a community so far away from the rest of civilization that it was very much on its own; it was up to the locals to make law enforcement work.

Down through the years, the system did work; certainly with less sophistication than in the metropolitan areas, but it did work, although it always seemed to have a rough hewn character about it. This was remote country, and the people didn't "cotton" too much with interference from the outside.

Lacking the body of statistical information that is available today, it can probably be said that Siskiyou County was as law abiding as any other. But this conclusion should probably be qualified by limiting the comparison to other similarly isolated more or less self administered counties.

In the forty-two years from the beginning of record keeping to 1895, there were forty-five murders in Siskiyou County. Considering the nature of the society in the first ten years or so, this figure on a per capita basis is probably low.

But a further study of the available data brings out some very obvious trends. Of the forty-five murderers, one had been lynched without trial; six had been legally tried and hanged. These six include one case wherein the defendant was tried one day and hanged the next, a dubious application of the term "legal." Fourteen received prison sentences, eight were acquitted, one escaped before trial, and the remaining fifteen were dismissed or there is no record of the disposition of the outcome.

The interesting factor in this listing involves the dates. The last of the six legal hangings was in 1863. All of the prison incarcerations were after 1860. It is obvious that sometime in the early 1860s the legal system had gone through a change in attitude insofar as capital punishment was concerned. It may be presumptuous to attempt to assign a statistical conclusion upon the data from a tiny corner of the state. The citizens may not even have been aware of statistics covering the subject. They had a feeling though. Here they were in 1895; in the first eleven years starting with 1852, there had been six executions of murderers. In the following thirty-one years, there had been none. In the public perception of things, they recalled that the approximate frequency of murders had never changed much since the very beginning and was still going on at the same rate. All those fancy changes in the state laws involving crime resulting in the practical elimination of capital punishment had done nothing to abate murder. It still ran at about one or more per year, the same as it always had.

Each time a murder took place, it always aroused considerable community discussion that something should be done. Nothing ever much but talk was ever done about it, but the talk was always there.

Then a catalyst arrived; it changed the nature and character of the entire county like nothing ever had before.

A Rash of Killings

On April 21, 1895, William Null murdered his mining partner, Henry Hayden near their claim at Callahan located at the south end of Scott Valley. Null was arrested and lodged in the County Jail at Yreka. On July 28th, Lawrence Johnson of Etna, in the central part of Scott Valley, brutally murdered his wife. He was apprehended and joined Null in the County Jail.

On August 5th at Bailey Hill, twenty miles north of Yreka just short of the California-Oregon border, George Sears and Casper Meierhaus were murdered. Louis Mareno was arrested and charged with murdering both men; Garland Stemler, who was not yet nineteen years of age, was charged with assisting Moreno in murdering Meierhaus at the same scene. Both of these defendants were also lodged in the County Jail.

There hadn't been a murder in Siskiyou County for two years; now suddenly, the community had four accused murderers in residence. The stage was set for violence. There was no talk of it in Yreka, but the stage was set, nonetheless.

On Sunday evening, August 25th, riders were saddling up in more than one community in Siskiyou County. Spring wagons were being hitched in preparation for a long pull into the night from several different locations. One group in the railroad town of Montague, six miles east of Yreka, prepared to make an evening run on a railroad handcar. These horsemen and wagon passengers were all men; at various times this night they headed out.

As many as two hundred men were on their way to one destination, Yreka. They came from Scott Valley, Callahan, Fort Jones, Shasta Valley and Little Shasta Valley, Montague, Hornbrook, Hawkinsville, Humbug and Greenhorn. They came from many directions, but they all had one purpose. To the last man, they were grim and determined.

If they met someone on the road they said little as they passed. If they overtook someone, they insisted that they accompany them until the mission was complete.

The ones from Scott Valley came via Forest House Road [Highway 3]. When they reached the intersection with Greenhorn Road, they paused and waited for the group to arrive from Shasta Valley. The men from Hornbrook and Hawkinsville paused at Butcher Hill to await the arrival of the riders from Montague and Little Shasta. It was after 12:00 midnight when both of the groups headed into Yreka to join up at the Siskiyou County Courthouse.

City Marshall Parks had been making his rounds that night without incident. At approximately 12:15, two men whom he did not recognize rushed up to him near Miner and Oregon Streets and shouted that a big fight was in progress at the foot of Miner Street. Parks took off on foot in a fast trot. When he arrived there, he found only two or three loiterers who quickly informed him that the problem was two or three blocks north on Main Street. Parks heard calls coming from that direction that would indicate someone was hurt.

When Parks arrived at his latest destination he found no one. Suddenly he realized that something was wrong. He whirled and took off again back over the same tracks he had just covered. He was now on his way to Engine House #1 at the corner of Miner and Third Streets.

Sheriff Hobbs some two weeks ago had instructed his men and the city officers that in case of a potential lynching, "ring the fire bells in order to arouse the citizenry."

When Parks arrived at the Engine House, he found that the bell rope had been tied up high, way out of reach.

Off again Parks went, this time at a full gallop. He had only two blocks to go in order to reach the courthouse park. Half way there, he could see what was under way. The yard was full of masked men. He fired two pistol shots into the air and charged in. In two minutes Parks was surrounded by a dozen men with pistols pointed at him. He was quickly disarmed and led away.

While Parks had been on his thoroughly orchestrated detour, the night riders had arrived at the courthouse. The jail itself was a separate building detached from the courthouse proper. The Sheriff's Office was located in the courthouse and it was here that the masked men first turned their attention.

Undersheriff Radford was sleeping in the Sheriff's Office when he was awakened by voices outside his door demanding the keys to the jail. His reply to this request was instantaneous and authoritative.

"The first man who tries to enter this office by breaking in the door will be shot to death."

Radford was known to be tough and competent. The group then switched operations to the jail itself. In a trice, they had scaled the fourteen foot stone wall that surrounded the brick building and were now in the jail yard itself.

Deputy Jailer Henry Brautlacht had been sleeping inside the jail building when he was awakened by a noise outside. He opened the outer door and found himself looking down the barrel of a Winchester rifle thrust into his face. He surrendered the keys to the outer and inner doors along with those for the stone wall. But he did not have the keys to the individual cells. He was told that they would not be necessary anyway.

They then unlocked the inner door and called a dozen more armed men into the cell area. These men carried sledge hammers, pry bars and other types of blacksmith tools. They first went to the cell of Lawrence Johnson, the Etna wife murderer. With the tools they carried, they made short work of prying open the padlock on the cell door and bending back the sliding "row catch."

A Chilling Scene

Johnson was ordered to dress and be quick about it. When he got his shirt and pants on, his hands were tied behind him. A rope with a hangman's noose was placed over his head and he was led out of the jail.

In the meantime, a fourteen foot long railroad rail had been placed in the forks of two close-by trees in the courtyard. Johnson was told to stand under the rail. He pled for mercy but the lynchers would have no part of it. The lynch rope was thrown over the rail and Johnson was hoisted upward and commenced his "dance on air."

Before Johnson had ceased struggling, his assailants had turned their backs and started for the jail again. This time it was the turn of William Null who had murdered his mining partner at Callahan.

The scenario was the same. When they got Null outside and under the rail, he asked if he could make a statement. He was told they had no time for that and up he went to join Johnson hanging from the rail. Johnson had already ceased to move.

Back into the jail went the "committeemen," this time for Moreno the murderer of Meirhaus and possibly also George Sears. Moreno took it stoically without uttering a single word.

Garland Stemler had been saved for the last. There had been some discussion among the lynchers about omitting the eighteen year old lad from the proceedings. He had not yet even had his preliminary hearing in court; this was scheduled for the following Monday. His older brother had arrived

The 1895 lynching took place on the grounds of the courthouse outside of the jail. The original photo was labeled "Western Justice" and was dated "Monday August 26, 1895, 1 a.m." (Siskiyou County Museum)

in Yreka this very day in company with a lawyer in order to put up some kind of a defense for the boy. But in the end, the extremists in the group won out and Stemler was taken to the rail like the others. Just before his tormentors pulled him up by the rope he was heard to shout, "Tell my brother to tell my mother I am innocent!"

After the lynchers departed a hand printed message was found pinned to Johnson's shirt. It said:

CAUTION

LET THIS BE A WARNING! IT IS HOPED THAT ALL COLD BLOODED MURDERERS IN THIS COUNTY WILL SUFFER LIKEWISE.

RESPECTFULLY, TAX PAYING CITIZENS

P.S. OFFICERS: BE WISE AND KEEP MUM

Thirty-nine years later in 1934, Siskiyou County Court Reporter Ralph McMurry's youngest son came to him with a question. It seemed that some of the kids at school had been talking about the "big lynching in 1895." He wanted to know all about it.

"Well, that was twenty-six years before this family came to Yreka," the father replied. Of course I have heard about it to some extent, but I am not by any means familiar with it. I have heard it mentioned from time to time down through the years, but no one much was really ever talking about it after the time that we came here. I'd suggest that you ask Barney about it."

The boy went right out the back door of the house, across the back lawn and right into the next door neighbor's house without knocking, as was their custom.

Mr. and Mrs. Barney Neilon had been their neighbors all of the boy's life. At this time, Barney was the Siskiyou County undersheriff. When the boy appeared, Barney was in the living room and motioned him to come on through.

"What can we do for you, Son?" said Barney. The boy posed the same question that he had asked his father.

Barney eased back in his big easy chair and thought for a long pause. The boy understood this and politely waited.

"That was a long time ago," said Barney. "Let's see. I was thirty-one years old then and I'm sixty-nine now. Yes, that was a long time ago."

"Did you see it?" asked the boy.

"I didn't actually see them hang those men, but they were still swinging from that steel rail by the time I got over there," replied Barney. "That was of course many years before I ever worked for the sheriff's office."

"How did all the people feel about it?" the eager boy asked.

"Well, right at first I would say that it was just about evenly split," Barney said. "It seemed like half the people approved of it and the other half didn't. But after a few years when everyone had more or less cooled off, I realized that my previous impression was probably wrong. I realized that I had been hearing from only those people that were eager and willing to discuss the matter."

"It finally dawned on me that the real count was that the biggest majority of the people did not approve of it but had not been among the 'talkers' about it at the time," explained Barney.

"So, in answer to your question, I now believe that most of the people disapproved of it. But it is important to mention that even if I am correct, there were still a whole lot of people out there that just passed it off according to the old saying."

The boy seemed somewhat perplexed. "What do you mean," asked the boy. "What do you mean by 'the old saying?'"

"I meant that they would just pass it off by saying that it was a good thing to have **just a little lynching now and then**."

This early (1910) view of "Courthouse Square" in the county seat of Yreka shows the county jail on the right hand side. This was the scene of the 1895 lynchings and the site of the trials in which the shooters in the 1930s crimes were convicted and sentenced. Originally built in 1856, wings were added to the north and south sides and a cupola added to the roof in 1897. The cupola had been removed by the time of the 1930s trials. (Siskiyou County Museum)

Why Here?

One might wonder why the three murderous crimes covered in this book were carried out in a backwoods county basically in the middle of nowhere.

The first two; George Hall's deadly downtown Yreka rampage and Clyde Johnson's fatal shooting of a Dunsmuir cop following a nearly fruitless hold up; could have unfolded similarly in scores of other small towns. Still, they happened here. During the Great Depression people took to the roads and the rails, looking for work and sometimes looking for trouble, and the main north-south route of travel along the western edge of the continent cuts right through the middle of Siskiyou County. Both the railroad line and the major highway, at the time US99, now Interstate 5, run more or less parallel to each other all the way from Los Angeles to Seattle.

These criminals were transient. In the case of George Hall, Yreka was the first town he encountered as he drove south on Highway 99 after the authorities became aware of his nefarious activities, so this is where the confrontation erupted. In the case of Clyde Johnson, he and his partner just happened to jump off the freight they'd been riding in Dunsmuir, following a lead given them by a fellow traveler.

The case of the Brite brothers, the third crime in this story, is more complicated. John and Coke, in their mid twenties, came here with their parents. They had been living in Oklahoma, Colorado, Arizona, and finally Jacksonville, Oregon before landing in Siskiyou County. This was a time when the local population, which had sharply declined after the Gold Rush, increased, as rural areas came to be viewed as lands of opportunity by people with no job prospects but with plenty of "roughing it" skills, or hopes of learning these skills. The draws and hillsides filled with little cabins housing the poor, transplants who preferred scraping by out in the woods to breadlines in the city. The Brites and many others like them grew large gardens, maybe raised a few animals, fished, hunted and poached deer, and did a little gold mining on the side, as the price of gold rose from $20.67 to $35 per ounce in 1935. For them, this was a pretty good way to live while waiting for things to get better.

Jill Livingston

Cast of Characters

E. L. Ballenger – U.S. Customs inspector from Washington state

George Hall aka "Manning" – kidnapper and shooter

"John Doe" Joe Clark – Hall's kidnapping accomplice

Paul Newcomb – "The Hitchhiker"

Fred Oller – Ballenger's rescuer

Andy Calkins – Siskiyou County Sheriff

Charley Calkins – Siskiyou County Deputy Sheriff (and Andy's son)

Steve Kent – local California Highway Patrolman, and victim

Lester Quigley – Steve Kent's friend and some time ride-along, and victim

Martin Lange – Siskiyou County Deputy Sheriff

Dr. A. H. Newton – Siskiyou County Physician

Les Chase – telephone company employee with a choice to make

Charles Johnson – Siskiyou County District Attorney

2

George Hall's
Ill-conceived Plans, 1933

Fred Oller got out of bed at 5:45 a.m. the morning of March 9th, 1933; he did this every day at the same time in order to get out and get started on his morning chores. Day in and day out it seemed always to be the same. Only last night he had discussed this with his wife. They both realized that times were hard all over the nation but "they" were getting by. When you had a small ranch you were way ahead of everyone else. Most of the food was raised right on the place; the excess was sold locally to bring in enough cash to cover their needs. Yes, they both agreed that they were not too bad off compared to others. But Fred complained that it was so damned boring it was hardly worth it. To him it was just the same old thing, day in and day out, year after year. He told her that it was too bad nothing ever happened around here to create a little excitement.

At exactly 6:00 a.m. Fred stepped out the door and immediately heard a faint sound that seemed like someone calling for help. He hesitated momentarily and then he heard it again. He quickly turned and took off up the little draw into the brush and scrub oak in the direction from where the cries seemed to be coming. At less than a hundred yards from the house he came upon a man that appeared to be tied to a small oak tree. As he approached closer he realized that the man was beaten and nearly unconscious. He wasn't "tied" to the tree; he was handcuffed to it.

Fred recalled the conversation with his wife when he had lamented the fact that nothing ever happens around here. Now by golly he thought, this is something; he was relishing every minute of it.

He could see that the man was badly beaten and needed help fast. The man was able to tell him that he had been kidnapped and that these were his handcuffs but his assailants kept the key. Fred rushed back to the house and brought back a saw with which he cut down the small tree. He then half carried and half dragged the fellow along the gully and on down to the house where his wife could be of help.

In the hands of Mrs. Oller it was no time at all before she had hot coffee in the man, his wounds washed off and a few bandages here and there. Little was said until she had him resting comfortably propped up in a rocking chair and apparently in much better shape. Then and only then did she allow Fred to ask him who he was and how on earth he had come to be handcuffed to an oak tree in the middle of the night one mile south of the Oregon border in Siskiyou County, California.

Yreka is the county seat of Siskiyou County. It lies twenty-two miles south of the California-Oregon border in a sort of protected bowl surrounded on three sides by lofty mountains of which the most prominent is the great snow covered peak of Mt. Shasta. It is one of California's Gold Rush towns with a history as long as most of the oldest settlements in the state. By 1933, gold mining was still active but had begun to give way to agriculture and lumber as leading industries. With its many fine old Victorian homes and "turn of the century" downtown architecture, it at that time consisted of a population of about 2,800 people. It was a picturesque self-contained community that enjoyed its position of leadership over the other four incorporated cities in the county.

In 1921, Ralph McMurry took the position of Siskiyou County Court Reporter at the courthouse in Yreka and brought his wife and two young sons to live there. In a short time the family was blessed with another son and a daughter; life was good and it seemed a correct decision to have made the move. When the Depression came in the late twenties it was almost as if those great high mountains seemed to insulate the little community from many of the problems that were being encountered elsewhere throughout the land. Rural people seem to always do better in trying times such as these. There was little cash money around but these hardy northern California country people seemed to know how to manage. In 1933, things were going well and the family was firmly established as an integral part of the community.

The Sound of Gunshots

In the early evening of March 10th, the day after Fred Oller had the fascinating experience of freeing a man handcuffed to a tree just twenty-one miles north of Yreka, Court Reporter McMurry's youngest eleven year old son had just gone to bed in the "boys' sleeping porch" downstairs. They referred to it as "downstairs" though it was only two steps down from the rest of the house. It was a large room with windows going full along three sides and

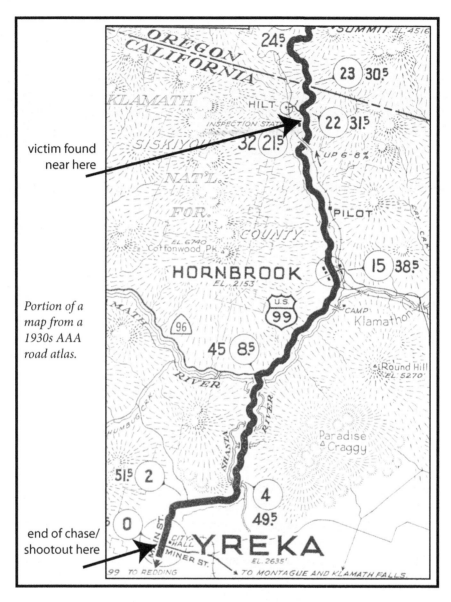

victim found near here

Portion of a map from a 1930s AAA road atlas.

end of chase/ shootout here

all three boys slept there. The weather had been nice this day and it was still somewhat warm; most of the windows were open. He had had a busy day as boys that age always seem to have. His mother had suggested he turn in just after dark. As the boy was just dozing off about 7:00 p.m. he thought he heard gunshots. It sounded as if it was a rapid series of small arms reports followed by some loud rolling shots coming from a shotgun. One thing for sure is that people living in the mountains know a gunshot when they hear one. Guns are a part of life in communities such as these and most everybody—man, woman or child—instinctively knows the difference between a gunshot and a car backfire or other similar noise. The boy didn't think too much of it and drifted off to sleep. In a half hour he was awakened by the ringing of the hand crank telephone mounted on the wall in the dining room upstairs. Just a few minutes later he heard the front door bang shut and this aroused his curiosity. He got up, went upstairs and asked his mother what was going on. She had a very serious look on her face.

"Don't worry about it," she said, "It's just that there has been some trouble downtown. The district attorney has called Daddy on the phone and asked him to come down to the courthouse."

The boy then told his mother that he had heard shots and asked her if someone had been hurt.

"Yes," she said, "there has been a shooting downtown and someone has been shot. I don't know any of the details yet. You go on back to bed now and get your sleep and when Daddy gets home we will find out what it's all about."

About four hours later the boy was again awakened. This time he heard heavy conversation coming from the kitchen. It sounded as if there were a lot of people in the house talking with each other. He noticed that neither of his brothers' beds had yet been slept in even though he knew it was very late in the night. Rubbing the sleep from his eyes he again went up the two stairs into the kitchen.

There sitting around the kitchen table having coffee and rolls were his father and his two older brothers with several other men. There was the next door neighbor, Barney Neilon, District Attorney Charley Johnson, Gene Dowling and a couple of others that the boy didn't know so well. He knew that all of these men worked at the courthouse. His mother and Mrs. Neilon were serving the refreshments. When the boy entered, everyone seemed to stop talking as if they were not sure that he was supposed to hear.

His father sensed what was happening and said, "It's alright. My wife tells me that he heard the shots. We can go right on with our discussion, but first we must tell my son what has happened."

"OK Ralph," said District Attorney Johnson, "you have taken down all the facts as we know them so far. Why don't you go ahead and tell the boy about it and we will interrupt if we detect any errors. It will be a good exercise for us anyway in order to insure that we have it all straight in our minds."

His father slowly took another sip of coffee and began to tell this story:

E. L. Ballinger lived in Bellingham, Washington; he was a U. S. Customs Service inspector at the Canadian border. On March 7th he had received orders to proceed the next day to Seattle Heights in connection with an on-going investigation of the Hillman case. Hillman was a rancher in that area who was under heavy suspicion as being involved in illegal border smuggling of liquor and possibly drugs. The Customs Service had reason to believe that a smuggling operation might be using Hillman's ranch as a drop and redistribution point for their smuggled goods. On the morning of the 8th, Ballinger was in position and had the ranch house under surveillance. At approximately 12:15 p.m. he observed a blue 1933 Ford V8 roadster with a Washington license plate coming from the Hillman residence. Ballinger let the car go for about three minutes and then followed it with the intention of determining its destination. There was one occupant in the car. After following the car about three miles it turned off the highway onto an abandoned wood road situated in a cutover forest. As Ballinger came around a curve he suddenly found himself right on top of the car which had stopped. The driver was out of the car and had the top of the "rumble seat" up; he seemed to be unwrapping a brown paper package.

Inspector Ballinger brought his car to a sudden stop, being careful to park it so that the other car would have no possible way of getting out. He stepped from his car, identified himself and proceeded to make an inspection of the contents of the suspect automobile. In the rumble seat compartment he found three more packages wrapped in the same brown paper that the man was holding when he had arrived on the scene. Two of the packages contained six automatic pistols and the others contained Thompson submachine guns. He questioned the man, who would say nothing except that his name was John Doe. He was about forty-five years old, five feet five or so, about 175 pounds. He had a very brown complexion, a round face, amber colored protruding eyes; the left eye was badly cast outward. He was wearing a grey slouch hat with a black band and a cheap overcoat of a peculiar brown color. His hands were heavily callused with broken nails. The man spoke in a raspy voice in a sort of "Chicago" slang.

These weapons, including the machine guns, in those days were not illegal in themselves, but Ballinger knew he could nail this fellow with something else for sure. He thereupon placed John Doe under arrest and put the handcuffs on him; he then ordered him back into the Ford car. Inspector Ballinger moved his own car out of the way with the intention of bringing in the suspect in the suspect's car and returning later for his own. As he started to enter the suspect's car he was hit with a blinding crash on the back of the head that dropped him to his knees but didn't completely knock him out.

His assailant had apparently been hiding in the woods where John Doe was to pick him up. Ballinger had not previously seen the man but now a furious scuffle began. He was struck over the head four or five more times with the butt end of a pistol, but he was able to recognize the man when he saw him again later that afternoon. Ballinger then was finally knocked unconscious.

When Ballinger regained consciousness about 2:30 that afternoon, he found himself handcuffed with his own cuffs and blindfolded in the rumble seat compartment of the suspect car. With the back of the seat closed down, the back cushion lay right against and on top of the seat so that Ballinger was crammed down on the floor into the space between the seat compartment and the separation wall of the driver's front cab. The car was moving rapidly. They drove until about 4:30 p.m. at which time they pulled off the road into a concealed parking place in the country where they stopped and opened the compartment door. Two men came out of the car, one being the man first seen with the car, and the second being Ballinger's assailant. The assailant was about thirty-five years old, five feet ten inches, about 180 pounds. He had a very blond complexion, grey eyes, with a white scar about the width of a cigarette running from immediately behind the point of the right cheek bone to near the corner of the mouth, being about two and a half inches long. He was quite handsome, but had a distinct undertone of yellow on his skin. He looked to Ballinger like an opium user. He was dressed in a derby hat, a black coat with velvet collar, and a grey suit made in Montreal, Canada. This label on his coat was noticeable when he would open it to display a large roll of currency which he boasted was $2,000. He repeatedly offered Ballinger the currency as a bribe to forget the whole incident. They also threatened to kill him. Quite a conversation was held at this time during which the assailant gave his name as Manning. After considerable verbal jockeying around in which it appeared to Ballinger that the two suspects didn't seem to know just what to do with him, the guns were transferred from the back compartment into the front part of the car. Ballinger's handcuffs were loosened upon his request in order to restore circulation and then he was returned to the rear compartment and the door was again closed and locked.

Ballinger could hear the men reenter the car and off they went again. He could faintly hear his two captors talking from time to time. Both of them seemed very nervous and frightened. All along the road he often heard them discussing what they should do with him. One of them regretted they had not dropped him into the Columbia River as they crossed the Interstate Bridge.

This time they traveled about four hours before the next stop somewhere in the country. By then it was dark and raining a little; Ballinger had no idea where they were. Here they transferred him to another roadster, either a 1931 Model A Ford or a 1932 Model B of about the same color as the first car. This car also had a rumble seat but the seat cushion had been removed giving Ballinger considerably more space. John Doe alone now entered this car with Ballinger in the rear rumble seat and they started rolling again. The engine of this second car missed badly at low speeds; Ballinger did not see his assailant, Manning, again.

John Doe drove fast nearly all night. He stopped several times to talk to someone and three or four times for gasoline. When he stopped for gasoline, he would drive a block or so by a service station and then walk back to it on foot carrying a gas can. After getting the can filled he would bring it back and empty it into the car's tank. He talked a few times with Ballinger. These conversations consisted mostly of promises to put him out near a hospital or about all the bad luck he had been having. The man seemed to Ballinger to be of very low intelligence and extremely crude in his vocabulary. At one time he heard him loudly cursing to himself up in the front cab, at which time he stopped the car and turned it around. As he started again in the opposite direction, Ballinger feared that this wild long trip was coming to a climax.

The kidnapper cuffed Ballinger to an oak tree not far from the Agricultural Inspection Station (aka "Checking Station" or "Bug Station") which was located close to Hilt at that time. This is also where the phone call was made to the Sheriff's Department after Ballinger was found as the rescuers had no phone. (Livingston collection)

Sure enough, in just a few short minutes, the car stopped again and he heard the rumble seat being unlocked. John Doe told Ballinger that he was now in California. Ballinger stole a glance at his watch; it was 5:20 a.m. He then led Ballinger away from the car, down an embankment into some brush and small trees, constantly holding a gun on him. Ballinger was convinced this was "it." About two hundred yards from the highway, John Doe unlocked one side of the handcuffs. He pointed to a small oak tree and told Ballinger to put his arms around it; he snapped the loose cuff back on Ballinger's wrist. He said not another word, turned and started back up the hill toward the car.

Ballinger was cuffed to a tree somewhere in California but he was greatly relieved to still be alive. He felt himself becoming sick as the pain from the beating he had received so long ago renewed itself. He remained very quiet for the time that he estimated it would take his captor to get back to the car. Then he managed some faint cries for help but he knew he had to conserve what store of energy he still had. He put his head down and promptly passed out.

Rescued!

When he awakened it was daylight but he had no idea what time it was. He was still sick but he felt he had to try some calls for help, spaced out to conserve his strength. He called out several times. He had no idea whether or not he was near any habitation, but regularly he called out again and again. He was beginning to despair as he knew he was growing weaker. Then suddenly he heard something down the hill; it sounded like someone moving through the woods. Then almost instantaneously he saw a man come out of the brush right towards him. It was Fred Oller.

As soon as Mrs. Oller got him into the house she went right to work on him in a methodical professional manner. Ballinger stated afterward that Mrs. Oller was a remarkable woman. Her ministrations made short work of binding his wounds and releasing him to a considerable extent from the nagging pain that had set in again since he was first cuffed to the tree. When she pronounced him somewhat fit he asked her if she had a button hook. She immediately brought one to him and Ballinger showed Fred how to pick the lock on the cuffs and he was finally freed.

After explaining to the Ollers who he was and how he had come to end up handcuffed to a tree on their property, he asked them if they had a telephone. They didn't have one so he asked Fred if he would take him to the California Agricultural Inspection Station which they had told him was close by. In learning this, it immediately explained the reason for the loud cursing coming from John Doe before he had turned the car around and headed back up the road to find a place to cuff him to a tree. Apparently John Doe didn't know about the Inspection Station and when he saw the signs for it he realized that he could not go through there with Ballinger in the back compartment of the car.

These Inspection Stations are located on all of the highways where California borders adjoining states for the purpose of inspecting all vehicles for the presence of plants or fruits that may contain insects harmful to agriculture. He knew that the station would have a telephone and that was what he needed the most at that time; the sooner the better. Fred was most willing to cooperate and in a few minutes they were at the Inspection Station.

Ballinger called Chief Customs Patrol Inspector Cozza in Bellingham and advised him of the situation. Mr. Cozza ordered Ballinger to make arrangements to see a doctor locally if possible and then go north to Medford, Oregon and report in to the police headquarters there and await further orders. Ballinger then called the Oregon State Police at Medford, who in turn broadcast warnings and descriptions of the men to Oregon and California state authorities.

Before leaving, Ballinger did one more thing that turned out to be critical in the case. He took the two men that were on duty at the station to one side and gave them a complete and thorough description of his two captors right down to the last detail. He told these men that he realized they did not have police powers nor authority to attempt apprehension of criminals.

He said that he was certain that John Doe had already gone through the Inspection Station early that morning but he had a strong suspicion that Manning, in a second vehicle, would be coming through sooner or later. He told the men that Manning would probably be alone but he may be wrong about John Doe having already gone through. Perhaps he didn't go through and had gone back the other way. It was improbable but possible; if this was the case, they would be coming through together.

But mainly he asked the men to watch for Manning. He asked them that if Manning came through, just pass him on but then call the police in Yreka. Neither of the men had been on duty at the time that Ballinger estimated it was that John Doe might have gone through so there was no evidence of just which was the case.

The last thing that he told the men was that if either or both of them came through, be sure to advise the Yreka police that they were heavily armed and dangerous.

Fred Oller then took Ballinger into Hilt, California, which was a little saw mill hamlet about two miles west of the Inspection Station. Here he went to see Dr. Langer, the mill company doctor, and received additional first aid. The Oregon State Police then sent a State Trooper to Hilt in order to pick up Ballinger and take him the thirty-four miles back north to Medford, Oregon.

It had turned out to be quite an exciting day for Fred Oller after all.

Downtown Shootout

Yreka weather during March is usually not very predictable. The town is located at an elevation of about 2,600 feet so the March evenings have a tendency to be a bit nippy. But the ring of mountains that surrounds the town had apparently served its purpose well on March 10th, the day after Ballenger had been freed from the oak tree twenty-one miles north of the town. It had been almost like a spring day, and the evening seemed as if summer had arrived.

About 7:30 p.m. the telephone rang in the home of Siskiyou County Sheriff Andrew "Andy" Calkins. His wife answered the phone and told Andy that Norman Colson, one of the Inspection Station inspectors, was on the line and wanted to talk to him.

When Andy got on the line, Colson told him that a man matching Manning's description had just gone through the Inspection Station, along with another man. He said there was no question about who it was. He was not too sure about the other fellow but there was no doubt about Manning because he saw that scar on his face and he was dressed exactly as per the description he had been given. He said they were in a brand new 1933 blue Ford two door sedan with no license plates. Colson said he had been instructed to be sure and tell the sheriff that these men were heavily armed and dangerous.

Calkins told him he had been warned by other law enforcement people that there was a possibility they might be coming through.

The city of Yreka had only two peace officers; a night man and a day man, neither of whom had a car. The Sheriff's Department had but five men, including jailers. The department had only one car, a 1929 four door Buick known as a "bulge sided Buick." Sheriff Calkins, a member of a pioneer Yreka family, was in his fourth term as Siskiyou County Sheriff and was thought of very highly throughout the entire county. His #1 assistant was his twenty-nine year old son, Deputy Sheriff Charles Calkins.

Upon hanging up the phone, Sheriff Calkins immediately called his son, Charley, and advised him of what was coming down; he told him he would

Highway Patrol officer Stephen Kent poses proudly beside the patrol car that he was required to purchase himself (along with his uniform and firearm) in the Shasta River canyon north of Yreka. He started out on the Siskiyou Traffic Squad and made the transition to the Highway Patrol when it was formed in 1929. He lost his life in the line of duty while pursuing one of Ballinger's kidnappers.
(Officer Down Memorial Page, odmp.org)

pick him up right away. He then called State Highway Patrolman Steve Kent and advised him of the situation; the two men agreed to meet immediately on the highway at the north city limits.

When Sheriff Calkins and his son Charley arrived at the rendezvous point on Highway 99 a few yards north of its intersection with Blake Street at the city limits, Steve Kent was already there in a regular "white-side" Highway Patrol car. Traveling with Kent was his long time pal, Lester Quigley, who happened to be visiting with Kent at the time the call had come from the sheriff. This was not unusual because Quigley often rode with the patrolman even though he was not a peace officer of any kind. Quigley had been for many years a Yreka resident, a garage mechanic and auto salesman, who was well known and universally liked in the community.

The timing was very tight. It was but a half hour drive from the Inspection Station to Yreka and a considerable time had already been consumed in the telephoning and traveling to get to the rendezvous point. The four men held a quick conversation concerning the situation, with the sheriff in charge. He

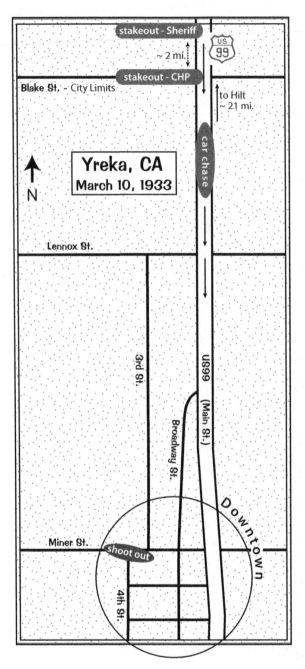

instructed his deputy to stay there with Kent and Quigley and he would go on down near Hawkinsville, some two miles farther north. The plan was for him to attempt to identify the car when it passed after which he would follow behind it. Hopefully, after he turned on the siren and red light, the fugitive car would be slowing down and stopping between the two police cars. Sheriff Calkins then took off at a fast clip and positioned himself on a dirt road that intersects the highway a small distance toward Yreka from the Hawkinsville road.

In what seemed like just a few minutes to the three men waiting at the city limit, they saw the Ford coming at a high rate of speed with the sheriff in hot pursuit, siren wide open and red light flashing. The Ford was not slowing down one bit as per the plan. As it went sailing by, the sheriff slowed down to almost a stop and signaled Charley, his son and his deputy, who was standing outside of the Highway Patrol car, to get in.

With the two officers in the Buick now and the Patrol car behind with its siren and lights going, the chase continued on south down the highway toward the center of town. It was not totally dark but night was falling fast.

The center of Yreka was at the east end of the main business district, at the intersection of Miner Street and Highway 99 (Main Street). At approximately this point the sheriff's car had made up the space lost when he had slowed to pick up Charley. The Ford sailed on by that intersection without slackening speed, with the sheriff's Buick right on its tail.

The next intersection, Center Street, is but a hundred or so yards south of Miner Street. All of a sudden the blue Ford made a wild screeching right turn off of Main Street, to head west on Center and deeper into the town. Sheriff Calkins was right behind it on the highway but he could not make the turn with the big Buick and continued on to the next intersection at Lane Street. Kent, being farther back, saw what was happening and was able to decelerate enough to make the right turn onto Center.

The Ford was now headed west on Center Street with Kent and Quigley close up. Two short blocks sped by and the Ford made another fast right turn on to Fourth Street, heading north with the Patrol car following tightly behind.

One quick block and the fugitive car was now approaching Miner Street. Just before it reached the intersection, as it appeared to be starting another right turn, it seemed to jam on all its brakes and come to a screeching halt near the right hand curb. Kent wheeled his car right up behind and stopped.

Kent got out of the left hand door and Quigley the right; both proceeded forward to the left and right sides of the suspect's car. Meanwhile, the sheriff had made the turn at Lane Street and again at Fourth Street and was coming up behind the Patrol car.

As Kent and Quigley were walking forward, Manning got out of the car on the left hand side, leaving the door open and was just standing there. The other man had just opened the door on the right hand side when Kent and Quigley arrived at the car.

The city street lights had come on and Kent was wearing his state badge in full view on the outside of his jacket when he said to Manning, "This is the Sheriff; get back in the car."

Manning said, "You get in the car."

Kent spoke again very sternly, "Get back in that car."

In a flash, Manning's right hand came up with a 45 caliber pistol in it that seemed to appear from nowhere. A shot went off with a thundering explosion and Kent went down, shot through the heart.

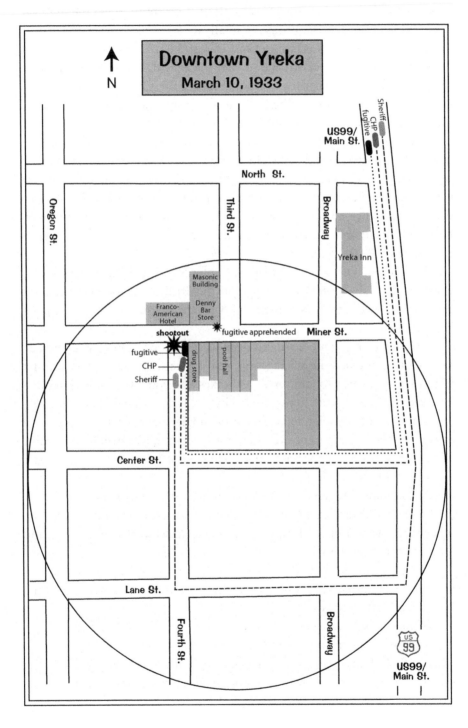

When the blast went off, the other man bolted out the door of the car, brushed past Quigley and ran around the corner into a drug store. He charged in, dived behind a counter, threw his gun on the floor and shouted, "Get the police!"

As Kent went down, Manning turned a half turn to his left and touched off three rapid fire shots into Quigley on the other side of the car by shooting right through the two open doors of the Ford. Quigley staggered back and sank to the pavement as Sheriff Calkins brought the big Buick screeching to a stop behind them.

Manning started to run across Miner Street as Charley Calkins alighted from the skidding car, and he too was on the run carrying a sawed off pump action shot gun loaded with bird shot. Just as Charley got the gun up to fire, Martin Lange, an off duty Deputy who just happened to be in the drug store, came charging out of the store as a result of what the other fugitive had shouted. Charley almost fired right into him but managed to hold back just in time. Manning was almost across the street when Charley got off his first shot. It shattered the glass in the Denny Bar Department Store but lodged some pellets in Manning's lower torso and legs. Manning whirled around and fired a shot at oncoming Deputy Lange. That shot creased Charley's neck just under the jaw bone but didn't slow him down one bit.

Manning was now running a bit slower from the load of bird shot he was carrying and was attempting to make for Third Street. (Third Street comes into the other side of Miner Street just forty yards east of where Fourth Street intersects it but the two incoming streets do not line up with each other.) Charley fired off two more blasts on the run and these laid another dose of bird shot into Manning. The fugitive whirled again and pulled the trigger but the pistol was now empty. Deputy Charley Calkins saw this and quickly overhauled him with a flying tackle, and down the two men went, all rolled up together. In the scuffle, Manning got the butt end of the pistol into action and bashed a terrible gash in the Deputy's skull. Charley quickly pinned him as Sheriff Calkins came up and put the handcuffs on Manning.

A total of six minutes had elapsed between the time that Kent and Quigley got out of their car and the time that the handcuffs clicked shut on Manning. One good police officer lay dead in the street; a popular local citizen was dying in the gutter; a heroic deputy had a superficial neck wound and blood was pouring out of his scalp; a nationally known desperado was handcuffed and pinned to the ground and another was lying on the floor of Maguire and Green's Drug Store babbling that he was "just an innocent hitchhiker."

Court Reporter Ralph McMurry then stopped talking. He was a compassionate and emotional man. There was complete silence in the room. With a sort of sad look on his face he reached up and very lightly brushed a tiny tear from the corner of his eye. Steve Kent had been the family's neighbor; he had lived two doors away.

After the shooting had died down it suddenly seemed as if everybody that lived in Yreka converged on the corner of Miner and Fourth Streets. There was a large group of younger fellows that usually "hung out" in Cooley & Pollard's billiard parlor on Miner Street two doors up from Fourth Street; all of them came out into the streets. Likewise a group of older men who usually spent evenings at Con Brown's Place, another pool room three or four doors down from Fourth Street, emerged into the streets. People from all around the close by neighborhoods who had heard the shots also rushed to the scene. People in cars that knew nothing of the shooting and happened to come along all stopped to see what it was all about. All these people were just milling about looking into the fugitives' car and viewing the bodies still lying where they had fallen.

Looking west up Miner Street in the 1930s. The shootout took place one block up on the SE corner of Miner and Fourth Streets. A brass plaque on the outside wall memorializes Steve Kent and Lester Quigley. Most of the buildings are still there although the large building in the foreground is now a parking lot. (Siskiyou County Museum)

Dr. Pius, whose office was on Miner Street just happened to be there at the time, came out and looked over Charley's gun-butt scalp wound. He then bundled the Deputy into his car and took him to the hospital, where he sewed it up with four stitches.

Before Deputy Calkins would even let Dr. Pius work on him at the hospital he immediately called his home in order to reassure his wife that he was OK and that neither he nor his father had been shot. This had been bothering him very much because both of their homes were located within gunshot hearing distance from the location of the shooting. His wife had no sooner hung up the telephone when it rang again and it was Mrs. Andy Calkins on the line to tell her that a woman had called her and said that Charley had been shot. Charley's wife then told her that it was not so because she had just talked with Charley and both he and Andy were OK.

Meanwhile Martin Lange, the off-duty deputy, had gone back into the drug store and taken the other fugitive into custody. When he emerged back into the streets with his captive, one of the partners that owned the drug store, Maguire & Green's, followed him out. Sheriff Calkins told the druggist, Bill Maguire, to call County Physician Dr. A. H. Newton. He said to tell him what had happened and have him come down here and have a look at the bodies. He told Maguire to also call the coroner but make sure that Dr. Newton had made his examination before the coroner took the bodies away. Sheriff Calkins and Martin Lange then departed for the jail with the two captives.

Lynch Talk

When the crowd was first forming in the streets, it was merely a curious crowd coming to see what all the excitement was about. But after awhile when they began to take in the enormity of the tragedy, the mood of the people began to change. After each had viewed the scene of each area of action on the premises, they were soon standing around in little knots conversing. At first it was shock at the loss of two men who were undoubtedly known by most everyone there; then it seemed to turn to indignation and in some cases, outright anger.

Inevitably the word "lynch" was heard in somewhat subdued tones. This kind of talk was coming from two differently motivated groups. One group was incensed at the loss of a friend and seemed to be seeking retribution with this idea. The motivation for the other faction appeared to be concern over the fact that these "big city" gangsters could come into a little peaceful community such as this and kill our peace officers right out in the open; they felt an example should be made to show the world that this conduct was not acceptable here.

These conversations were just talk; not much more than just "griping" as a result of their frustration. No raucous leader had arisen; there was no shouting or "mob action" as such. As the bodies were removed and a tow truck took away the fugitives' car the crowd began to drift along Fourth Street toward the courthouse. The jail was all lit up and many of the court-house lights were on as various public officials had been called out.

When Sheriff Calkins had taken Manning into the jail office for booking, he asked the fugitive, "Just who are you anyway?"

Manning replied, "You will find all about who I am as soon as you get a report back on my fingerprints."

Manning was woozy from the approximately two hundred bird shot pel-lets that were still lodged in his rear quarters. He asked the sheriff if they had a doctor that could get them out. Andy told him that he had already called for the county physician to come to the jail and take care of it.

The other man seemed to be very frightened and was still maintaining that he was merely an innocent hitchhiker. He asked the sheriff not to put him in the same cell with Manning because he was afraid of him.

Dr. Newton had made superficial examinations of the bodies in the street and confirmed of course that the two men were indeed dead. Now he was on his way into the jail to help the man that had killed them. It occurred to the doctor that this was somewhat ironic. When Dr. Newton entered Man-ning's cell and began treating the bird shot wounds he asked him, "If you had it to do all over again, would you have shot them?"

Manning's answer was, "If you corner a rat, the rat will turn and bite you. If you don't corner the rat, he won't bite you."

By the time Charley got back from the hospital everything was under control in the jail but he found that his father was becoming very much concerned about the mood of the crowd that had formed in the courtyard outside the jail. There were approximately 200 people out there milling about and there was talk a plenty about a lynching. The crowd at that time had not really assumed the nature of a "mob" but it was obvious through the barred window of the office that one person had more or less emerged out there as the leader. The sheriff well knew that he himself had the reputation of being a "no-nonsense" sheriff but he certainly didn't want to have it put to the test.

He said to Charley, "I'm going out and have a talk with them. You stay in here and be prepared for anything that might develop."

He then unlocked the office door and stepped outside. Immediately the leader of the more belligerent group came up to him and told him that there was a strong feeling out there that the sheriff ought to take a walk and let them see that justice was done in fast order.

In just a loud enough voice so that the ringleaders standing close by would be sure to hear him, but not loud enough to reach out into the crowd which might tend to incite a bad feeling in those who heretofore had not been in on all the tough talk, the sheriff replied, "Now you fellows just calm down here. You all know me and know me well. You know that you might take these prisoners out of here but bear in mind that you are going to take them out over my dead body."

He quickly turned away and went back through the door and that seemed to be the end of that kind of talk for one night anyway. It was now very late and the crowd began drifting away.

The Hitchhiker

The next day, District Attorney Charles E. Johnson commenced questioning the two suspects. Very early in this process attention became focused on the "other man."

Johnson had contacted Norman Colson at the Inspection Station near Hilt and obtained in detail the description of E. L. Ballinger's "John Doe." The other man did not in any way at all fit that description. The man, who gave his name as Paul Victor Newcomb, had been continually complaining that he was merely a hitchhiker that Manning had picked up earlier in the day of the killing. In the meantime the man was being referred to in the press as "a desperate criminal" and "one of the killers."

He stated that he was a San Francisco jewelry salesman and that he was hitchhiking to that destination when Manning picked him up near Drain, Oregon the afternoon of the day of the shooting. He said that not much conversation was carried on with Manning during the ride. When they approached the state line Inspection Station, he said that Manning told him to take the two pistols from the dash compartment of the car before the officers inspected it. After they passed through the station Manning told him to hang on to one of the pistols and give him the other. At this point he stated that he became very frightened and nervous.

When the officers overhauled them as they approached Yreka he said that he shouted to Manning, "Stop, those men are officers!" But Manning speeded up.

He went on to say that after Manning made the two turns in Yreka and was coming up on Miner Street with the police car right behind them, he reached down and pulled on the emergency brake as hard as he could and then jumped out and ran into the drug store near the corner.

All of this was beginning to appear plausible to District Attorney Johnson; especially so when the victim, E. L. Ballinger himself arrived in Yreka and definitely established that Newcomb was not "John Doe." This was proof enough for Johnson that Newcomb was not one of the kidnappers of Ballinger, but the information did nothing to disprove that Newcomb and Manning were somehow connected.

Johnson had been astounded by Newcomb's claim to having stopped the car with the emergency brake. He felt if this could be proven it would show that this was the act not of a fleeing criminal but the act of a frightened man being held against his will who wanted it all to be stopped and be protected by the police.

Enter George Hall

By Monday morning Manning was still refusing to talk. But via telephone and telegraph a great amount of information on Manning was reaching the authorities in Yreka from all over the western states. It turned out that Manning was only an alias for the man who was actually George Hall. Manning/Hall was wanted in at least three states for kidnapping, bank robbery, and drug running, to say nothing of a rap sheet a yard long listing prior arrests for armed robbery and several previous incarcerations.

When the district attorney faced George Hall with all of this information, the suspect began to talk. The first order of business on Johnson's mind was to get the matter of Newcomb settled. Without having been exposed to Newcomb's story as told to Johnson, Hall recited essentially the same one in so far as any relationship with Newcomb was concerned. He even volunteered the information that it was Newcomb who actually stopped the car by pulling on the emergency brake. He also added that Newcomb had attempted to turn the vehicle ignition key off just before he pulled the emergency brake.

Late in the morning, Miss Jean Uhl, half sister of Newcomb, arrived in Yreka with additional information to the effect that there was no way that Newcomb had any prior connection with Hall. This satisfied Johnson and he thereupon released Newcomb, the unfortunate hitchhiker.

In the afternoon District Attorney Johnson filed murder charges against George Hall.

When the news went out that Newcomb was in fact the innocent hitch-hiker that he had proclaimed, there was more than one man in Yreka who flinched at the news and took a new look at his inner self.

These men were asking themselves, "What if all that talk and threats of ours about lynching had been carried out on the night of the killing; an innocent man would have been a victim of vigilante justice." This was something that wasn't even considered in the heat of the moment that evening in the courtyard.

Taking Precautions

For the next few days the wheels of justice began to slowly turn as the District Attorney and the sheriff commenced formalizing the case against their famous gangster now safely ensconced in the county jail. Most of the "lynch" talk had died down but Sheriff Calkins was taking no chances. He and his son Charley were personally guarding the prisoner. Neither of them ever carried the keys on their person outside the jail building. They each were pulling twelve hour shifts; the door was never unlocked without positive identification from one or the other on the outside. Each night they changed Hall's location by moving him to a different cell.

The sheriff had put on two extra night men. He had one stationed in the district attorney's office and one in the courtroom. Each of these rooms had windows overlooking the jail entrance. The men were armed with shotguns and rifles; they were instructed to keep constant watch on the yard below for any trouble that may develop.

On Tuesday, March 14th, a double funeral was held for the two victims of the shooting. A crowd estimated at 2,500 people was in attendance. The Masonic Lodge handled the ceremony and many of those present were law enforcement people from all over the western states.

But after the ceremonies, as people stood around the old subject of "lynch" was heard in more than one group. Not a big movement; it might be said that it was but a little trickle of thought floating around the populace. No shouting; just some serious but quiet discussion. There was really nothing much to it, but it was there!

Les Chase was a young man that worked for the telephone company in Fresno, California. In 1931 he was transferred to Yreka and he and his wife moved there. He was the new General Manager/Wire Chief. By the time of the murder, which occurred right across the street from the telephone company office, he and his wife had become very well integrated into the community and found that they liked Yreka very much. Thirty-eight years later he wrote a little paper that he entitled *Three Hours of Fright*.

Here is what Les Chase had to say about whether or not "there really was nothing much to it" in regard to these "quiet" conversations that were held after the funeral about a lynching:

As I recall it, the Friday evening of March 10, 1933 was lovely. We were at the Vestry House, learning our lessons required for membership in the Episcopal Church. Suddenly, we heard a barrage of shots! Heavy shots as well as light ones were heard by everyone. They sounded mighty close! The rector offered a prayer for the safety of everyone. (We were two blocks south of the site of the shooting.)

The county courthouse and jail are located across the street from the church property. Soon, a great number of people were present at the site. A great deal of commotion took place at the jail.

On joining the crowd, my wife and I learned of the tragic deaths of two popular young men in the community. Steve Kent was a Highway Patrolman, and Lester Quigley was an automobile salesman. They had been buddies; when you found one, you usually found the other. This accounts for them both being together and shot this fateful evening. More people were not killed because the killer ran out of ammunition and was subsequently subdued by a deputy sheriff.

The city was in a state of shock. Two popular and well-respected members of the community's family had been taken from us. Emotions ran high and "lynch law" talk began immediately. Formation of a vigilance committee for action was planned. To live through a circumstance such as had taken place, was to learn how high and how quickly emotions can be aroused. Even without rapid ways of travel and communication, most people of the community and the state knew what had happened in this isolated mountain area.

When a group of sober, stable and serious men banded together for action to correct wrongdoing, you had a Vigilance Committee. This was the case! It was felt quick justice must be executed.

During the following week emotions continued to build and a course of action was decided upon. The killer had to pay for his crimes. One afternoon of that week, I was called upon by a member of the committee. I was told that inasmuch as I knew how to cut the wires for the communication circuits to the jail that was to be my job in the vigilante action. The killer would be taken from the jail the night I cut the wires, and hung. I would be told later when I was to execute my job. I was too stunned to ask any questions and he left quickly.

During the 1930s, the law enforcement agencies did not have the sophisticated equipment that they have now. My job would be a comparatively easy one, if I did it.

I didn't believe in mob justice and still don't, regardless of the crime or how, apparently, justified. I felt, we are a nation of laws and everyone should have his day in court. Without this right, in my mind, we soon would be a nation of anarchists.

I sat at my desk, stunned. I remember breaking out in a cold sweat and shaking. My mind was in a muddle. What course of action should I take? Fright entered my mind due to my feelings of law and order.

My two bosses were located 175 miles away in Chico, California. I called the plant manager, but he was out. His secretary did not know how to reach him. Next, I called the business manager. He listened to my story and, on conclusion, said, "You, son, have a problem! Use your own judgment."

More fright built up in my mind! Time was running out for my decision as to what my actions would be. I continued shaking and sweating.

Community emotions were known to be very high. It was felt that the killer was no doubt guilty. He was; he was caught in the act of killing. I remembered San Francisco's vigilance committees in their early history. If you were with them, you were safe. If you were against them, you were considered one of the lawless and treated accordingly. I wondered, if I refused their request, how this local committee would treat me.

If I followed their plans of cutting the wires, I would be tampering with law enforcement communication facilities. I might go to jail when the authorities learned of my actions. If the criminal wasn't hung, he might kill more innocent people in the streets.

I decided against my concepts of justice. I would do what

was asked of me. Better to lose the life of the killer than any more members of our community family. My immaturity and fright were uppermost in my mind. I wondered if my company would fire me when it learned of my actions.

Sometime, near 5:00 p.m., the same committee member again called upon me. He was in a terrific hurry and obviously upset. He told me to forget the whole thing; the hanging was not to take place. He gave no details.

It's an understatement to say I was feeling relieved as I went home. I told my twenty-five year old wife what her twenty-seven year old husband had almost done against his better judgment. It was good to be young, when emotions can return to normal quickly.

Later I learned that the action had been canceled upon the sheriff's learning of the plans. He had learned who were involved to carry out the plan. He reached the members of the vigilance committee, and told them that his prisoner would be protected. He told the citizens they had helped elect him to do his job of preserving law and order, and he would be doing just that! If they persisted in carrying out the plan, someone would get hurt; he regretted to have to take such action, as they were all his friends. He was taken for his word.

Thank God for such a man at particularly such a time in my life! As I grow older, sixty-seven, I often wonder how my life might have been affected had the vigilante action been success-ful. To carry the knowledge that I might have contributed to the success of action, and the death of another human being without his day in court, still frightens me. I am thankful that a higher authority, which seems to control our lives, prevented the action.

John Doe Exposed

On Friday, March 17th, a message came into the district attorney's of-fice concerning "John Doe." The message from George Hubbard, Collector of Customs at Seattle, stated that the other man that had participated with Hall in the kidnapping of Ballinger had been identified as Joe Clark. The message further reported that both Clark and Hall were wanted by Canadian authori-ties for bank robbery.

Upon receiving this message, District Attorney Johnson remarked,

The marble and brass plaque mounted on the outside wall on the southeast corner of Miner and Fourth Streets in Yreka.

"That's some progress anyway on that fellow John Doe. But where is he?"

Johnson got his answer to that question the next day but the answer was good for only a few hours.

Late Friday, Joe Clark had been captured at Los Angeles and booked into the County Jail in Glendale for his alleged participation with George Hall in the kidnapping of customs officer Ballinger. Thrown into the same cell with Clark was an intoxicated man. A few hours later Clark boldly assumed the identity of his cellmate held on a drunk charge. Clark called for a bondsman who supplied $250 bail. Then, as the intoxicated man whose name he had "stolen" lay in the cell in a stupor, Clark walked out of the jail to freedom.

Police Chief John D. Fraser of Glendale explained the escape as follows:

"Clark apparently stole his drunken companion's property slip, having obtained from the intoxicated man his name, address and information as to where he was employed. Then after calling a bondsman he arranged for bail, presented the slip and received the other prisoner's property and left the jail. So smooth a worker was the fugitive that the officers who released him believed everything to be in order. He even simulated a hangover."

When E. L. Ballinger was told of this development, he stated, "I'm sorry that I said that fellow was of low intelligence!"

Hall's trial was set for Monday, April 3rd at 10:00 a.m. District Attorney Johnson, due to some technicalities, was charging Hall only with the murder of Kent. His main reason, however, was that he wanted to keep his options open to try him again for Quigley's murder in case anything went wrong the first time around.

In the meantime Hall had retained local attorney William V. Cowen, who then brought in L. Luke Howe and O. Francis Meldon, both prominent criminal lawyers from Sacramento. The feeling around the town was that these two attorneys had volunteered their services without fee due to the notoriety of the case.

Johnson enlisted the local law firm of Allen and McNamara to help his office with the case. Joseph P. McNamara was to actively assist during the trial.

George Hall Goes to Court

On the appointed day, there was a huge jury panel on hand consisting of 100 individuals. Examination of the panel was commenced and just before 5:00 p.m. on Wednesday, the third day, the final member of the jury was impaneled.

The next day in his opening remarks, Johnson gave a very detailed description step by step of all the facts in the case insofar as the prosecution was concerned. He then, alternating with attorney McNamara, put on the stand a long list of witnesses attesting to these facts. It was a very easy case for the prosecution because of the adequate number of apparently reliable witnesses that testified confidently and thoroughly.

The defense did very little questioning of all these prosecution witnesses. The capacity audience in the court room was surprised and wondered why the defense wasn't more challenging and aggressive with these witnesses. But people with experience and knowledge of trial tactics began to slowly realize what was going on here.

That evening at home, Court Reporter McMurry was questioned about this by his oldest son. He replied, "I am not completely sure yet, but as soon as the defense takes over I believe we will have the answer to that question. My hunch now is that we will have a very short defense effort when it becomes their case. I think that the lawyers for the defense realize that they have no case at all and that the only hope for their client is to ride out an endless succession of appeals until they can literally wear out the system and possibly escape the noose somewhere several years down the road. I believe you might see them send up a couple of trial balloons in order to have something to ride on with endless appeals, but I look for a very short presentation when they come on stage."

The prosecution's testimony with the witnesses took all of that day and the next, at which time Johnson rested his case. It then being Friday evening,

Judge C. J. Luttrell recessed the case for the weekend.

When the trial resumed the following Monday morning the defense astounded the audience by calling none other than Hall himself as their first and only witness.

After Hall was sworn in, Mr. Howe asked him to please state the circumstances relating to the death of Mr. Steve Kent only, which occurred at the corner of Fourth and Miner Streets in Yreka:

A. Well, as the car stopped at Fourth and Miner, Mr. Newcomb and myself got out. As we got out of the car there was someone come around who I learned after was Mr. Kent. He asked where in the hell we were going. And I asked him what he wanted. And he says, "Never mind what I want, get back in the car." And he made as if to draw his gun. As he did so, I reached in the car and got mine and shot him."

Q. At that time when he made the motion to draw his gun, did you believe that your life was in danger and that he was about to shoot you?

With this question out in the open, Johnson stole a glance at McNamara and both of them had a kind of knowing look on their faces and sort of tossed their heads toward the ceiling in a resigned shrug. Both of them knew that as far as the defense was concerned, this question was the key one of their whole case and would be the vehicle upon which they would ride through the endless thickets of the appeal process.

A. I did.

Mr. Howe: The defense rests.

In the closing arguments McNamara took over. He again reviewed the facts as they had been presented, using but a few minutes. Knowing now that the defense was relying only on a position that Hall didn't know that Kent was a police officer and had shot him in self defense when Kent had reached for his gun, McNamara dwelt on the wild chase that led to the shooting. The implication that the defendant was unaware that his pursuers were police officers seemed ludicrous when one considered the sirens and flashing lights as Hall had continued to try to escape. McNamara also pointed out that Hall ran from the scene of the killing which indicated that Hall knew full well that he had shot not in self defense but in order to kill a police officer in hopes of escaping arrest.

When the defense presented its closing arguments it was exactly as Johnson and McNamara, and Ralph McMurry too, had expected. Attorney Cowan said that he believed Mr. Kent forgot for the moment when he walked up to the car that he was not wearing his traffic officer's uniform, and that he believed both men acted without giving full consideration to their acts. He stated that he did not believe that Officer Kent told Hall and Newcomb that "This is the Sheriff," as testified by Newcomb. He said that it was not a natural thing for Kent to say under those conditions. He pointed out that it was quite dark at the scene of the shooting and that it was quite possible that Hall did not see the star Steve Kent was wearing.

Mr. Cowan then said, "That concludes our case, Your Honor."

Judge Luttrell gave his instructions to the jury and they retired to the jury room for deliberations.

While the jury was sequestered, Johnson, McNamara and Court Reporter McMurry were having coffee in the district attorney's office.

Johnson said, "Let's see if we have a consensus between the three of us on what we think the tactics of the defense were."

The three men were in complete agreement. Their assessment was that under appeal, the defense would use the consideration that the defendant had no way of knowing that he was confronted by a police officer and had therefore acted in self defense. Hence, no premeditation; this, if successful would be at worst (for the defendant), a reduction in charges to manslaughter or at best, an outright reversal. There was no question though, in the minds of the three men talking in the D.A.'s office, that this jury here today would bring in a guilty verdict of murder in the first degree.

In less than ten minutes after the jury had retired, the three men were astounded to hear the court summons bell go off.

"I wonder what that's all about," said Johnson, "Let's get going."

When they were all reassembled in the court room again, the Judge signaled to the bailiff and the jury filed back in. In no time at all, it was all over.

Guilty of murder in the first degree!

It was April 10th, thirty days to the day after the crime had been committed.

"This must be some kind of a record," Johnson was heard to say.

In a few days, court was reconvened and Judge Luttrell sentenced Hall to be hanged at Folsom Prison on June 23rd, 1933. As the two prosecutors and the court reporter had predicted, a long series of appeals, motions, requests for transcript, requests for stays of execution, along with all the legal delaying tactics began falling like snow flakes from the offices of the defense lawyers. The ponderous movements of the slowly turning wheels of the judicial system were sorely being tested. As time went on, the case began to slowly fade from the public consciousness as one execution date after the other was postponed by higher authority. Month after month, George Hall sat it out on death row in Folsom Prison. He was still there in 1934. He was still there in 1935... ...

1985: Deputy Calkins Reflects Back

Fifty-two years later, a hale and hearty eighty-one year old Charley Calkins said, "Several people gave me a lot of flack about that Hall Case. They said that I shouldn't have shot him with that shotgun. This hurt my feelings. You know, in sixteen years as a deputy sheriff, I was paid $150 a month; never got more than five hours sleep a night; I was shot at six times; got a bullet crease on my neck and a four inch gun-butt cut on my head. Only a few people ever said thanks but plenty of them handed me a load of flack. I shouldn't have had to take that."

The shooting took place just around this corner. The surprised and innocent hitchhiker ran from the scene and took refuge in the drugstore. Maguire and Greene was still there forty years later. (Siskiyou County Museum)

45

"My Twenty Four Hours of Hell!"

…screamed a title printed on the cover of the June, 1936 issue of *Official Detective Stories*. Inside, an eight page story dramatized the abduction of Customs Agent E. L. Ballinger (Chapter 2) in the twice-monthly magazine.

In *Daring Detective* (date unknown), "The Case of the Fashion Plate Killers" tells the tale of the Dunsmuir area robbery/murder (Chapter 3), the title apparently referring to the perpetrators' "double breasted blue serge suits and new stiff brimmed straw hats," attire assuredly unusual in that time and place. We do know that the two men wore straw hats during the heist as a part of their ploy, a distraction technique. But the suits beg a question; was this detail artistic license? And where, traveling on freight trains as they were and short of cash, would these dapper suits have been purchased or stored?

The 1930s, the decade in which the crimes covered in this book took place, was a decade rife with crime. For one thing, the 18th Amendment, or "Prohibition," was still on the books, and it seems to have fostered more crime than it prevented. (The amendment was repealed after 14 years, in December, 1933.)

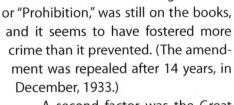

A second factor was the Great Depression, which displaced many people, prompting some to commit crimes that could easily escalate from, for example, a relatively benign small-time robbery into something as serious as a murder.

The rampant unemployment and discontent of the times also left people eager for cheap entertainment. Thus the 1930s became the Golden Age of crime and detective magazines, a genre akin to dime novels and pulp fiction. Perhaps it was especially gratifying in that era to read about the misfortunes of others, and you could get a lot of diversion from your own nagging situation for the 10 cent price.

Criminals and cops alike found themselves turned into stars as local newspapers were scanned for new story lines to fill the pages of the plethora of crime magazines. Here are some other *Official Detective Stories* cover stories from 1936: "The Torso in the Pillow Slip." "The Riddle of the Headless Milliner." "Sold into White Slavery." "New York's Bathtub Slaying." "The Crimes of a Love-mad Playgirl." Other magazines in the same genre included *True Gang Life, Real Police Stories, Startling Detective, Master Detective, Racketeers and their Methods, Scientific Detective Monthly*, and many more.

There was as well a notable prurient element to these magazines; not quite "girlie" magazines, nevertheless, an attractive woman, scantily clad, was generally on the cover. The cover girls were pictured either as hapless victims or as the ruthless wielders of the weapons themselves. The covers of the various crime and detective magazines were usually colorful renderings done by skilled illustrators, a sort of low brow art form that can be appreciated today.

Jill Livingston

A magazine rack on Miner Street in Yreka in 1942. Photo by FSA photographer Russell Lee. The world war being fought was the most important subject of the newspapers and the magazines by this time, but there were still a number of detective magazines on display. (Library of Congress)

Cast of Characters

Robert Miller Barr - hobo arriving in Dunsmuir by train

Clyde L. Johnson - hobo arriving in Dunsmuir by train

George C. "Molly" Malone – California Highway Patrolman stationed in Dunsmuir

Frank R. "Jack" Daw – Dunsmuir Chief of Police, and victim

Steve Abgaroff – member of the Dunsmuir posse

Charles Tracy – member of the Dunsmuir posse

W. G. Chandler - Siskiyou County Sheriff, recovering from surgery

Ed Mathews –Siskiyou County Sheriff Deputy and Acting Sheriff

Martin Lange –Siskiyou County Deputy Sheriff

Felix J. Kunz – Siskiyou County Coroner, present at murder inquest

Lloyd Noble - Siskiyou County Deputy Coroner, present at murder inquest

James Davis – Siskiyou County District Attorney, present at murder inquest

Ralph McMurry – Siskiyou County Court Reporter, present at murder inquest

Fleming "Hank" Martin – hapless witness to the jail breakout

Dr. A. H. Newton – Siskiyou County Physician

"Snappy" Goodrich – local crime photographer

3

Hobos Stage a Holdup, 1935:
Clyde Johnson and Robert Barr

It was a time of drifting throughout the land. It seemed like everyone in the world was going somewhere while at the same time not really getting anywhere. Robert Miller Barr and Clyde L. Johnson rode a freight train into Dunsmuir the night of July 27th, 1935. This was in the time that the Great Depression had reached its lowest depth. There were as many as a hundred men "riding the rods" on that train that day so Barr and Johnson had plenty of company.

Many of those men on the train that day were solid upstanding citizens who had been dealt a rough deal by the economic conditions that seemed to be devouring the social structure of the nation. They were on the road seeking work; any kind of work; anywhere.

Others were just drifting. They had given up looking for jobs and had no other place to go. With them, riding the rails had become a way of life. Some of them had adopted crime as a way of financing this aimless meandering. Even for these, expectations were very low. People that had jobs had little money; it was hardly worthwhile to rob them. But a "stickup" of a bar or an occasional burglary could keep a man going on the rods. It didn't require much. There was always the possibility of making a big score sometime. This was all that really kept them going.

Barr and Johnson were young men that had very spotty and frustrating records in the crime business. Barr was but twenty-five years old and had already served a five year term in the state reformatory at Ione, California. He had been in numerous jails throughout the state and had a string of aliases. He had been arrested in Redding, California as recently as February of this year.

Johnson was a little older. He was originally from Alabama. He had drifted west like so many of the other young men driven by hard times. Just in the past month he had committed robberies in Hollister and Roseville, California. He and Barr had become acquainted while both were serving a hitch in the Santa Rosa jail.

Robert and Clyde were traveling together now but they were getting very low on funds. As the train was slowly making its way north up through the valley that warm afternoon they talked together and assessed their situation. They knew that they were approaching the twisting Sacramento River Canyon and long after dark the train would be pulling into Dunsmuir, where there would be a fairly long delay. Dunsmuir, they knew, was a major railroad headquarters where an additional "helper" engine would be connected in order to make the steep pull over the Siskiyou Mountains. They decided that they should "roll" off in Dunsmuir and get some long needed sleep in a hotel. Then they would check out the area and see if they could make a score there.

Any man worth his salt in the robbery business would know that Dunsmuir, California was probably the worst choice in the whole country to pull off a holdup. Dunsmuir is the southernmost town in Siskiyou County, the northern-most county in the state. It lies in the bottom of the rugged steep-sided Sacramento River Canyon. Escape routes from Dunsmuir are north or south only. Both directions involve but one road which is Highway 99 (now I-5), also lying in the bottom of the canyon. No one can go east or west because of the steep canyon walls. For sophisticated criminals, Dunsmuir's lack of alternate escape routes would place it at the bottom of any list of feasible

Barr and Johnson hopped off a freight in the railroad town of Dunsmuir on July 27, 1935. After a night in a hotel they hiked a few miles south to Castella and proceeded to rob a saloon. (Siskiyou County Museum)

locations for a heist. But these men were not sophisticated criminals.

By the time the train rolled into town the quiet citizens of Dunsmuir had sometime ago rolled up the sidewalks and retired. But like all railroad towns there was an all night diner and a hotel near the tracks. This is the nature of these towns due to the twenty-four hour activity of a busy railroad yard. But even so, it seemed this night as always there was a quiet hush hanging over the yards. Only the sound of a single hammer clanging on an anvil from the depths of the machine shop floated out into the night punctuated now and then by the release of steam from a yard engine sorting cars way out on a distant spur.

One and a half hours after midnight, Clyde Johnson and Robert Miller Barr checked into the hotel near the tracks in Dunsmuir. The night clerk hardly noticed them when he gave them the room. They were just two more of the same gaunt, searching faces that came wandering in after nearly every freight train arrived in town. Johnson and Barr went on upstairs and got a good night's sleep.

The two men slept till nearly noon the next morning. When men are riding the rods they get out of the habit of observing the more formal sched- ules that the rest of society observes. They just sleep whenever they get the chance and eat to the extent their bodies call for sustenance. They had a good breakfast, or really a brunch, in the diner and then headed south on foot on Highway 99 bound for Castella. They each wore stiff-brimmed straw hats and they had a plan.

Castella is a tiny little hamlet several miles south of Dunsmuir, just over the county line in Shasta County. Their objective was to rob the bar or pool hall, whatever it was, that Johnson had been told about during one of the many "bull" sessions around the camp fires in the hobo "jungles."

Sleeping in a hotel as they had the night before and eating in a restaurant was a definite treat for a hobo. The standard fare to be had in the jungles was canned beans and boiled coffee followed by sleep on the ground in a "roll." Around the fire before sleeping there was always the talk. The subjects discussed were women, home, railroad "bulls" and how to get some money; in that order. Generally these groups of men were mostly strangers to each other but if one floated around the jungles for any length of time he often met familiar faces. Talk was free and easy and it wasn't long before many of the hobos developed a "reputation." In other words, if a man was a stickup artist it was generally known in the jungles. This was the reputation carried by both Johnson and Barr. There was no danger from a "squealer" because the code of the jungle forbade it. Besides, it was definitely not healthy. Sometimes when two or more of the men that carried similar reputations found themselves around the fire, they talked quite openly about business. They bragged and sometimes joked about previous heists and even discussed potential future ones. It was in one of these sessions down south when Johnson had heard another hobo mention Dunsmuir and Castella.

"There are too damn many people in the bars in Dunsmuir," he said. "You want to stay away from those places where there's a lot of action. You want a quiet cozy little place where there's not much coming and going. In a railroad town like Dunsmuir where those trains are coming and going all the time, there are a lot of those railroaders doing the same thing in and out of the joints."

He failed to mention the lack of escape routes in Dunsmuir but he went on talking.

"There's this little town about ten miles south of Dunsmuir," he said. It's called Castella. Just a little dump between 99 and the river. There's a real quiet joint in that town. Most of the customers are regulars and there's not a lot of traffic through the door. Probably not as much cash available as in some of the larger places but a lot safer. If I found myself low on dough around Dunsmuir, that's where I'd make my play."

This was absolutely all that Johnson knew about Castella. But with his lack of sophistication in such matters he knew that the fellow who told him about it was an old pro and he meant to heed his advice. It looked like a good proposition to him and it had been no trouble to convince Barr. Besides, they both had guns. What could go wrong?

Stick 'em Up!

They slowly walked the nearly seven miles that afternoon along the highway. There wasn't much traffic; it was Sunday; just two nondescript men walking along the road. If anyone saw them they didn't remember it. Johnson and Barr arrived at the place where the road that goes on into Castella turns off to the left about 5:30. They just sat down by the highway and waited until dark. About 9:30 or 10:00 o'clock they went on into "downtown" Castella in order to get on with it. The place turned out to be a pool hall. There were a few cars parked outside; it was called Padula's, also known as Mike's Place. They just strolled in, no big thing; two strangers in the pool hall wearing straw hats.

There were about five or six other men there. A couple was playing pool and the rest were at the bar. Johnson pulled out his 30 caliber Luger and Barr

Barr and Johnson robbed Padula's, or "Mike's Place" in Castella then drove away in a stolen car. It's almost as if there was no Prohibition in out of the way Castella, making it a popular destination for people from the Bay Area and even Hollywood. The saloon was still standing in the 1980s. (Shasta Historical Society)

produced his 38 Colt.

"Alright, stick'em up!" Barr shouted.

The other men looked a little surprised but no one seemed particularly excited. It was almost like a routine event. Clyde and Robert ordered all the men to place their hands on the bar. They then proceeded to lift each man's wallet and clean out the cash register. Barr put the money in his pocket and threw the wallets on the floor. They then ordered everyone into a back room that had no other exit. They got the key from the bartender and locked them in and went out the front door. They had told the men not to break out of there for a half hour.

When they got outside they looked around and picked out a car that had the key in the ignition. Barr got in the car first and started the engine. When Johnson opened the door to get in they noticed that there was a man asleep in the back seat. They politely aroused him and Barr escorted him at gun point back in through the front door of the bar, unlocked the back room and ordered him in with the others.

When Barr came back to the car they drove out the Castella entrance road to the highway and headed north back toward Dunsmuir. Before reaching town they took a right turn onto a side road and continued straight on through into North Dunsmuir. They then ditched the car out of sight on a side road. They also ditched their stiff-brimmed straw hats along with the car and started walking back south toward Dunsmuir. The hats were part of their "plan." They figured that these straw hats were a little bit unusual in this region. The idea was that all the witnesses would have noticed the hats which would distract them from noticing much of anything else in the way of a description. They figured that when the news of the holdup was out, everyone would be looking for two men wearing straw hats; of course they were very cleverly no longer wearing them. Their plan was to hide out in the Dunsmuir hobo jungle until the next freight train came through. If they were lucky there might even be one along before day break. This way they would soon be safely out of town on a train while any pursuers would be looking for the stolen car on the highway traveling north.

Robert and Clyde had worked out the final details of this plan while waiting for darkness beside the highway at the Castella turnoff. To them it all seemed perfectly logical. Now, as they strolled along the road back toward Dunsmuir it appeared that it had worked like clockwork. They practically had it made, or so it seemed.

George C. "Molly" Malone was the California State Highway Patrolman in Dunsmuir. It had been a quiet evening this night with nothing much at all happening within his jurisdiction. At about 10:30 p.m. his phone rang. It was a man named Lutman calling from Castella. He said he was the attendant at Padula's Pool Hall and that they had just been held up by two armed robbers. Malone asked him if he had any idea as to which way they went. Lutman told him that he thought they were headed north toward Dunsmuir.

Malone was an "old pro" and far from the excitable type even though an armed robbery was more than the usual run of calls that came his way. Inasmuch as it appeared that the robbers may be heading to ward Dunsmuir he decided to ask Dunsmuir Chief of Police Jack Daw if he would like to go with him to Castella to investigate the matter.

Frank R. "Jack" Daw was the Chief of Police of Dunsmuir. Being the "chief" hadn't given him command of much of a force but it was a position of honor and respect in the local community. Daw was a World War I veteran and had been in Dunsmuir for fifteen years. He had been a fireman on the Southern Pacific Railroad prior to his appointment as police chief. He had originally come from Oregon and was very well liked in Dunsmuir as well as throughout the county. He had a wife and three young children. When

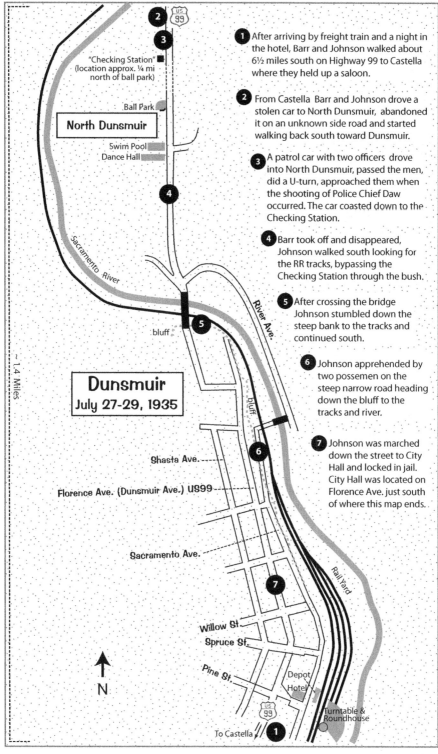

1 After arriving by freight train and a night in the hotel, Barr and Johnson walked about 6½ miles south on Highway 99 to Castella where they held up a saloon.

2 From Castella Barr and Johnson drove a stolen car to North Dunsmuir, abandoned it on an unknown side road and started walking back south toward Dunsmuir.

3 A patrol car with two officers drove into North Dunsmuir, passed the men, did a U-turn, approached them when the shooting of Police Chief Daw occurred. The car coasted down to the Checking Station.

4 Barr took off and disappeared, Johnson walked south looking for the RR tracks, bypassing the Checking Station through the bush.

5 After crossing the bridge Johnson stumbled down the steep bank to the tracks and continued south.

6 Johnson apprehended by two possemen on the steep narrow road heading down the bluff to the tracks and river.

7 Johnson was marched down the street to City Hall and locked in jail. City Hall was located on Florence Ave. just south of where this map ends.

"Checking Station" (location approx. ¼ mi north of ball park)

Ball Park

North Dunsmuir

Swim Pool
Dance Hall

Sacramento River

River Ave.

bluff

Dunsmuir
July 27-29, 1935

bluff

Shasta Ave.

Florence Ave. (Dunsmuir Ave.) US99

Sacramento Ave.

Rail Yard

Willow St.
Spruce St.
Pine St.

Depot
Hotel

Turntable & Roundhouse

To Castella

N

~ 1.4 Miles

US 99

US 99

he took the call from his friend Molly Malone he considered it routine as he willingly agreed to participate. He told Malone to meet him at the police station. When Officer Malone arrived, they both took off in Daw's car for Castella.

Two Officers Heed the Call

When the two officers arrived in Castella, they questioned all of the witnesses and looked over the ground. They learned that the robbers were young and had been wearing stiff-brimmed straw hats.

They learned that the two robbers had made their getaway in a 1929 Chevrolet belonging to John and Elmer Hall of Redding. By examining tire tracks on the dirt-surfaced Castella access road, they were able to ascertain that the fleeing holdup men had turned right onto Highway 99 and headed north toward Dunsmuir.

These two officers were very thorough. As they retraced the route of their bandits north, they stopped at each and every intersecting road, all of which were unpaved, and searched for the already established tire track patterns. Sure enough, they found where the robbers had turned off the highway just north of Castella at the old box factory and proceeded north on the old county road to the Castle Crags intersection where they had rejoined the highway and continued on to Dunsmuir. The two officers missed the tracks of the getaway vehicle where it had turned off to the right just before entering Dunsmuir.

When Malone and Daw arrived back in Dunsmuir they stopped at the local police station and notified night officer Joe Roderick to be on the lookout for the two fleeing bandits. The two officers, with Daw still driving, then proceeded north on 99 into North Dunsmuir.

When they reached the Robin Dell Gardens, two miles north of Dunsmuir in the North Dunsmuir area, they passed two men who were walking toward them on the right hand side of the highway. After they had passed they wondered if these two men might be the ones they were seeking.

The men they were after were supposed to be wearing straw hats and these two were bare headed. Also, their quarry was by all reasonable reckoning supposed to be racing north on Highway 99 in a stolen car, surely not peacefully strolling along the road in the middle of the night walking toward Dunsmuir. They decided to question them anyway. It was a definite long shot, but you never could be sure.

Daw made a slow U turn and then crossed the center line again. Traveling on the left hand side of the road, he eased the car along side of the two men. As Daw stopped the car, not a word was spoken but Malone immediately sensed danger. The two men came across up to the open window on Jack Daw's side. Malone reached down beside him for his submachine gun that had recently been issued to the Patrol on an experimental basis. He was preparing to get out when he suddenly heard Daw's voice.

"Get your hand away from that belt, Buddy," Daw commanded.

Daw's command went unheeded, and Malone's attempt to get room to operate his machine gun was too late.

Boom! Boom! Boom!

Officer Down

It was Johnson doing the firing. Daw was immediately hit; at impact he collapsed to his right, sprawling across Malone. Daw hadn't taken the car out of gear and when the shooting had started, his foot slipped off the clutch and the car lunged forward. As the car went forward slowly, Johnson waited for the rear fender to clear and then jumped up on the rear bumper. He used his gun barrel to break out the rear window and then continued firing through the glass. Bullets were rattling around everywhere inside the vehicle; the noise was deafening.

Malone then realized that the car was picking up speed and was about to crash against a service station located on the right side of the road. He was able to shrug Daw off of him enough to reach over and get control and swerve by the service station. By this time, Johnson's Luger clip was empty and he had jumped off the bumper. Malone raced down the road a short way to the Highway Patrol office, locally known as the "Checking Station," where he managed to stop the car.

He jumped out. No one was in sight; all was quiet. Not a bird whistled or a cricket chirped. All was still.

Malone was sure that Daw was dead. He rushed into the Checking Station and quickly told the night man to call Dr. Steele in Dunsmuir and tell him to come immediately and tend to Chief Daw. Malone went back outside and half lifted and dragged Daw from the automobile and got him up on the porch of the building. He then went back in and called Charles Carlquist at the Smoke Shop, instructing him to sound the fire alarm and commence organizing a posse from the group of volunteer firemen that would respond. Then he finally had a chance to check himself over. One of the bullets had grazed his left temple and two had pierced his hat, but otherwise he was unscathed.

It was now 12:45 a.m. and Dr. Steel arrived with an ambulance not far behind. Daw was taken to the Dunsmuir Hospital where Dr. Steel called on Dr. J. R. U. Campbell for consultation and examination. Daw was bleeding profusely from wounds below the left eye and left forearm, and several small wounds on the left side of the face. He had a gaping wound on the back of his head where a bullet had either entered or emerged.

Police Chief Frank R. "Jack" Daw died at 2:15 a.m., July 29th from multiple gunshot wounds fired from a 30 caliber Luger handgun. He was thirty-eight years old. His killers had gotten $35 in the holdup.

More Fateful Miscalculations

When Johnson had been standing on the rear bumper of the car and blazing away with his Luger through the back window, he was sure that he had killed both of the car's occupants. He had seen the driver take a hit and flop over against the other man. The car had begun to swerve and pick up speed as though it was totally out of control. He decided at any instant it was going to crash into that service station and so he jumped off.

He was utterly astounded when the car seemed to come back under control, turn and miss the station and proceed down the highway. This couldn't be. In his mind he had filled that car with lead; no human being could have survived. But there it was before his own eyes; someone in that car was still very much alive. He felt a terrible feeling of fear and frustration.

And where in hell was that damn Barr. He was nowhere to be seen. He was no help at all in the shoot-out and the last Johnson had seen of him, Barr was running across the road and disappearing down over the steep bank to the west. Johnson retraced the route of the careening car back to the place where the shooting had started. There on the ground he saw Barr's Colt 38; he picked it up and inspected the chamber. The chicken son of a bitch hadn't fired a shot. Johnson flung Barr's gun back to the ground in disgust. On top of everything else, Barr had the money from the holdup. Johnson knew he was in a real jam now and that he better make tracks out of there.

His first impulse was to start running up the highway to the north away from Dunsmuir. He could hail a passing car if one ever came along. If he was able to get in a car headed north, he could go a short way up the road, pull his gun, rob the driver and put him out. He could then take over the car. He would make a fast run on up the highway and as soon as he could get out of eyesight from the driver, he could seek a side road. He could go on it a

Dunsmuir Police Chief Daw's car after the shootout. (Siskiyou County Sheriff's Department)

short distance, ditch the car and make his way on foot to the railroad tracks and climb on the first freight that came by. He reasoned that all the pursuers would be in automobiles and would soon be converging on the spot where he now stood. But they would assume that he had fled north up the highway and that was where they would rush to look. They would soon find the ejected motorist and he would tell them that his assailant had headed north fast in his car, and that would be where the search would continue. This would give him time to make it to the tracks and hop a freight.

In all of Johnson's heavy thinking about the caper, this plan was perhaps the only sensible and logical one he had considered. It just might have worked.

Escape Route Dilemma

He started to trot along the highway to the north and then he suddenly stopped. Wait a minute, he thought. This might be the worst thing he could do. His mind was working like a trip hammer. I've already set it up for them to assume I have headed north on the highway, he reasoned. He figured that they were all going to rush into that assumption anyway based on what they would know at that point. What if no car at all came along the highway? He might just be delaying his chance to catch a freight. What if a train went through while he was fooling around with the car and making the entire planned detour? The thing to do, he figured, was to abandon such a complicated wild idea, get back to the tracks and get on a train as fast as possible while his pursuers were fooling around, searching the highways north of here. Also, he thought, he didn't know the territory. What was he going to find up some side road that he may select? Maybe he would go up one of these and get himself in the middle of some houses with no place to conceal the ditched car. No, that wouldn't work at all. He had to get back to the railroad and do it fast.

He spun around and took off with a fast pace heading south on the highway back toward Dunsmuir. It was downhill and easy going. He realized that if his new plan had a flaw, it was the bridge.

The highway bridge constituted the unofficial landmark delineating the line between Dunsmuir proper and North Dunsmuir. In Dunsmuir itself the Southern Pacific tracks lay east of the highway and the Sacramento River east of them. All run parallel north and south. At the extreme north end of Dunsmuir, the river and the parallel tracks make a 90° turn to the west, while the highway continues north over both of them on a very high concrete arch bridge.

By this time, Johnson knew enough of the territory to know that he had

Johnson walked across this long bridge over the Sacramento River as he sought access to the train tracks and a freight ride out of town. (Siskiyou County Museum)

to cross this bridge in order to get on the "track" side of the river. As far as he knew, it was the absolute only way that one could get there. He knew it was a potential bottleneck but he reasoned it was a chance he had to take. His only hope was to get to the bridge as fast as he could and get across before the alarm had gone out. He realized that the whole bunch of his tormenters would soon be crossing that bridge and he just had to get to it before they did.

Almost immediately as he started his race for the bridge he rounded a curve in the highway and there was a little building ahead all lit up with lights blazing and there in front of it was parked the Hudson automobile all shot up with the glass broken. There were men in the building. It was the Checking Station.

He knew instinctively what those men inside were doing. But he had to get by it because it was the only route to the bridge. He swerved off the road as fast as his legs could pump and dodged into the brush thickets on the west side. Hunched over, stumbling and falling, he made his way past this island of activity in an otherwise quiet and peaceful scene. About fifty yards beyond the checking station he emerged from the brush and continued his headlong pace down the road toward his goal.

He arrived at the north side of the bridge breathing heavily. He gazed across. As he stood there in the night at the north abutment of the bridge he could see the shiny top surfaces of the railroad track glimmering in the moonlight way down below but across the river. He had to cross the bridge even though he would be exposed to view with no place to retreat. He didn't know that all he would have had to do at that point in order to reach the tracks was to take a little side road that branched off to the left of the abutment. This road went down into the bottom of the river canyon and followed along the river bank; it was known as the River Road. It only went a short way around the great bend in the river and then crossed on a low level bridge which brought it to the tracks. But Johnson didn't know this. Even though this flight back through Dunsmuir had been in the original plan, they hadn't done their homework.

No one was on the bridge. There was a good chance left. Just as he was at mid-span, he looked up and here came the headlights of an automobile. He pulled out the reloaded Luger and waited. The car approached, seemed to slow down, and then went right on by him. So far, so good. He quickly made his way across the remainder of the bridge. Now he was on the same side of the river as the tracks were. He quickly scooted around the end of the bridge railing and over the bank he went. It was nearly straight off. He slid, fell, bounced and slid some more and suddenly he was right in the middle of the rail road track. With a sigh of relief he picked himself up and started down the tracks toward the great curve which he knew would lead right into the freight yards. But the freight yards were not his destination.

The plan, which in fact seemed to be working, was to get himself back through town to a point south of Dunsmuir. Here he could station himself at a point where he figured would be well out of the excitement of a manhunt effort. If he could get between the tracks and the highway he could attempt to hitch a southbound ride in an automobile. If a southbound freight came along before he could flag a ride, he could hop the freight. So in accordance with the plan, his immediate objective was to reach an area undetected that was south of town. He figured that in order to do this he must leave the tracks temporarily because it was too risky to attempt the trip through the middle of the freight yards.

Johnson remembered the night before when they had come into the town and got off the train. It seemed so long ago. And then when they left the hotel and walked up the hill to get on the highway, they had checked the lay of the land. That hotel, right across the street from the tracks, was on a street named Sacramento Avenue. That avenue was really a very narrow street that traveled north and south. It lay in the bottom of the canyon at the same elevation as the tracks. He remembered looking north up that street and saw that it immediately went up a steep hill until it disappeared from sight. When he and Barr had left the hotel, they had gone up a very steep street traveling due west in order to get up on the highway. He remembered that at the point where this steep street they had gone up reached the highway, Highway 99 itself was called Florence Avenue.

In thinking back over what he had earlier observed, he now reasoned that the two avenues at that point ran parallel, north and south. He had already traveled north in the stolen car along Florence Avenue and knew that eventually it made the big curve to the left and then another one to the right in order to go across the bridge. Therefore, he figured, Sacramento Avenue had to continue up that hill he had observed from the hotel and then eventually go on down to the canyon bottom again to the tracks. As Johnson now walked along the tracks it was Sacramento Avenue that he hoped to find. He knew it would be impossible to get through town on the highway because it would soon be full of people looking for him. Besides it was too far from the tracks. He figured that he could stay out of sight on Sacramento Avenue and keep his desired position between the highway and the tracks. He kept walking and soon the tracks began to make that big bend to the south. That street had to appear soon or he would be in the freight yards.

He began to lose faith in his reasoning. He pressed on further and finally he saw it. Or was that it? It was just a little narrow road coming down off the hill to the bottom of the canyon. Here it crossed the tracks and then crossed the river on a low level bridge, the bridge he unknowingly could have used off River Road to cross the river. Beyond that it seemed to curve upstream but he wasn't interested in it beyond this point. He looked it over very thoroughly. It was too rough and crude to be an actual street but what else could it be. At least, he figured, it must be an extension of that street. If he followed it up the hill toward town it was bound to get him onto Sacramento Avenue.

He started walking up the road. It was steep going. He stayed in close to the high cut-bank on the right side to avoid casting a silhouette. Suddenly he saw a pair of headlights approaching. A car had come over the crest of the hill and was coming toward him. He felt for the Luger in his pocket. It was coming very slowly. One person, alone. He was ready, but it went right on by with the driver hardly glancing at him. After it passed, he heard the driver shifting down the gears in order to break the speed.

Nothing to worry about; just a lone motorist going somewhere in the night. Johnson continued up the hill. He began to figure that he had it made. By golly, he thought, he was going to show this hick town a thing or two. But he hadn't figured on the likes of Charles Tracey and Steve Abgaroff.

Charley Tracey, a Southern Pacific Railroad employee, and Steve Abgaroff, a local taxi operator, had teamed up together and reported to the city hall as posse volunteers. They were the last of the many volunteers that had checked in. When the police department swore them in, they were handed shotguns. Abgaroff refused the offer of the shotgun remarking that he wanted to go home and get his personal Luger pistol. The two men then drove to the Abgaroff residence in south Dunsmuir before undertaking their search for the hunted men.

Upon obtaining the pistol, they traveled northward with Abgaroff driving through the business district of Dunsmuir on Florence Avenue. As they did so, they discussed their strategy. They figured that all the other posse men that had gone out ahead of them would have converged on the scene of the shooting in North Dunsmuir. That area must be teeming with people speeding up and down the highway or beating the brush on either side. When they reached the intersection of Florence and Sacramento Avenues, they stopped momentarily. They had figured that with the North Dunsmuir area probably over-staffed, they ought to get themselves in a location where they could watch the bridge and tracks. If those gunmen were still in North Dunsmuir and heading south, they would undoubtedly cross that bridge; the fugitives would have no way of knowing about River Road and the low level bridge. If they were trying to make their getaway on a freight train, they had to get near the tracks. Tracey and Abgaroff knew of a place where they could watch both the bridge and the tracks.

Sacramento Avenue is east of Florence Avenue with the two streets running parallel. The two possemen were now sitting where Sacramento Avenue veers to the west and ends itself at a sort of "Y" intersection with Florence. Florence Avenue, being Highway 99, continues northward. Not far beyond the intersection, Florence veers to the west and again to the right and crosses the bridge.

Right at the Sacramento and Florence Avenue "Y" there is another narrow extension of Sacramento Avenue which takes off slightly to the northeast. It goes down a steep hill and finally reaches the bottom of the canyon near the tracks which it crosses. It then crosses the river and becomes River Road. At that point the highway bridge off to the left is in full view but high overhead. It was down this road that Abgaroff now headed the car. It was less than twenty minutes since they had left the city hall; little did they know that they had a "rendezvous with destiny" half way down Blacksmith Hill.

"We'll Let You Have It!"

The road was quite rough and very quickly rolled off into a steep incline. It was the kind of road that called for a slow speed. Abgaroff and Tracey had just cleared the intersection of the two avenues and were slowly approaching the point where the steepness begins when there appeared in the headlights a young man walking toward them on the left side of the road close in to the high cut bank. He appeared to fit the description of one of the gunmen that had been given to the two men only a short time ago at city hall. Only this man was hatless.

When they saw the approaching man on foot, Tracey ducked down on the floor of the car so that he wouldn't be seen and spoke to Abgaroff. "That has got to be one of them. He'll be watching for two men. I'll stay out of sight. Go on past him a little ways and slow the car down but don't stop; I'll slip out and take him unaware."

As they went by the walker, he seemed to merely glance into the car without undue interest and continued his journey up the road. Tracey quietly eased himself out of the right hand side of the car. Abgaroff then made a lot of noise with the gear shift to indicate that he was merely shifting down in order to continue on the steep downhill grade. As soon as he was over the crown of the hill, Abgaroff stopped the car and also quietly got out.

When Tracey had stepped out of the car he went right to work. He quickly crossed over to the other side of the road and headed back up the hill directly behind the suspect. In a calm but firm voice Tracey said, "Stick 'em up and stand where you are."

Johnson's hands went up. Abgaroff in just a few moments arrived to help his partner. The two men ordered Johnson to start walking up the hill and to keep his eyes off them. Johnson obeyed.

At one point Johnson started to lower his hands but this was met with the stern command, "Get out in the center of the road and keep 'em up or we'll let you have it."

Johnson began to lose hope. Just a few minutes ago he was thinking that he had it made. Now, here he was stumbling up this crazy road with his hands up with two local yokels holding a shotgun and pistol on him. And yokels or not, these two guys seemed to know what they were doing. If I could just get to my Luger, he thought, maybe there was still a chance. Just then he looked forward to the top of the hill. There was a street light or something up there, and it was the goddamn highway that this road was coming into. What in hell had become of Sacramento Avenue? He knew that up in the light with a lot of highway traffic would be no place to be making a move for the pistol. He had to do it now.

Johnson said out loud, "Well, you might as well come over and take my gun off me."

Tracey and Abgaroff knew better than that. It was dark here. If they tried to disarm him here, he would probably attempt to make a lunge for the gun and get it into action. They knew he was now a desperate man and that this was what he had in mind when he had suggested it. No, they didn't buy that one. They told him to just continue on up the road.

When the three of them arrived at the top of the hill where the road joined the intersection of Florence and Sacramento Avenues, his two captors very methodically disarmed Johnson under the illumination of a street light. They took his Luger pistol and a clip of ammunition. Johnson now knew that he had bought it; there was no escape from the likes of these two.

The three of them still had a considerable distance to go in order to get to the city jail at the police station. Abgaroff and Tracey knew that there were supposed to be two gunmen. They feared an attack yet from the second man. It was now after three o'clock in the morning and there was little traffic on the highway. Obviously the two gunmen had somehow become separated;

but what if the other one had stolen a car and happened to come along as the three of them were marching down the street?

Well, if this happened, surely he would be coming from the north. As they had been all evening, the two possemen were very cool and logical in their manner of handling this potential problem. They started a single file march right down the center of the highway with Johnson in the lead, his hands still held high. Abgaroff was a few feet behind with his gun at the ever ready. Several yards behind him Tracey came with his gun out and observing careful vigilance.

Abgaroff was constantly telling Johnson to keep his eyes forward. This way Abgaroff could glance from side to side in case the second gunman might make a run at them. Tracey was holding back any traffic that might come up behind them on the theory that Johnson may try to jump on a car as it went by. It seemed like an eternity to Tracey and Abgaroff, but this procession finally arrived at City Hall.

As they approached their destination, Tracey began to think of his friend Jack Daw. He said to Johnson, "I've got a notion to let you have it."

In a sort of resigned voice, Johnson replied. "Go ahead."

But without incident, Johnson was turned over to jailer W. J. Stevenson and lodged in the city jail. At least one of Jack Daw's killers was now behind bars. This would give the citizens of Dunsmuir some relief.

Safe Behind Bars?

But ironically it seemed to give Johnson some relief also. He was almost happy to be free of those two characters that had apprehended him. He had misjudged them. He admitted to himself that they were not "yokels". Those men knew about guns and how to handle them. And they knew how to handle themselves too. At least, he thought, he was now safe behind bars; safe from the two men who had taken him and safe from any irate citizens that may be inclined to take a pot shot at him. These were the thoughts running through Johnson's mind as the cell door clanged shut.

He figured that he could work something out later about escaping from this "hick town" jail. But then he had second thoughts. He had been wrong before when he underestimated these "yokels." He decided that he had better play it very cool from here on out. He decided that he had better be very cooperative with these people while he carefully devised a plan. These "country boys" could very well turn out to be more than he had bargained for.

Before eleven o'clock that Monday morning the *Dunsmuir News*, nor-

Johnson in handcuffs at the Siskiyou County Jail, with only hours left to live. (Siskiyou County Sheriff's Department)

mally a weekly that came out on Fridays, was on the street with an "extra." The *News* staff had been busy since the first call for a posse had been sounded. The extra carried all of the facts concerning the hold up, the killing and the capture in a very thorough manner. Copies had been dispatched to the neighboring towns of Mt. Shasta City, McCloud and Weed. It was a complete scoop for the *News*. It was so complete in content and so lucid in description of all of these lurid, exciting and tragic events that little could be added or changed when the competing papers in the other cities in the county later came out on their regular publication days.

When Johnson was questioned in his cell that morning he admitted that he had done the shooting. He went so far as to say that he didn't think his partner had fired a shot. He did claim that when he walked up to the car the officers had started shooting first. Of course Malone disputed this vehemently. It was later found that Daw's gun contained three empty cartridges but there was no way to ascertain whether or not they had been fired that night or sometime prior. At any rate, Malone held steadfast with his version of that particular consideration and the question was not pursued further at that time as it was felt by the interrogators that it was immaterial to the case.

By Monday afternoon a sizeable crowd of friends of Jack Daw was gathering around the city jail. Epithets a plenty were directed toward the occupant of the jail. There was much discussion of the fact that George Hall who had murdered a peace officer and a civilian in cold blood at Yreka just two years earlier was alive and well. He was still successfully avoiding the execution to which he had been sentenced.

There were also in this group some members of the rowdy element whose jeers and catcalls in the direction of the jail helped tighten the growing tension. By this time Deputys Ed Mathews and Martin Lange were on the scene and taking note of the explosive atmosphere that was building up. They decided that they could not wait another day or two for an inquest to be held. They therefore made arrangements for the immediate removal of the prisoner to the County Jail in Yreka. This was safely accomplished before any real leadership in the gathering crowd emerged.

But Where is Robert Barr?

As soon as Abgaroff and Tracey had checked into the police station with the captured fugitive the word went out. By daylight, most of the posse had come in. All of them had the same report. No trace of the other man. From that time on the city hall became a veritable command post for an army of searchers for the fleeing Barr.

When a citizen is murdered in mountain country there is never a shortage of gun toting men eager to offer their services in a manhunt. But when a police officer is murdered, the response from the contiguous police forces results in a large additional layer of added personnel available for the task at hand.

Captain George Daley of the California Highway Patrol squad headquartered in Yreka immediately responded in person with four of his patrolmen in addition to Officer G. C. Malone. Highway Patrol Inspector Fred L. Goodloe of Redding, Shasta County, brought in Captain H. F. Foster and four of his officers. Soon to arrive was Officer Royal Trimble from neighboring Trinity County, Redding Chief of Police H. F. Riley, Sheriff Lowe of Klamath Falls, Oregon and Shasta County Sheriff W. W. Sublett.

The Southern Pacific Railroad Company furnished two of their private officers and of course the entire Dunsmuir police force was on hand. Siskiyou County Sheriff W. G. Chandler, himself a former Southern Pacific Company officer and previous resident of Dunsmuir was recovering from an operation in Yreka and unable to personally be on hand. His entire staff from the county office was made available under the leadership of Acting Sheriff Ed Mathews. In addition to all this professional help, a thoroughbred tracking bloodhound was brought in from Oregon.

Most of the possemen who had participated in the first search were still on the job after an hour or two of sleep. As the word had gone out, many additional local men reported to the City Hall for posse duty. This large group of volunteers was quickly organized into a manageable body with the professional officers in leadership roles.

The main focus of the search for Barr started from the site of the shooting. From questioning of Johnson it was determined that Barr had fled to the west, downhill over the embankment behind the Robin Dell Gardens. The dog was taken to this point and soon picked up a scent. Down through the tangled brush and trees the dog led the pursuers, but this was to no avail. The scent soon petered out and the chase evolved into merely a systematic brush beating operation. The entire manhunt was then reorganized into a zoned foot by foot ever expanding circle from the murder site outward. This took the searchers into almost impenetrable brush fields, through steep mountainous timber terrain, across deep gullies and over rocky promontories. But nary a sign of their man could be found.

Officers interviewed anyone they could find that might have been on the highway or the streets during the events in question. People living in homes all along every conceivable escape route were interviewed. A thorough search of the railroad yards and the hobo jungle was conducted. Nothing was found.

Forest Service lookouts were notified to be on the watch for unidentified camp fires that might crop up within their viewing area. William Randolph Hearst, the San Francisco newspaper publisher, had a summer home [Wyntoon] on the nearby McCloud River. His private airplane was enlisted in the search. Rumors came pouring in from people that thought they may have seen the fleeing fugitive. All of these were checked out. But still nothing useful was produced.

This activity continued at a feverish pace for two days and nights and then slowly tapered off. In the meantime, Owen Kessell, investigator for the State Department of Criminal Investigation, had arrived in Dunsmuir. By means of ballistics tests, he had determined that the bullet that killed Daw had come from Johnson's Luger pistol. With this testimony available, an inquest was scheduled for Tuesday afternoon.

The inquest was conducted by County Coroner Felix J. Kunz of Fort

Jones, Deputy Coroner Lloyd Noble of Mt. Shasta City, District Attorney James Davis and Court Reporter Ralph McMurry of Yreka. A large crowd was in attendance but the proceedings proved to be anticlimactic. By this time all of the pertinent facts in the case thus far were well known by all in the community. *The Dunsmuir News* had performed such a complete reporting job on the facts of the killing and capture of Johnson that nothing new could be added. As all of the principals in the case were local citizens, word of mouth took care of spreading any information that may have come out since the *News* extra had appeared on Monday morning. The confessed suspect was in custody and Kessell's ballistics tests had definitely tied him to the actual killing. The inquest was just a formality.

But afterward, outside the hearing room the muttering and cursing by the crowd in vilification of Johnson resumed. The name of George Hall, the still unexecuted cop killer from two years ago, was overheard again and again in these epithets. Some in the crowd viewed these remarks as being ominous of something yet to come. It was not loud or boisterous; there was nothing to indicate a potential riot. No call to action; no demagoguery. Just a little thing, but it was there.

Funeral services for Chief R. F. Daw were scheduled for Friday afternoon. His sister and three brothers together with their families had arrived in Dunsmuir from various cities in Oregon and California. His mother was on a visit to Iowa at the time of the shooting and had left immediately for California. All were there together with the wife of the deceased and his three young children. The huge crowd that overflowed the facilities in the Dunsmuir Masonic Temple together with the bountiful number of floral offerings was testimony to the high esteem in which Chief Daw was held. Suitable eulogies were read, with ceremonies conducted by the Odd Fellows Lodge. Methodist services were offered with the American Legion Honor Guard standing by.

Rumblings of Retribution

But when the services were over and the bereaved family had left, the crowd outside began again the talk of retribution; just quiet discussions among little knots of people gathered outside the hall. These were protestations of the tragedy of a senseless killing of such a fine man. And again there were the criticisms of a legal system that allowed killers of this kind to escape indefinitely the ultimate punishment for their crimes. Here again this talk was quiet and low keyed; entirely understandable under the circumstances. Surely not something that could lead to anything beyond the frustrations of

Police Chief Daw's funeral procession down Florence Avenue in Dunsmuir. (Siskiyou County Sheriff's Department)

the mood and the moment.

But notwithstanding the low-keyed, quiet discussions that were evidenced in the sunshine of that balmy summer afternoon after the funeral, there had been other forces at work.

The murder had taken place in the early morning hours of Monday, July 29th. Four nights had gone by since then until the afternoon of the funeral on Friday. On one or more of these nights, furtive clandestine gatherings had been organized. These were meetings of more determined men, men sterner and harder in nature than those participating in the idle conversations after the funeral. These meetings included men of respect and leadership in the community. These were the men that were accustomed to demanding action and then seeing that it happened. They were men that were driven by one or both of two considerations of the events that had transpired. Some were driven by their anger over the senseless slaying of a friend and honored member of the community. Others were motivated by the even larger issue of the injustice inherent in the "system's" apparent inability to bring appropriate punishment down on the perpetrators of such crimes. They were convinced that the wheels of justice served as no deterrent and this case in particular would be no exception, as evidenced by the facts of the Kent/Quigley murder case in Yreka two years prior.

Probably most of them were driven by convictions based on both of these considerations. It can be said that these men had no sympathy for so called "mob" action. They were men of considered judgment who rightly or wrongly arrived at a decision and then organized a plan for its implementation. There were few among them that would condone lawlessness in general, but all of them felt that sometimes in the affairs of mankind it was up to the people themselves to act to see that justice was meted out. And at their last meeting on the night after the funeral, they firmly decided to do just that.

Deputy Sheriff Ed Mathews was now serving as Acting Sheriff due to the illness of Sheriff Chandler. These added responsibilities during the manhunt had been keeping him on the run. On Friday, the day of the funeral, both he and Deputy Sheriff Martin Lange were in Dunsmuir in the same automobile. Mathews had been actively engaged for a stretch of seventy-two hours without sleep. While in Dunsmuir he had heard from Mt. Shasta Chief of Police Jack Roberts that there was a report that someone had been raiding a private citizen's vegetable garden near Mt. Shasta. Chief Robert's idea was that this could possibly be Barr. He felt that maybe Barr was still holed up somewhere in the area and had been raiding that garden for food. He suggested to Mathews that they stake it out that night and maybe they could nail Barr. Mathews agreed.

This created a problem because the time was fast approaching when the jailer in Yreka had to be relieved. Either Mathews or Lange was scheduled to take the night shift at the jail. So Mathews and Lange came back to Yreka and flipped a coin to see which one of them would take the jailer's shift and which one must return to Mt. Shasta for the stakeout. Lange won the toss and chose the jail shift.

Mathews called Tex Harmon in Dunsmuir and asked him to participate in the stakeout that evening. Harmon was a railroad employee and one of the original posse volunteers. He had been giving the sheriff's department nearly round the clock assistance during the manhunt.

The Garden Raider

Mathews then grabbed a couple of hours sleep in Yreka and by nine o'clock he was on the road again. He met Chief Roberts and Tex Harmon at the vegetable garden. Each of them took a different angle of view and commenced the long vigil. Sure enough, about 12:30 a flashlight beam came approaching the garden. As the man entered the fenced garden the three officers jumped out. It was not Barr. It was a very young man, not much more than a boy. His story was that he had heard of the midnight raids on the vegetable garden and had the same idea as the officers. He had decided that it must be Barr and was conducting his own posse. The officers sort of believed him; at least they knew he was not the fugitive that they were after. They had no time to be fooling around with a "garden raider" under these circumstances, so they let him go.

Mathews was very tired and sleepy in spite of the little cat nap that he had in Yreka but he still wanted to do one more thing while he was in the area. He wanted to go back down to Dunsmuir and check out the train schedule. It seemed that there was some doubt about exactly what time the train was to go through, but he wanted to try and be on hand if one did. He and Tex Harmon bid Chief Roberts good night and headed for Dunsmuir. After checking in at the depot several times without getting positive information from the railroad, they decided to go into the diner for coffee, after which Mathews would mosey on home to Yreka for a long awaited sleep.

As Mathews and Harmon were seated in the diner, they looked up and saw Joe Roderick, the Police Night Officer, come in the door. Roderick seemed greatly surprised to see Sheriff Mathews.

"What are you doing down here in Dunsmuir tonight?" Roderick said. "The word around here is that there's going to be some big action on this case in Yreka tonight. I hear that a bunch of cars left here together about 11:30 bound for Yreka."

Mathews was dumfounded. Every muscle in his body tightened. His brain was pounding against his temples.

"Jesus Christ!" he exclaimed. As he whirled for the door, he shouted over his shoulder, "Call the sheriff's office!"

He leaped for the car, switched on both red flashers and shoved the throttle to the floorboard. With the siren on full blast he commenced a wild fifty mile dash for Yreka. As he started to roll he glanced at his watch. It was 2:40 a.m. He realized he was too late. The phone call was too late.

Back in Yreka

Deputy Sheriff Martin Lange had gone on duty at the jail in Yreka at about the same time that Mathews had headed back down the highway toward Mt. Shasta. Night duty at the jail was always a quiet time. Lange had made the rounds of the cell blocks in the South Annex and had found everything in order. He returned to the office in the north wing and sat down. It had been a long day and he was tired. He sat down at the jailer's desk, removed his shoes, and leaned back to catch some shuteye. He readily drifted off to sleep.

About 1:30 a.m. Fleming "Hank" Martin was walking past the jail on Oregon Street. He lived across the street from the jail and was returning home from his job as night cook at the Broadway Lunch Cafe. He saw a long string of headlights approach the area and come to a stop in the yard between the jail and the courthouse. He was awe struck and alarmed, but he realized immediately what was happening and paused to watch the excitement.

Approximately thirty-five masked men very quietly alighted from the cars and gathered near the jail office door. They held a whispered conversation and two of them come over to where Martin was standing.

"Don't be alarmed," they told him. "We have a little job to do here and we just want you to stay with us for a little while."

Without making another sound, someone in the group lightly knocked on the wooden office door. Deputy Martin Lange opened the door a few inches against a loose chain-stop and said, "Who is it?"

"We've come to get Johnson," one of the masked men called back. "Give us the keys to the jail."

"You'll not take my prisoner," was Lange's response.

With that, a heavy shoulder crashed against the door easily tearing out the chain. Lange had been standing behind the door when it flew open mashing him against the adjoining wall; he was effectively trapped behind the door. The crowd then rushed into the office and began ransacking it for the keys. Soon a large ring of keys was found and everyone came out of the office back into the yard where the cars were parked. They forcibly brought Lange with them. He was still without his shoes as they tied his hands together and down to a rope around his waist. He was ordered to get into one of the cars.

Two men got into the car with Deputy Lange and took off. At very high speeds, they drove him six miles east to the little town of Montague. There they turned south on the Montague-Grenada road and traveled another eleven miles on through the hamlet of Grenada.

In the excitement of the high speed ride under way, Lange said to his abductors, "You don't need to kill us all just because you're going to hang a man." There was no response.

Stranded and Shoeless

At a point approximately two miles south of Grenada, they stopped.

They cut Lange's hands loose and let him out on the graveled road and drove off back toward Yreka. As the car pulled out, Lange looked at the rear license plate. It had been removed. Still in his bare feet, Lange took off toward Grenada as fast as the sharp gravel allowed. When he got there he commenced banging on a few doors but his story seemed so far-fetched, no one would believe him. He gave up this effort in exasperation and took to the road again. Soon a passing car approached and he was able to stop it with the use of his police whistle, which was still in his pocket.

Deputy Martin Lange, looking a bit bewildered after his ordeal, had been kidnapped from the jail and stranded, shoeless, near Grenada. (Siskiyou County Sheriff's Department)

He said later, "That was a hell of way to treat a man."

While Lange was urging his commandeered driver for more speed back to Yreka, Acting Sheriff Ed Mathews was roaring in the same direction with lights, siren and throttle wide open. Lange, like Mathews, was now also too late.

When the car bearing Lange and his two abductors had left the court yard, the remaining masked men turned to the steel exterior door of the South Annex of the jail. As they tried each and every key on the ring, none would work. With some minor cursing they went back to the jail office door and found that in the excitement of getting Lange out, the door had been slammed shut and it was now locked and latched. They again tried all the keys on the ring and none would work in that door either. This was a small problem easily solved with heavy shoulders banging against the wooden door when it burst open. A frantic search through the office soon produced another huge ring of keys; this one was the right one.

As the masked men opened the main jail door and went in, a feeling of great agitation among the prisoners was immediately apparent. There were some in the center "tank" and some in single cells. All of them knew exactly what was happening. All of them knew exactly who it was that the men wanted. But all of them were also absolutely petrified with the fear that there would be some mistake in identity. Every last one of them immediately raised his arm and pointed to the prisoner in the southwest corner single cell, the same one in which George Hall, the killer of Kent and Quigley had been held.

Several of the other prisoners called out with remarks such as, "there's your man" or "that's him over there" or "that's Johnson." Even with all this help, the masked group was very thorough and took the time to question a few of them so that no mistake would be made. Some of the men seemed to know Johnson anyway. His picture had been in the various county papers and surely some of them had actually seen him in person.

There was otherwise little talking inside the jail and Johnson himself resisted only feebly without uttering a sound. They quickly opened Johnson's cell door, bound his wrists and led him outside. They forced Johnson into one of the cars and all of the vehicles began moving out. The occupants of the last car told Hank Martin, the hapless observer, that he could go home now but "keep your mouth shut."

Strung Up

There are no known witnesses to what happened next with the exception of the participants; and none of them has ever uttered a word about it. We know that the group had obviously had the lay of the land well cased. They all drove to a spot approximately where there was an open-air dance floor known as the Moonlit Oaks. At a point just south of it and a few hundred yards from where the Ft. Jones road branches off from Highway 99, there stood beside the road a tall lonely pine tree. Here they took Johnson out of the car, stripped the shirt from his back, tied his legs and put a noose around his neck. Willing hands then pulled him up until his legs dangled four feet off the ground. They tied the other end of the rope to a fence post and Clyde Johnson danced on air.

The auto caravan quickly loaded, reassembled and drove back to the intersection, where they got on the highway and headed south. Again, no one was in sight. Not a bird whistled or a cricket chirped. All was still.

Meanwhile, Acting Sheriff Ed Mathews had been sailing along the highway as fast as his car could travel. When he passed the 99 Ranch, a roadhouse just north of Weed, with his lights flashing and siren blaring, he met an oncoming string of headlights headed south. Some of the drivers in the caravan honked their horns at him as he sailed by. It was here he became convinced that he was really and truly too late.

When he came roaring to a skidding stop in the courthouse yard it was exactly 3:20 a.m., precisely forty minutes after he had left Dunsmuir. All the lights in the jail buildings were blazing brightly. Both the office and the main jail door were wide open. Deputy Lange, who had arrived back just a few minutes earlier, came ambling out of the office shouting, "Oh God, they got him."

Lange looked a sight. He had retrieved his shoes from the office by that time but had still not gotten around to tying one of them. His shirt tails were hanging out and the rope that had been tied around his waist was still there. He was ragged and dirty. The courtyard had begun to fill up with people and there was general pandemonium.

As ordered by the lynchers, Hank Martin had gone across Oregon Street to Mrs. Haight's boarding house where he lived with his brother, "Dutch" Martin. He had immediately aroused his brother and told him the tale. After a short while, the Martin brothers had taken their car and driven south of town in an attempt to figure out where Johnson had been taken.

They got it right the first time and discovered the body hanging from the tree. They then rushed back to town and told all in the boarding house of what they knew. From there, the news traveled fast throughout the community.

The Martin brothers then took Florence Smith, one of the other boarders in the house, along with two other girls back out to the hanging tree to view the results of the exciting evening's events. When this party was at the lynch site there was still no one else there.

Mathews ordered Deputy Lange to get the jail locked up and make a count of the remaining prisoners. He went on into the office and called Sheriff Chandler, who was still recovering at home from his operation. Mathews related all he knew about the event and Chandler instructed him to call the other authorities. Mathews accordingly called the county physician, Dr. A. H. Newton, the deputy coroner, Frank Bills and as per Chandler's suggestion, he also called "Snappy" Goodrich, the local photographer. Mathews and Lange then proceeded to the hanging site.

Upon their arrival there at the site they waited for the others. In due course, Dr. Newton arrived and pronounced the victim dead. Goodrich took several pictures of the body hanging from the tree. Then Mathews and Lange cut the rope and the body was taken away by Frank Bills in a hearse.

Clyde L. Johnson had died by the noose at approximately 3:00 a.m., August 3rd, 1935 as a result of the murder of a Siskiyou County police officer. The whole train of events had been started by a $35 holdup. Johnson hadn't even gotten the $35.

77

The Aftermath

Robert Miller Barr wasn't captured until the following year. The interesting and unusual twist in connection with that event will be covered with its relationship with another case later.

On August 5th, Kunz & Bills Undertaking Parlor received a telegram from Johnson's father, C. L. Johnson, Sr., at Greensboro, Alabama, requesting information as to the charges for shipping the body to Alabama. Upon receiving the requested information he wired that he could not raise the money. Johnson was buried by the County in "Potter's Field."

On August 9th, Undersheriff W. J. Neilon, acting for ailing Sheriff Chandler, issued a statement to the effect that "the sheriff's office will do everything in its power to identify the members of the mob and will assist in every way possible in furnishing information and evidence to the Grand Jury. At this time, however, due to the absence of witnesses at the county jail and at the scene of the lynching, no member of the mob has been identified." Nothing ever came of this effort.

On August 10th, Coroner Felix Kunz and Court Reporter Ralph McMurry convened another inquest to inquire into the death of one Clyde L. Johnson. At this inquest, District Attorney James Davis participated. No new information was obtained.

The events related here of course had tremendous political and social impact upon the people of Siskiyou County. In fact these events had effect upon all serious and thinking people throughout the United States who were aware of the case. If it is true that the editorial efforts of a community's newspapers reflect the attitudes of their readers, a perusal of the relevant local articles and editorials is worthwhile.

On Monday afternoon the *Siskiyou News*, which was published in Yreka, was first out with the news coverage of the lynching. What follows appeared on the front page as a "news" article even though it appears to be more "editorial" in nature.

VIGILANTES AGAIN ACTIVE AS SLAYERS OF
JACK DAW LYNCHED EARLY SATURDAY
Masked Mob of 35 Men Leave
C. L. Johnson's Body
Hanging in Pine Tree Three
Miles Southwest of Yreka

..... There can be no appeal from the "Lynch Law" sentence given C. L. Johnson, confessed slayer of Frank R. "Jack" Daw, popular Chief of Police of Dunsmuir, who was shot to death on the night of July 28 while attempting to question Johnson and his companion, later identified as Robert Miller Barr, in connection with the robbery of a beer joint at Castella. Nor will Johnson evade execution of the sentence for a period of years as has George Hall, convicted slayer of Stephen Kent, popular member of the Highway Patrol, who was shot to death along with Lester Quigley, well known garage man, by Hall on the evening of March 10, 1933, and who is still awaiting the outcome of an appeal.

Johnson is dead. His body left swaying at the end of a rope from the limb of a pine tree three miles southwest of Yreka on the Fort Jones road by a vigilante committee which took him from the county jail about 2 a.m. Friday, escorted him in a caravan of automobiles filled with grim men, their faces covered with handkerchiefs, to the wind swept flat west of the Moonlit Oaks, where they hanged him. Finis has been written to one career of crime, and a summary notice served on gunmen that Siskiyou citizens will not stand idly by while officers of the law are shot down in cold blood .....

On Thursday, August 8th, the *Mt. Shasta Herald* featured a lengthy statement released by Siskiyou County District Attorney James G. Davis. This was a very scholarly effort that seemed to say it all. It was felt by many to be the majority view of the entire community. It reads in part as follows:

The lynching of Johnson came as a surprise to me although I noted at the funeral of Officer Daw, who leaves a wife and several children, the tendency of the citizens to casually ask of me the status of the Hall case, referring to George Hall, alias George Manning, who shot and killed Deputy Sheriff Lester Quigley and Stephen Kent, highway patrolman, in March 1933. On numerous occasions since I took office in January of this year, citizens have asked me the question, when Hall would be hung and why he had not been hung before. The average citizen, with full knowledge that Hall had shot down two Siskiyou County officers in the streets of Yreka and within the sight of dozens of citizens,

The sobering sight of Johnson hanging from a pine near Moonlit Oaks just south of Yreka. Local photographer "Snappy" Goodrich photographed the scene. (Siskiyou County Museum)

cannot understand the delay in his execution. To me, the Hall case and the attendant delay and the failure of his execution in the face of the facts is the direct cause of the lynching of Johnson.

As District Attorney of this county, I want to say here and now that the apathy of the supreme court of the United States and of the federal courts through which the George Hall case is being processed by slow manipulation, has created, in the citizens of this county, a distrust of the legal machinery represented by the upper courts of this country.

In the case of the People vs. George Hall, I find on the examination of the record in this county, that the order allowing appeal to the supreme court of the United States was made on the second day of April, 1934, Officers Quigley and Kent were killed on the 10th day of March, 1933. The defendant, Hall, was quickly convicted in Siskiyou County and sentenced to be hanged. It took practically a year for the machinery of the upper courts of this state to function in an atrocious case of this kind. This case, and this case alone, has created an uncontrollable unrest among the citizens of this county and I believe, rightly so. The dilatory tactics resorted to by shyster lawyers in the upper courts who base their pleas upon trivial technicalities leads directly to mob violence. It is my opinion, that in cases such as the Hall case, and such as the case in which Johnson was hanged, the duty of the District Attorney is to properly enforce the law and it is equally his duty to see that the penalty imposed by the law is quickly carried out.

Something must be done in this country to create respect for the law and to suppress the criminal element, not by appointing commissions to investigate and make speeches before the bar association and reports to congress.

So far as the lynching of Johnson is concerned, it will be the duty of this office to follow the law. If any evidence is disclosed warranting an action by this office, such evidence will be presented in due time to the grand jury of this county.

So far we have been unable to establish the identity of anyone who participated in the lynching.

News concerning the Hall case came out in the San Francisco papers on August 7th and was later covered by the *Dunsmuir News* on their regular issue date of August 9th. The *Dunsmuir* article reads as follows:

MORE DELAY LOOMS IN HALL CASE

Monday the Federal District Court denied a petition for a writ of habeas corpus for George Hall, who was convicted at Yreka in April, 1933 of the murder of Stephen Kent. Since that time the execution of Hall has been put off from time to time, as attorneys took advantage of delay after delay offered by law.

On top of this, the circuit court, in affirming the denial held that Hall had not exhausted the state courts. In effect it instructed his attorneys to begin the cycle anew—to ask the superior court, appellate court and state supreme court for the writ and then, if refused, to come into the federal courts.

On August 8th, the *Siskiyou News* came out with a hard hitting piece. It would be interesting to know whether or not it happened to have been read by Governor Merriam:

LET THE GOVERNOR ACT

To residents of this county, Governor Merriam's insistent demand for an investigation by state authorities into the lynching of C. L. Johnson, confessed murderer of Jack Daw, appears, to say the least, a bit incongruous. The Governor appears considerably wrought up because a man, who in cold blood shot and killed an officer of the law, has been summarily dealt with by a group of ordinarily law abiding citizens.

This newspaper agrees with Governor Merriam that lynchings are bad and that there should be a most searching investigation by state officials, but disagrees as to what should be investigated. Approximately two and one half years ago two men were shot down on the streets of Yreka before the startled gaze of residents of this city. George Hall, the man who did the killing was captured, tried according to law, convicted and sentenced to hang, all within thirty days of the killing. There was no cry at the time for outside officials to step in and handle the affair. Siskiyou officials demonstrated convincingly that they were able to handle matters of this kind. However, George Hall, who killed two men, has yet to pay for his crime.

If ever there was a situation that required investigation, this one does, but we have yet to hear of Governor Merriam raising his voice to demand an investigation to ascertain why this killer has not been given justice. Hall killed two men. Neither of these men had committed murder, neither were sought for a previous felony, in fact both gave up their lives in support of the laws of this state and nation, yet no investigation of the affair has been sought by the Governor.

Siskiyou vigilantes took the life of but one man. That man had admittedly murdered an officer who sought to arrest him for staging a holdup, and hardly had news of the affair reached the executive ear before the Governor demanded an investigation by outside agencies. Siskiyou officials were apparently considered capable of dealing with Hall, twice a killer, but according to Merriam, not capable of dealing with those who have hanged Johnson. A week elapsed between the killing of Officer Daw at Dunsmuir and the hanging of Johnson, yet there was no executive wail for an investigation of that killing.

When men in high places, representing the government, wake up to the fact that officers of the law and respectable citizens are entitled to at least the same consideration and protection that is furnished criminals and killers, then and no sooner will respect for the law be established. A dozen officers of the law can be shot down by organized gangsters without creating a tenth of the commotion created by the hanging of Johnson.

Again we say we are wholeheartedly in favor of an investigation. A most thorough investigation into the Hall case. Let the Governor show the respectable citizens of his state that he is interested in their welfare. Killers and gangsters are looking out for themselves.

Officials of this county are sworn to uphold the law. They have many times demonstrated that this they can and will do, and there is no question but that a thorough investigation will be made by them into the lynching of Johnson. While this is going on, if the Governor is in earnest about wanting an investigation into a brutal killing, let him turn his attention to the Hall case. Siskiyou County has done her part in that case and done it well. She will do her part in the lynching investigation.

Attorney General Webb is to be complemented on his stand, namely to act only should local authorities fail to do their duty. Webb is familiar with the functioning of Siskiyou County officials, and knows that they are capable of handling this situation. If the Governor will turn his attention to obtaining justice for George Hall, any possibility of future lynchings in this county will be remote indeed.

In the August 9th issue of the *Dunsmuir News* there appeared a statement released by Mrs. Jack Daw, widow of the slain officer. It was a poignant statement and demonstrated a heartfelt thought and attitude that should have moved even the bombastic editorial writers. It read as follows:

I do not believe always in an "eye for an eye" course. Two wrongs never make a right. I do believe, however, that Mr. Johnson was a dangerous menace to society and something should have been done with him soon. I appreciate the feelings of the citizens when they took things into their own hands in view of the fact that the law is often obstructed in taking its course of justice. Something must be done to aid the law in giving some protection to honest society. I would never sanction an act such as was carried out this morning, for I believe that the law should take its course. However, as long as it was done, I feel that speedy justice was carried out. My hope is that no one will get into trouble over the affair. My feelings are that justice was done.

There is no question whatsoever that the general attitude of the citizens of Siskiyou County was one of approval. But there was still many a serious individual that was very much troubled by the event.

Court Reporter Ralph McMurry, a kind and gentle man, was one of these. He had been very busy by the series of events that had unfolded. There had been two inquests within days of each other along with his required work in connection with repeated statements by witnesses and other principals, all of which had to be recorded. During the excitement he was asked by his teenage son if he felt that the vigilantes had done the "right" thing.

"No," he replied, "no man has the right to try, convict and execute another man under any circumstances outside the law. If a man objects to the inequities of the law, his quarrel is with the law, not the case or the defendant. There are remedies available to him to get redress for this. Any course outside this principle will lead to chaos in the end and then we lose all of the protection that the laws give us."

This answer bothered the son for a long time. Many years later when he was in college he discussed the question with a famous professor of philosophy. He outlined the events and then asked the professor if he thought the vigilantes did "right."

The professor replied, "You have asked one of the very few really unanswerable questions in all of philosophy. Some men do what they think is "right" because they believe it is right. Other men do what they think is "right" because they must. Still others do what they think is "right" only because still others think it is right. But unfortunately, whatever is "right" in the minds and hearts of all these men for whatever reason, there are others that feel the same thing is wrong. Therefore, each right is wrong, and vice versa. In other words there is no absolute answer, but it is my personal opinion that through deductive reasoning an assessment of the consequences of an act

NEAR THIS SPOT AT 3:00 AM AUGUST 3, 1935 CLYDE JOHNSON, NATIVE OF ALABAMA, WAS LYNCHED BY A YET UNKNOWN GROUP OF MASKED MEN FOR THE MURDER OF DUNSMUIR CHIEF OF POLICE FRANK R. (JACK) DAW, AFTER ROBBING PADULA'S BAR IN CASTELLA, SHASTA CO. OF $ 35.00

THIS MONUMENT DEDICATED AUGUST 3, 1991 BY HUMBUG CHAPTER # 73 E CLAMPUS VITUS

The plaque on a monument memorializing Clyde Johnson's lynching placed near the site on Moonlit Oaks Road in Yreka by E Clampus Vitus in 1991.

can be weighed against the act of not acting. Thus a course that is probably right may be determined. As for the case you describe, only you can make that decision for yourself. My background, attitudes and values are undoubtedly different from yours; my answer may not be acceptable to you at all. You must decide for yourself."

The young man was somewhat confused by this "answer" but he thought about it for a few more years and finally reached a decision.

Have you, the reader, reached yours?

Leaving that aside, these events had created one opinion that was universally held throughout the entire county. This was the firm belief that the lynching will serve as a deterrent; surely now there will be an end to the killing of Siskiyou County police officers.

We shall see.

Epilogue: Trying to Save George Hall

All through 1935 and well into 1936 the lawyers for the defense in the George Hall case [see Chapter 2] continued their never ending search for the technicality in the judicial system that might free, or at the very least, save him from the gallows.

There was a motion for a new trial that went before the State Supreme Court where it was denied; it went on to the United States Supreme Court to meet the same fate. New dates were set by the Siskiyou County Superior Court for Hall's execution. A petition for writ of habeas corpus was filed in the federal court in Sacramento charging that Hall had been imprisoned illegally in Siskiyou County. The writ claimed that Hall was not allowed to defend himself. This procedure again worked its tortuous way up to the U. S. Supreme Court which again refused to intervene.

New appeals were filed on behalf of Hall with the claim that he had been denied the opportunity to plead insanity. This move started again on the road to its eventual demise at the hands of the United States Supreme Court. Motions; petitions; re-hearings; stays; on and on these procedures wound and ground throughout the system.

Time and further delaying procedures eventually appeared to be running out. The execution date was reset for March 27th, 1936, three years and seventeen days after the murder of Steve Kent and Lester Quigley.

A Failed Getaway

On March 8th one last appeal was set into motion, but this one could hardly be attributed to the cumbersome nature of the proceedings.

Hall's twenty-three year old wife, Ann, appeared at the visitors' booths at Folsom prison for her usual visit with her husband. To the guards it appeared to be routine without incident until the termination of the session was announced.

In the last available instant, Mrs. Hall leaned close to the screen and seemed to be whispering something as they both stood up for her departure. Two guards then came over to escort Hall back to his cell.

As they cleared the row of visiting screens, Hall broke from the guards and made a dash around the end. His wife dashed toward him; when they met he seemed to reach into her blouse where she had secreted a fully loaded 45 caliber pistol. She herself began fumbling in her purse where she had a

32 automatic. They were both moving toward the visitor area secretary's office when the secretary, having witnessed the development, came out and muscled them both to the floor. The two guards then jumped in and quickly subdued them. Mrs. Hall was arrested on the spot and her husband was hustled off to solitary confinement.

It now appeared that the procedures involved with Mrs. Hall's arrest would result in yet another postponement of her husband's execution date. She had to be booked, questioned, brought up for arraignment and other procedures. Hall's attorney, Luke Howe, immediately set into motion a request to the Governor for a stay of Hall's execution on the grounds that his wife was now entitled to whatever help her husband's testimony would be in her own upcoming proceedings.

In refusing Howe's request, Governor Merriam said, "The law provides for taking depositions in cases of this kind, but that makes no difference to me. I am not going to grant a reprieve. I cannot see how he could help his wife. It would be cause for delay and might give him another opportunity to make a break for freedom. There has been a great deal of delay already in this matter and see no justification for interference."

Ann Hall ultimately received a sentence of "one to five."

On March 27th, Charley Calkins along with approximately fifteen other Siskiyou County citizens including relatives and friends of Kent and Quigley, reported to Folsom Prison. At 10 a.m. they witnessed the final close of the case as George Hall dropped through the trap door and did his "dance on air."

The general talk around Yreka afterward seemed to revolve around two themes:

1. Hall wouldn't even have been executed as early as 1936 if Johnson hadn't been lynched. The so-called Judicial System had finally gotten the message.

2. If George Hall had been hanged within two years instead of three years, Clyde Johnson would never have been lynched.

Two very interesting hypotheses, but no one will ever know for sure.

Rural, remote Siskiyou County was making headlines. The lynching, as described by a participant to a San Francisco newspaper, was as brutal and cold blooded as the murder it was avenging.

San Francisco Examiner
August 4, 1935

Lyncher's Own Story – How Man Died!

Dunsmuir, Aug. 3 (Saturday). Here is the first complete account of the actual lynching of C.L. Johnson by one of the raiding party, as told to the *Examiner* today. The man must necessarily remain anonymous.

"There were exactly 30 of us in the group – all Dunsmuir citizens.

"We had carefully planned every detail of the lynching, and the plans worked with clocklike precision.

"We left Dunsmuir at 12:30 a.m. in seven cars and arrived at the county jail just before 2 o'clock.

Jailer Taken Away in Car

"After breaking into the office of the jail, we overcame the jailer – all of us were armed – and drove him away in a car.

"Then we got the keys to the cell block and after some difficulty finally found Johnson.

"He was extremely cold-blooded about the thing, asked us to 'wait while I put my pants on.'

"We dragged him out to an automobile and then drove about three miles south of Yreka on the Fort Jones road. A rope was tied around his neck while the car was on the way.

"He never said a word to us after that first remark and died in the same fashion.

Johnson Beaten Severely

"While the car was being driven to the scene of the lynching some of the men – personal friends of Chief Daw – beat Johnson severely. He was almost unconscious when we arrived at the lynching place.

"He was dragged from the car and over to the side of the road where there was a pine tree. The rope was thrown over a limb about 20 feet above the ground and he was pulled about 10 feet up in the air.

"The other end of the rope was tied to a nearby fence post and the group stood off to watch him die. His neck wasn't broken. He strangled to death.

Johnson Tries to Grab Rope

"It took about 10 minutes for him to die.

"At one time, his hands came loose – we'd tied them behind his back – and they twitched for several minutes as he tried to grab the rope.

"It took so long for him to die that some of the fellows wanted to shoot him. They'd been cursing him all the way from the jail.

"One raised his gun in fact, but it was knocked out of his hand with the remark, 'Let him die the toughest way.'

Slayer is Pronounced Dead

"Finally, when all movement had ceased one of the men who had medical experience climbed on a post and felt his pulse. He pronounced him dead.

"Then we all left. The job was over and the brutal murder of Jack Daw had been avenged."

Cast of Characters

Coke Brite, 31– accused killer of three

John Brite, 35 – accused killer of three

"Ma" (Martha) and "Pa" (Archie) Brite – parents of Coke and John

Charley Baker - Brite neighbor having a troubled relationship with the Brites

B. F. Decker – Brite family neighbor; "first on the scene"

Captain Fred Seaborn – Baker's friend and hunting partner; victim

W. G. "Chan" Chandler - Siskiyou County Sheriff

Martin Lange – Deputy Sheriff; victim

Joe Clark – Deputy Sheriff; victim

Chester Barton – "Mayor" of Horse Creek and owner of general store

Judge Rainey – local Horse Creek constable

Dr. Roy Schalappi – Yreka doctor who performed the autopsies

Felix Kunz - Siskiyou County Coroner

James Davis– Siskiyou County District Attorney

Charley Johnson - former DA who always had a witty comment

Horace F. Frye – Brites' defense attorney, from Sacramento

James Allen – Special Prosecutor, mysteriously replacing D. A. Jim Davis

Joseph Correia – Assistant District Attorney

Frank Merriam - California Governor at time of trial

Culbert Olson - California Governor at time of reprieve

4

The Brite Brothers
Put Horse Creek on the Map, 1936

Siskiyou County is one of the largest counties in all of California. Its economic base is about equal between agriculture and lumbering. Even though it contains some of the highest yielding farm properties in the west, these areas seem small in size when compared to the vast expanse of mountains, mountains and more mountains.

If a person gains the top of any one ridge in this great tangle of peaks, ridges and alpine valleys and looks west, he will see row on row of wild forbidding wilderness ranges running in all possible directions with no apparent organization to them. There is only one common denominator that comes into view; this is the Klamath River that somehow finds its way through this huge maze to eventually dump into the sea far off to the west.

The Klamath River originates at Klamath Lake near Klamath Falls, Oregon. It starts out peacefully enough in Oregon and quickly crosses the state line into California. But after that, it becomes almost frustrated in its attempt to find it's way downstream. In the tangled crisscross nature of the mountains through which it must travel it flows in every direction of the compass in it's never ending search for low ground. As it diligently works it's way through it's deep and sometimes dark canyons, the great mountains on each side dump in vast amounts of additional water from snow, springs, creeks and several sizeable rivers including the Scott, the Salmon and the Trinity.

As the river flows and grows from its origin in Oregon at Klamath Lake, it travels generally westward for nearly eighty miles when it suddenly makes a 90° turn to the south. Flowing in this direction for another forty miles in Siskiyou County, it finally passes into Humboldt County where it abruptly makes a "U" turn to continue its travels in a northerly direction. After crossing into Del Norte County it finally achieves its goal of meeting the sea.

The river courses through some of the most remote and spectacular scenery in the world. It is a "white water" river, a fisherman's paradise, a great hydroelectric producer. But first and foremost it is a "wild" river in every sense of the word. It is in this pristine and beautiful setting in 1936 that the Brite brothers suddenly found themselves to be the focal point in a great drama of life and death.

All along the length of the Klamath River, little settlements are to be encountered. Most of them date back to the great California Gold Rush in the 1850s during which each one had its boom times of short duration.

As the gold fever waned, most of the people departed from these little "wide places in the road" but a hardy few remain to this day. As the gold petered out, some of these places began to rely upon the then emerging logging industry, but they have always remained very small and sometimes very much isolated. Each of these little communities typically has its post office and a general store, often combined. Grouped around this "central" area are a few houses, mostly occupying one to three acres which increase to small farms and some to large ranches. But in nearly all cases, the geography determines the nature of the community. The river is in a canyon which means that the steep mountains are not far back from the river's banks on either side. But even then, as is human nature, people are living out in the little cabins and plots scattered throughout a great portion of the mountains. Some of these places are merely little shacks possibly on a gold claim, but others are fully developed homes with a few acres, steep though the sites may be.

So we have a "community" that becomes more or less cohesive in itself. The social and business life revolves around the post office and the general store and most everyone knows everyone else. These are "country" or "river" people and through the years have become highly self sufficient. They are generally on the low end of the economic scale but they "make do" in a sort of pioneer fashion. They live in these places not because they must, but because they want to; they are very loyal to their community and proud of it. They make few demands on the outside world and consequently are pretty much left to themselves.

A great portion of the food for these communities is raised right on each citizen's little plot or acreage. If they ever run really short of food, the river itself furnishes fish and the mountains abound with deer. The river people more or less look upon the natural game as "theirs." They would take all they truly needed but that would be the extent of it; they in fact by nature are fervent game conservationists. But game wardens beware! An over enthusiastic warden within their midst would not be welcome, to say nothing of the fact that he would have a frustrating time trying to get cooperation in obtaining evidence of a violation.

Horse Creek valley has been ranched since not long after the gold miners arrived in the 1850s. The low tech mining done by Charley Baker, the Brites and others in the mountains above the valley in the 1930s was in contrast to the large dredge (dredge and tailings visible on middle left of photo) working its way up the valley starting in 1935. Fortunately the topsoil was put back in place and the valley continues to produce cattle to this day. (Siskiyou County Museum)

Horse Creek is one of these little Siskiyou County river communities. It is reached by traveling eight miles north from Yreka down the Shasta River canyon and then turning due west where the Shasta meets the Klamath. After another thirty miles down the Klamath River the space between the canyon walls seems to widen a bit and therein lays the settlement of Horse Creek. The community itself is located near the mouth of Horse Creek, a rather large and swift-flowing creek that flows out of the high mountains to the north and empties into the Klamath River.

In 1936 Charley Baker was sixty-two years of age and lived with his wife in Horse Creek. Charley had been a carpenter in Long Beach, California before his retirement and moved to Horse Creek approximately eight years earlier. Though Charley could hardly read or write, he was a man of some fundamental intelligence and was enjoying his life of retirement in the northern wilds of California where he had always longed to be. He and his wife had a rather substantial cabin on the creek about eight miles up from its mouth.

When asked about his occupation, he would say that he was now engaged "in a little mining, raising a little garden but mostly doing work around the house." He and his wife were well known in the community but it seemed that they had no particularly intimate friends. In fact, Charley had a reputation for being a bit cantankerous and not too sociable, but most people that really knew him felt that this was due to a minor hearing impairment that he had. Mr. and Mrs. Baker were teetotaling, God fearing and useful citizens who pretty much kept to themselves. They were entirely acceptable as conforming members of this independent minded community.

In the 1930s Hollywood produced a movie based on the great Steinbeck novel, *The Grapes of Wrath*. Had the producers of the movie only known, they could have saved a lot of time and effort in the casting process had they located the Brite family to play the part of the Joad family. The members of the Brite family in real life looked like, talked like, acted like and albeit, actually felt like the famous Joads.

The Brites Move to Horse Creek

Archie J. Brite, sixty-five, and his wife Martha, "Ma Brite," sixty-four, together with their two sons, John and Coke, were authentic characters in that novel as developed by Steinbeck. As with the Joad family in the book, it was the mother who was the power in the family structure. Ma Brite knew very well that times were bad; she knew that life was a struggle, but "by God" she meant to hold that family together "come hell or high water." She realized that her two "boys," thirty-five year old John and thirty-one year old Coke, tended to be wild and high spirited. She was well aware that "them boys" had served time for a felony in Arizona and that they had been in trouble with the law in Jacksonville, Oregon, where the family had last resided. She felt that these bad times would finally fade away and that if the family held together, "them boys" would eventually settle down and amount to something.

The four Brites landed in the Horse Creek area in 1935. It is not known what the arrangement was concerning a lease where they lived but it is highly doubtful that the rent was very high. Leaving the highway and the Horse Creek Store, the road going up Horse Creek eventually goes by Charley Baker's place. A quarter mile above that is another residence, and then the road ends abruptly. From the end of the road near this last place there is a foot path through the woods then known as the Government Trail. Approximately a mile and a half up that trail as it winds up a steep mountainside, was the mining claim with a cabin on it that the Brites occupied. Up there, as with

The Brite family's cabin site is in a pretty spring fed mountain meadow a mile or so up a trail from the main Horse Creek road. A few fruit trees there still produce fruit but there are no remnants of the cabin that Ma, Pa, Coke and John lived in.
(photo by Jill Livingston)

Charley Baker, the Brites did "a little mining and vegetable gardening."

The Brites had an old Model T Ford touring car with no top; the tires were entirely shot. The whole contraption could be classed as a living wreck looking for a place to die. The boys did most of the traveling down the road to the community of Horse Creek in order to obtain what few supplies were needed up on the hill. It was a tough hike from the cabin down to where they always left the car at the trail head and an even worse one back up the same trail after returning from the auto trip into Horse Creek. So Ma and Pa Brite avoided this as much as possible. After hiking down the trail and picking up the car it was less than half a mile before they would pass the Baker cabin on their way down to the store or post office. On the way home they would leave the car in the same place and commence that long pull on foot back to the cabin, often carrying a heavy load. As a matter of fact that "heavy load" frequently consisted of something other than supplies. The boys liked a touch of wine and they never left the store without a bottle. By the time they started their climb up the hill on foot, the bottle was usually empty.

The Bakers often saw the Brites go rattling by the house in that old Ford. The boys always waved as they went by and seemed friendly enough. Charley Baker had met Coke Brite at the store a couple of times and he always seemed cordial to Baker. He had never had occasion to actually talk to John but he felt that he knew him.

On one occasion Charley's horse had gotten out of the little pasture near the house and Charley noticed that the upper gate was standing open. He assumed that the Brites had left the gate open because it was located near the place where the Brites always left their car. The next time Baker saw Coke Brite in Horse Creek Store he spoke to him about it. Coke seemed to be slightly disgruntled that Baker would think that he had done such a thing but he didn't make an issue of it. Charley gave it no further thought. As time went on, Coke Brite would often stop at Baker's and just sit in the car and visit with Mrs. Baker. Once in awhile he might make a purchase at the store for her and drop it off on the way back up the hill. The word was out that those Brite brothers could get really mean when they were drunk but neither of the Bakers was ever exposed to them under that circumstance. It couldn't be said

The Horse Creek Store and Post Office was the center of the community and proprietor Chester Barton was a respected community leader. Coke and John would often pick up a bottle of wine for themselves along with a few grocery items for their mother or Mrs. Baker. The bottle was usually empty before they got home. (Livingston collection)

that the Bakers and the Brite Brothers were close friends; it could better be described as a "nodding acquaintance." The Brites were there and the Bakers were there; they were all part of the Horse Creek community and this gave them something in common.

Rumble at the Baker Place

In June of 1936 Charley Baker was out in his meadow irrigating. He saw the Brite's old Ford coming up the narrow winding Horse Creek dirt road and stop in front of his house. This time the car was driven by one of the Maplesden boys, a member of a pioneer Klamath River family; Coke Brite was in the passenger's seat. Charley noticed that Coke was talking to his wife as Charley walked up. Coke had previously stopped by on his way "downtown" and Mrs. Baker had asked him to pick up two loaves of bread for her. She had given Coke a quarter for the purchase but it turned out that the total cost was twenty-six cents. Coke had told her that he still had a penny coming.

Mrs. Baker said, "Alright, I will run in and get it."

Just as Charley came walking up, Coke said, "Mrs. Baker, I am drunk; I am drunk as hell."

Charley's wife replied, "You ought to be ashamed of yourself, Mr. Brite."

"No, goddamn you Mrs. Baker," Coke shouted at her, "I ain't ashamed of what I done!"

Charley then stepped in and said, "Don't you dare talk that way to my wife. You're on our property and you're at our gate. You don't talk that way."

Coke then began cursing out Charley who had swiftly stepped through the gate and was attempting to close it. Coke grabbed the gate and jerked it open again and followed right on through behind Baker. As the two men scrambled up on the porch, Charley reached into a rose bush and pulled out a three foot long heavy stick that he had there to help support the bush. He took one wild swing at Coke with this "club" and caught him just above the left elbow. Maplesden then came charging out of the car, through the gate and up the steps where he threw both arms around Charley and shouted, "Don't strike him any more! I'll get him out of here; I'll take him out!"

"Take him out and keep him out!" Baker shouted as his wife began to cry out the same thing.

Maplesden let go of Baker and tried to get his arms around Brite but Coke wasn't cooperating. He said, "I'll kill the son of a bitch!"

Baker then made his way down the steps and began backing around the corner of the house. Coke kept coming on, sort of dragging Maplesden along with him, cursing and blackguarding Baker as they went.

Finally, Maplesden was able to cool Brite down enough to get him back to the car. Just as they pulled away, Coke shook his fist back at Charley and shouted, "I'll getcha!"

The next day Charley got in his car and drove the eight miles down the road into Horse Creek. He was going down there to arrange to have Coke Brite arrested. He knew that Justice of the Peace Rainey was the person to issue a warrant but he drove right on by Rainey's farm home because he first wanted to get the advice of his friend, Chester Barton, the owner of the general store.

Chester Barton and Justice of the Peace Rainey were probably the co-leaders of the Horse Creek community. It is the nature of these little out of the way hamlets that one or two of their long time residents emerge as the unofficial civic and social leaders. Both were men of principle and carried the respect of most everyone in the community. It was a very common thing for people to seek advice and counsel from either one of them when most any type of problem came along.

Don't Call the Sheriff

After Charley related the incident, Barton told him, "No Mr. Baker, Coke Brite will sober up and eventually apologize the next time he sees you. My advice is to just forget it. You know, those of us who choose to live way out in places like Horse Creek must learn to take care of our own problems. That is one of the things that makes living out here so attractive. We don't ask for much from outside authorities and they more or less respect us for it. In order to survive down here we must take care of each other and refrain from being entangled in all the woes and troubles that can come to us by always running for outside help. This thing will blow over and we will all be better off for not calling in the sheriff."

So Charley took his friend's advice and went on back up that old rough dirt road to his home. He did meet Coke Brite on various occasions afterward. Coke was cordial at all times and never brought the matter up again. Brite continued to stop frequently at the house and visit with Mrs. Baker when she was working in the garden. He even invited her up to visit his mother; he told her that his mother was up on the hill and hadn't been out of there in six months. Both of the Bakers reasoned that it must have just been the wine "talking" when Coke had acted so badly and let it go at that.

On the afternoon of August 29th, Charley Baker was repairing his roof. He had been postponing the project for some time but he finally decided he had better get up there and do it because deer hunting season was to open the first week in September. As a matter of fact, there were husbands all over the river settlements engaged in all manner of such postponable projects on the last weekend before deer season. Their wives were seeing to that. Everyone residing in these communities knows that when deer season arrives it is impossible to get any routine chores done. Horse Creek was no exception. Deer hunting was something in which every person became involved. It dominated everyone's life for almost a month and was the subject of social conversation practically throughout the year. So Charley had his orders; that roof was to be fixed before deer season because "the rainy season would be on us in October."

About 3:00 o'clock, as Charley was fitting and pounding new shingles into the gaps on his roof, he looked down and saw a car pull up to his gate. It was his old friend, Fred Seaborn of Vallejo, California, who got out and shouted to him up on the roof. Fred and Charley had been hunting together the first week of the season for the past four years. When Fred departed last year he mentioned that he would be up a little early this year, hunting season 1936, so they could do a little reconnoitering around the hills before the season got under way.

Captain Fred Seaborn was fifty-one years old. He was a retired naval officer and at that time held the civilian position of Chief of Harbor at Vallejo. He was a cultured, educated and refined man. He was a person of many interests; one of his passions was deer hunting. The two men, Captain Seaborn and Charley Baker, seemed somewhat of an "odd couple," but somewhere along the way the two of them had come together as friends through their common interest in the sport of deer hunting. All things considered, however, the relationship made sense. Charley was very proud of the fact that his friend was such a prominent and successful man; surely Fred viewed Charley as a fabulous "country man" who was a real character and knew the woods and mountains backward and forward. The annual deer hunt and visit of the two men was anticipated with great pleasure by both of them and of course was the subject of considerable reminiscence throughout the year between seasons.

Charley told Captain Seaborn that he would be a little while longer on the roof and suggested that he go in and visit with Mrs. Baker until he was finished. By the time Charley came down and the two men had begun discussing plans for the coming hunt, Mrs. Baker announced that supper was ready. When the three of them were eating, she reminded Charley that the horse was missing again and that she had earlier seen him going up the Government Trail.

Gone to Find the Horse

After supper, Charley said to Fred, "You stay here while I go up the trail and see if I can't find the horse. It won't take me very long. You can finish unloading your things from the car; you probably need a rest from your long trip anyway."

"No, I want a little exercise," Seaborn said. "I've been sitting in the car all day. I'll just go along with you."

The two men started up the trail together. It was just a pleasant evening stroll after a fine meal, even though the trail very quickly became steep. They soon picked up the tracks of the horse and found where it had turned off the trail and headed downhill toward a little pasture that belonged to Baker's nearest neighbor who lived upstream. Darkness was coming on. As the two men came on the short connecting trail, they soon reached the creek at a point a few hundred yards upstream from the Baker house. Visibility was now becoming quite difficult.

As they stood near the creek, Captain Seaborn said, "I'm going to get a drink of water."

Seaborn stepped a few feet further on down to the creek bank and kneeled down on one knee. He then turned his head slightly to his left and saw an old Ford car sitting there.

"Whose car is that, Baker?" Seaborn asked.

"It belongs to the Brite boys up on the hill," Baker replied.

That innocent sounding answer to a casual question between two friends became the most controversial ten words ever uttered in Siskiyou County. There soon developed a considerable faction of people who are now both living and dead who claimed that Baker's reply consisted of fifteen words instead of ten:

"It belongs to those two sons of bitches, the Brite boys, up on the hill!"

"You're God-damned right it does," a loud voice suddenly resounded from the direction where the old Ford was parked. "What are you sons of bitches doing in our camp?"

Baker immediately recognized the voice of Coke Brite just as an empty wine bottle came whistling through the air over Seaborn's head and thudded into the creek bank.

The Brite brothers had earlier driven to their customary parking place from a trip to the store in Horse Creek where, among other things, they had bought a bottle of wine. It was early evening and before starting the long pull up the hill to get home they had sat around and finished off the wine. By that time it was nearly dark; for the first time ever, they decided to unroll their bed, which was always in the old Ford, and sleep there for the night.

It wasn't much of a bed. They threw a tarp down on the ground and on that they put a "sleeping bag" of sorts that Ma Brite had made up for them. It was just two three-quarter sized blankets that were sewn together down one side and across the foot. They then put another wider tarp on top of that. The result was that John was reasonably comfortable between the blankets on the "sewed" side but Coke had to make do by being only half between what remained of the blankets with the rest of him on top of the bottom tarp and under the upper tarp. From the blanket roll, they had removed their 30/30 rifle and laid it at the head of the bed. They hadn't dozed off yet when they heard the talking between Baker and Seaborn.

Captain Seaborn straightened up and turned toward the direction of this new voice and apologetically said, "We're not bothering your camp. We are just out searching for my friend's horse. We didn't know you were here. Pardon us. I don't know you. If we have said anything that offends you, I'm sorry."

That last sentence spoken by Seaborn was destined to become the rallying point of the faction that believed the second version of Baker's answer to Seaborn's earlier question was the true version. They reasoned that the second version must have been the correct one, otherwise why would Seaborn have said, "If we have said anything that offends you?"

An Angry Confrontation

Both the brothers had emerged from the bed and came charging down the slope toward the creek bank where Seaborn stood, cursing and abusing him all the way. A veritable battle broke out. Seaborn commenced retreating diagonally back up toward Baker. As the boys caught him, Coke swung a fist but Seaborn was able to fend it off. Before Seaborn got back to where Baker was, John moved around Seaborn and landed a crushing blow right on his eye. Seaborn continued to move backward and sideways, moving closer to Baker. He continued to commiserate with his attackers, attempting to assure them that they meant no harm.

When Seaborn had finally gotten near Baker, who had also been backing up, Coke jumped around both his brother and Seaborn, and knocked Baker to the ground with a well aimed blow to the side of the head. When Baker went down he landed flat on his back with his feet sort of drawn up. As Coke attempted to close on him, Baker let fly with both feet and caught him square in the midriff, which nearly knocked the wind out of Coke.

In the meantime, John had been hammering on Seaborn, but he was not proving to be an easy prey. Seaborn was a large man and he was able to block most of the blows. Seaborn had seen the mighty kick that Baker had delivered but he noticed Coke was still going back for more. As Coke was about to pounce upon the fallen Baker, Seaborn whirled around and grabbed Coke with both arms and flung him aside. Just then John spied a sturdy stick on the ground; he snatched it up and charged around Coke. As Baker was attempting to get up, John laid into him, swinging the stick and put him right back on the ground. He then turned again on Seaborn and resumed beating him. But with the stick, it was no contest this time.

Seaborn finally ducked and dived enough to get a good grip on his friend Baker and began half dragging and pulling him along the trail as the two of them started a slow retreat in spite of the relentless pounding the brothers were administering. Seaborn continued to apologize to the Brites, trying to tell them that it was all a mistake.

After suffering several more blows from the "club," Seaborn was finally able to get Baker on his feet so that they could quicken the pace of the withdrawal. The Brites, with Coke still a little shaky from the blow to the stomach, appeared to feel that they had made their point. They gave up further pursuit as the two "intruders" hobbled down the trail toward Baker's house.

Seaborn Wouldn't Let it Go

Seaborn was determined to not let it stand there.

"No," Seaborn said. "Those fellows need to be taught a lesson. I am the man they hit first and they abused the both of us. That kind of conduct is totally unacceptable to me. If we let them get away with this they will make it miserable for you from here on out, long after I have left."

Baker was thinking of what Chester Barton had told him after the other altercation that he had with Coke Brite. But maybe Mr. Barton was wrong after all. It hadn't all been forgotten like Barton had predicted, even though it seemed so until this evening.

"Just forget it," Baker replied. "They will sober up and it will all be forgotten. There is nothing to gain by our carrying it any further."

Little was said as they approached the yard. But after releasing the horse it became obvious that Seaborn was very mad. He was absolutely incensed over the treatment they had just suffered at the hands of "those two drunken brothers." There was blood all over his shirt, he had a knot on his skull half the size of a goose egg, and one of his eyes was swollen nearly shut. "Wait a minute, Mr. Baker," Seaborn said as they approached the porch steps. "We are going to go down to that Justice of the Peace friend of yours and arrange to have those fellows arrested."

"Alright," Baker said. "Just let me go in the house and change my shirt. This one is all bloody and about half torn off me."

Seaborn said, "No, don't change anything. Just stay as you are so that we can show the authorities what a mess those fellows made of us. Don't even tell your wife what has happened because it will just upset and frighten her."

But before Seaborn had finished speaking, Baker had gone up the steps into the house.

As Seaborn waited outside, Baker told his wife what had happened. As Seaborn had feared, she was very much upset and worried. Baker told her that they were going down to Judge Rainey's and swear out a warrant for the Brite boys. This news upset her even more. As he observed her reaction, Baker wavered somewhat in his resolve. But Seaborn was the dominant character of the two and Baker knew that he wouldn't be able to dissuade him.

The two men got into Seaborn's car and started down the twisting mountain road to cover the six miles to Judge Rainey's. It was completely dark; the headlights were on.

Charley Baker and Captain Fred Seaborn were knocking on the front door of the Judge Rainey residence some time between 9:00 and 10:00 p.m. Mrs. Rainey, of course, was acquainted with Baker and invited them in. The judge was not at home but after ascertaining what the two men wanted, Mrs. Rainy was able to locate him via telephone and he soon arrived at the house.

After introductions were made, Seaborn described the incident to the judge and told him that he wanted to swear out a warrant for the arrest of the Brite brothers.

Judge Rainey, in seeing the beat-up condition of his two guests, offered no comment concerning the advisability of Seaborn's proposal. His only comment was to the effect that he wanted both men to sign the warrant inasmuch as they had both obviously been assaulted.

In view of this consideration, Captain Seaborn said, "No, Judge Rainey, I want to be the only signer of the warrant. I want it this way in order to prevent any future retribution against my friend Charles Baker after I have left the area. These boys are dangerous. Even if they serve time for this offense committed tonight, they might come back here and do harm to Mr. Baker. If his name does not appear on any of the documents, it might be a small factor that could prevent such a development."

The judge made no objection to this proposal. He turned his swivel chair around to his desk, reached into a cubbyhole and pulled out a blank warrant form. He asked several questions of Seaborn as he filled it out and then handed it to him for his signature.

The judge's act of extracting the form from the desk seemed to all present to be a routine and immaterial event. But further developments subsequently generated this innocent act into a major factor in the case.

In California in those days, Justices of the Peace were not necessarily required to be lawyers; this was especially the case in these small out of the way communities. These rural justices were often not too well acquainted with the legal technicalities involved in many of the actions the job required them to perform. At that time, issuers of warrants were provided with two similar but slightly different forms. One form was an order to the sheriff to arrest someone "as soon as convenient," or words to that effect. The other form was an order to the sheriff to make the arrest "forthwith and without delay."

In this particular instance, Judge Rainey gave it no thought; he paid no attention as to which of the forms he pulled from the cubbyhole in the desk. By the "luck of the draw," it happened to be the second type of form, the one that ordered the sheriff to make the arrest "forthwith and without delay."

Judge Rainey then asked his wife to see if she could get the Sheriff's Office in Yreka on the telephone. These were the days of the old crank telephone when all calls had to go through the central operator. Mrs. Rainey had a difficult time putting any call through. At first she couldn't raise "Central." She tried calling two different neighbors just by "crank ringing" on the line in order to ask them to try and reach Central. Finally, Central came on the line and Mrs. Rainey asked her to get the Sheriff's Office. Central then reported that she couldn't raise anyone there.

Mr. Baker suggested that Mrs. Rainey ask Central to see if she could locate the Yreka city policeman, Charles Doggett. Baker explained that he was a friend of Doggett and that he could most certainly find someone connected with the Sheriff's Office. All of this was taking considerable time but eventually Mr. Doggett was on the line from Yreka; he advised Mrs. Rainey that he would see what he could do.

After another short wait, the phone rang again and Deputy Sheriff Martin Lange was on the line. This was the same Martin Lange who had coincidentally emerged from the drug store and was nearly shot by Charley Calkins during the capture of George Hall three years before; the same man who had been the jailer the night that Clyde Johnson was lynched one year ago [see Chapters 2 and 3].

Judge Rainey took over the telephone and had a short conversation with Lange in which he explained the situation, after which he hung up.

He turned to the others in the room and said, "Deputy Lange says that he needs to come to the Horse Creek area on Monday in connection with another matter and that he will pick up the boys at that time."

Captain Seaborn, very surprised at this turn of events, said, "No, no, Judge Rainey, that won't do. I am going to insist that the arrest be made tonight. Who knows where those Brites will be two days from now. At best they will be on up that long foot trail at that cabin where they live and the officer's will be reluctant to hike all the way up there without even knowing if they are there. At worst they might have even left the country by then. Also, I happen to know from my experience in the Navy that the best law enforcement results when an arrest is made as soon as possible after the commission of the offense."

Judge Rainey suggested that if Mrs. Rainey could get Lange back on the telephone, Captain Seaborn should talk to him. Seaborn agreed. By comparison with the other attempts to reach Yreka, it was no time at all when Deputy Lange was back on the line.

When Captain Seaborn took over the phone, a lengthy conversation ensued. He essentially repeated his position to Lange, insisting all along that the authorities take action now. But Deputy Lange had a problem. It was getting very late at night; he was alone at the jail and he was unsure if he could get someone at that hour to take over if he came down the river. Secondly, if he was to make a night-time arrest out in the woods he would need at least another officer with him.

Seaborn, true to his nature, was courteous at all times during the conversation. But now he was finally beginning to show a subtle trace of exasperation. He said, "Deputy Lange, I understand your problems as you have so ably described them but I am looking at the sworn warrant for the arrest of these two men and it says here that you are directed to proceed forthwith and without delay. I must advise you that I therefore expect this arrest to be made tonight." After a short pause, Captain Seaborn said, "I appreciate that; thank you very much." He hung up the phone.

Deputies Head Downriver

"Deputy Lange will be on his way shortly. We are to wait here for him," Seaborn said. Just before Charlie Doggett had come in about 10:30 and told him that Judge Rainey had been trying to reach him on the telephone, Martin Lange had finished his last round of the cell blocks and was looking forward to a good night's sleep. He had already been on duty for more than ten hours and he was tired. He had been musing to himself about his situation as deputy sheriff.

"Here I am," he thought, "just a couple of weeks past my forth-eighthth birthday and after all these years as a deputy under two different sheriffs, I'm still pulling ten to twelve hour shifts. Most of the time I'm just babying these prisoners and only once in a while does a little excitement come up. And the pay is lousy; and the job's dangerous too. Look what happened to my ex-brother in law, Steve Kent. And look at that crazy ride to Grenada that those lynchers took me on. I'm really just a farm boy; that's where I should have stayed. I'll stick with Chandler till the end of this term but then I ought to look around for something different."

When Doggett came in with the message, Lange shook off his reverie and reached for the phone to call Judge Rainey. After that call was completed, Doggett said he had to complete his rounds on Miner Street and left. Then the phone rang again and "that fellow Seaborn" was on the line. While Lange was talking to Seaborn, his old friend Joe Clark walked in and sat down.

Clark had been the constable in Yreka for several years. Eventually he switched over to the Sheriff's Department as a deputy sheriff. He was then sixty eight years old and the other men on the force sometimes favored him when passing out the various assignments in deference to his age. This was not really necessary though because he was actually tough as nails and very active. He and Martin Lange were great friends.

When Lange hung up the phone he greeted his old friend and said, "Joe, how would you like to take a trip with me down the Klamath River and up Horse Creek a ways?"

"When," Clark asked.

"Now," Lange answered.

"Are you serious?" Clark asked.

"I'm afraid I am," Lange said. "That was a fellow on the phone from Horse Creek who has one of those 'forthwith and without delay' warrants that Judge Rainey issued and he is insisting that it be served tonight. I had to promise that someone would be there as soon as possible and you can guess who that 'someone' will be. I have to call around now and get somebody to come down here and take my place in the jail and then we would need to get rolling. We have to apprehend a couple of fellows in a camp by the creek and I figure it is a two man job. Will you go?"

"OK," Clark replied. "I am already bushed now; I was on my way home to turn in. But I suppose it must be done so let's get rolling."

Martin Lange got busy with the phone and soon had a man on his way to the jail to take over while he was gone. It was nearly 11:00 p.m. when the two deputies piled into one of the old 1930s vintage county cars and headed off into the night on a forty-eight mile ride. Down through the deep canyon of the Shasta River; then they would go down the even deeper Klamath River canyon; and then up Horse Creek canyon in order to locate the camp of a couple of errant citizens. Treacherous blind curves all the way and ruts and dust for the final eight miles lay ahead.

One last instant of reverie came over Martin Lange as they passed the Lange home on Oregon Street in North Yreka and cleared the city limits. He just shook his head a little, smiled to himself and mused, "This is the way it is; here we go."

Back in the Sack

After the fight earlier in the evening, the Brite brothers went back up the slope to the old car and sat in it for awhile. They weren't hurt a bit physically; in fact they were somewhat elated. In their world, it was a very natural thing to have a god knock-down drag-out fight once in awhile. They had emerged from this one the undisputed victors and they were proud of it.

The crumpled note found in Martin Lange's pocket with the names of the two men he was to meet downriver at Horse Creek.

Coke said, "It'll be a cold day in hell before that Baker tries to take us on again."

John replied, "I wouldn't be too sure of it. I don't think he has a lot of friends around here but he is pretty well known. He might try to get a bunch together and take us on again."

"Bullshit; he hasn't got the guts," Coke said. "You can count on it."

"I wonder who that big guy was that was with him. That man was plenty tough," John said.

"I don't know and I don't give a damn," Coke declared.

The two brothers crawled back in the makeshift bedroll. It was a beautiful cool summer night in the mountains. They soon drifted off to sleep.

Some time later both boys were awakened by the sound of a hoot owl. They couldn't see him so John just rose up a little in the bed and reached for the .32 automatic pistol that they had lying near the head of the bed. He fired off one shot in the general direction of where it seemed the owl was located and they heard him wing it off into the night. They again drifted off to sleep.

An hour or so after the visit from the hoot owl, the two sleeping men were again awakened. This time it was the dog. Whenever the brothers left the home up on the mountain their dog had soon learned that if he went down the trail along toward evening he would meet them coming up the road in the old car. The dog would usually be there where they parked the car awaiting their return to that spot.

Sometimes he would be over at Baker's neighbor's house. But as soon as he heard the engine of the Ford coming up the road he would race back over to the parking place. On this night, for some reason, the dog was very late in making his rendezvous. So some time later after the owl incident the dog appeared in the camp and was sniffing and walking around on top of the two men's bed. He did this long enough to awaken both of them and then jumped into the car and bedded down for the night. Again, drowsiness returned to the Brites, who finally dropped into a deep sleep for the last time that night. All the major players in the drama were now in place. The countdown had started and the clock was ticking.

It was after 12:00 midnight when the deputies arrived at the Rainey household. Judge Rainey introduced Seaborn and Baker. Seaborn related the whole episode to the deputies. They listened very attentively and when Seaborn finished, Lange asked for the warrant. Seaborn handed it to him and Lange gave it a quick glance; he folded it once and put it into the pocket of his vest.

Deputy Sheriff Lange wanted to get right down to business. He said to

Seaborn, "Do you know the men; would you recognize them?"

"No, never saw them before," Seaborn replied, "and it was dark up there at the time and I really never did see them very well. I certainly believe, however, that I could recognize their voices."

Lange then turned to Baker. "Do you know the men?" he asked.

"I do," answered Baker.

"Then we will need you to go along and point them out to us," said Lange.

The four men went out the door and got into two cars. Baker and Seaborn were in the lead in Seaborn's car and the two deputies in the county car followed a short distance behind.

As they neared the Baker house, Seaborn said, "You get out here at the gate and wait for the sheriff's car. I'll take the car on through the gate and put it away in the garage. I want to take off this white shirt and put on a darker one so that the Brites might not so easily recognize me. I have another shirt right here in the car."

Baker said, "No, you don't need to go on up there to the camp with us. He has asked me to point them out. There is no need to subject yourself to any more of this. Your eye is 'swole' plumb shut now. Just stay here with the wife and I'll be back shortly. I'll take the fellows up."

Baker got out of the car to await the arrival of the deputies as Seaborn said, "Don't leave until I get back out here."

By the time the sheriff's car arrived and the deputies were getting out, Seaborn came walking back up to the gate. He was wearing a darker shirt.

"I'm going up with you," Seaborn said to Baker, loud enough for the deputies to also hear.

There was no objection from the deputies and Baker said nothing further on the subject.

Captain Seaborn was carrying a Coleman gas lantern which he had lighted back in the garage. Deputy Clark said, "We will turn that out until we get there. Do you have a flashlight on you?"

"Yes, I do," Seaborn replied as he put out the lantern.

Clark and Lange also had flashlights. Baker had none.

The four of them started up the rather wide trail, Baker and Lange, side by side in the lead. They had to go through two gates on the way up. Baker opened each one and Seaborn closed them as he and Clark brought up the rear.

The journey on foot consisted of only a few hundred yards. Undoubtedly Baker and Seaborn were both thinking of the circumstances under which they had come down this same trail earlier that day. Or was it still the same day? It was really closer to 1:30 a.m. the next day.

With each step closer to their destination, the men seemed to move more carefully and quietly without being told. When the procession was about 50 feet from where the old Ford stood, Baker signaled for a halt.

Deputies Enter the Brite Camp

In a low voice he said, "They are right there about fifty feet farther."

Seaborn, in a similar quiet voice said, "They're dangerous; don't give them a chance."

The four men quietly walked forward. There was the rag tag "sleeping bag" laid out with the foot of it next to the running board of the old car and the length of it parallel to the creek. Both of the occupants appeared to be asleep with the covers pulled clear up over their heads. The group stopped about three feet from the foot of the bed.

Baker pointed his finger at the bed roll and quietly said, "There they are, lying right there."

All the flashlights were on. Lange moved around the foot of the bed and went a step or two closer to the head of it. In a loud and decisive voice, he said, "Hello boys! This is the law; this is the Sheriff. You're under arrest!"

One of the men, still under the covers, began to move around. It seemed almost as if he was searching for something under the covers. Then Coke's voice rang out from beneath the blanket, "The hell you say; no damn sheriff can arrest us!"

By that time Joe Clark had moved around to the head of the bed on the other side. He reached down and threw the covers back off of the head and shoulders of both the Brites.

With this, John started cursing and blackguarding the two men. Lange reached into his pocket and pulled out a little leather sap, or "billy," with which he gave John a couple of raps on the head. This quieted him down somewhat. Then Coke started to rise up from the bed and commenced cursing and yelling again. Clark quieted him down in the same manner with his billy.

With the billy still dangling from his wrist, Lange pulled his handcuffs off his belt. He stepped right over Coke and squatted down with his feet on the bed so that he was facing John in an attempt to put the cuffs on him. By this time, the bed covers had worked clear down almost to the foot of the bed. Coke was shouting and cursing with Clark giving him a little "billy-tap" once in awhile.

In a stern voice, Lange commanded, "Hold still, I'm putting the hand-cuffs on you!"

Still bellowing and cursing, John continued to resist. As Lange was astraddle of him, John tried to kick him in the groin. But John's feet were still just under the covers and this was not working.

Coke looked over at the situation that his brother was in and suddenly spied the billy dangling from Lange's wrist. He made a lunge for the billy and was able to grasp it. He gave it a mighty jerk; the leather thong broke and the billy flew through the air. Coke's lunge for the billy carried him on over against Lange, whom he grabbed in a bear-hug. He rode Lange right off the top of his brother into the dirt and commenced beating on him.

"Take the Brute Off!"

Lange shouted, "Take the brute off!"

Seaborn and Baker had been standing off from all this fracas about six or eight feet, near the end of the car. When Coke and Lange went down, they landed right in front of the old car. When Lange cried out, Seaborn wheeled and made a dash clear around the back end of the car and swooped down on the two scuffling men. He hit Coke two good whacks with his flashlight. Then he grabbed him from the back, chest high, picked him up off Lange and flung him back down on top of the bed.

At this point, Coke found the very thing that he had been seeking under the covers when the officers had first arrived. He looked down in the blankets where Seaborn's attack had landed him and he saw what he wanted. Quickly, his hand slid down into the covers and in that instant he came up with a 30/30 carbine rifle.

Just as Coke raised the rifle, Baker shouted, "Look out! He's got a gun! He's got a gun!"

Coke fired. He fired again.

Lange shouted something.

John, who was still on the bed, reached over and grabbed the rifle out of Coke's hands.

Baker took off on the run, headed for the "walk-log" that crosses the creek. As he mounted the log, the gun was continuing to go off. He saw a piece of wood fly up from under his feet.

He heard Coke shout, "There goes one of the sons of bitches; get 'em all!" Baker jumped off the log into the creek in order to keep the log between him and the gun, and went wading across as fast as he could go. As he charged up the opposite bank and back into the timber, he heard the gun still going off. He also heard a dog barking.

B. F. Decker lived 103 yards from the center of the Brite brothers' camp. He was Baker's closest neighbor, being located a few hundred yards upstream on the creek. His place was approximately a quarter of a mile from the Baker's home via the road. Decker was a retired contractor from Southern California and had been living on Horse Creek about five years. His house was quite a substantial one compared to others along the creek. On his property was also located a cabin in which his friend Bob Lanning lived. Lanning was a younger man and was Decker's partner in some small mining ventures on and near the property.

Decker was well acquainted with the Brite boys, especially Coke. He liked them both and considered them his friends. The boys had been in his home several times and they often visited when they met at the Horse Creek Store. As a matter of fact, on one occasion when former District Attorney Charles Johnson had been visiting Decker at his home, the Brite boys happened to also be there. Mr. Johnson, a former barber, often gave his friends haircuts; on this visit he had given John Brite one.

Decker was of course also acquainted with his neighbor, Charley Baker. The two of them were always cordial with each other but Decker really didn't care too much for Baker. He just sort of tolerated him but there was never any particular trouble between the two of them.

On the night of August 29th, 1936, Bob Lanning had come over to Decker's home and was listening to the radio. Decker himself was lying on the couch reading until after 11:00 o'clock when he went to bed. While he was asleep, Lanning had turned off the radio and gone back to his cabin.

About 1:30 a.m. Decker was awakened by what seemed to him as gun fire and a dog barking. His first thoughts were that somebody must be out there opening up the deer season two days early and shooting at his "pet" deer. A doe and two fawns had been making a habit of eating some of the plants in Decker's garden; he liked having them around and never disturbed them during their nocturnal visits to his yard.

Decker had been around guns all his life. As he got out of bed he heard what sounded to him like five or six shots from a small caliber rifle, then five or six more from a heavy power gun. He rushed to the kitchen window and raised it. As he did so, he heard sounds of utter confusion coming from a short distance down the creek. The dog was continuing to bark and growl as if he had hold of a deer; someone was hollering something that he couldn't make out, and the guns were still banging away. While this was going on he suddenly saw a shadow of something or someone that seemed to be running up the hill toward the house. Then he heard shouting again; one voice crying out something about "murder" and another was calling "Help!" The shadowy figure soon emerged into that of a running man who rounded Decker's garden fence and was headed for the house. Decker reached the door at the same time as the running man. He flung the door open, and there was Charley Baker.

"They're goin' to kill us all!" Baker shouted as he charged through the doorway. "Give me a gun; I think they've already shot the sheriff and my friend, Seaborn; let me have a gun!"

"Get hold of yourself, man!" Decker shouted. "Now what's this all about?"

Baker calmed a little and began babbling out the story of the attempted arrest. It was a disjointed rambling tale but Decker realized that he had more on his hands now than a couple of deer poachers.

"Sit down here and wait till I get back," said Decker. "I'm not giving you any gun. Those Brite boys wouldn't do that. I'm going down there and find out what it's all about."

"They'll kill you; don't go," Baker said.

"There are men down there hollering for help; I'm going," Decker said as he put on his overalls and then his shoes, without bothering to tie them.

"Sit right here and don't move a muscle until I get back," he said as he grabbed his flashlight and moved out into the night headed down the same route that Baker had so recently traveled in the opposite direction.

Baker began to panic again as soon as Decker stepped off the porch. He watched him go out of sight and then hurried over to Bob Lanning's cabin.

Lanning told him, "If Mr. Decker said to stay here, that's what we'll both do."

Decker went down the familiar trail and stopped at the near side of the walk-log across the creek. "Hello-o-o camp!" he called.

No answer. He went on across the log and stopped.

"He-ll-o-o camp!"

Still no answer. He moved on a little farther. He heard someone groaning.

"Coke! Are any of you on your feet?"

"Yea!" answered Coke's voice.

"This is Decker; I'm comin' into camp."

"Alright," said Coke, "come on in."

"I'm turning on my flashlight so I can see this trail," Decker said.

He walked right on into the camp. He saw John standing there holding what appeared to be a 30/30 rifle with the wooden stock broken off. John turned toward him but didn't raise the rifle or point it at Decker.

"Don't come into this camp," John said in a threatening voice.

"Well, I am comin' in," Decker said, "There's a man hollering for help. I'm comin' in."

Decker put the flashlight on John who was still a few yards away. John appeared to be in sort of a daze. Decker walked right up close to him, keeping the light in his eyes. When he was near enough, he just put his hand on the rifle and eased it out of the way and kept close enough so that John wouldn't be able to swing it around at him. John tried to step out of the light but Decker stayed with him. Finally he took John by the shoulder and gently shook him.

"Get your head about you," Decker said. "Look what you've done. There's one man, you see there, probably dead; there's two more over there. One's wounded and the other may be dead. My God, look what you've done."

Decker was both afraid and curious. From the moment he had turned on the flashlight he was able to make out a little of the scene in the camp. With some help from the moonlight filtering through the trees he had caught a glimpse of at least three men on the ground. One of them was moaning and the other two were either dead or unconscious. At the same time, he was carefully keeping his eye on John.

Coke was standing about four feet away from John. Coke was soaking wet; he had obviously been in the creek either sometime during the fight or after it had shut down. Coke was holding his left arm up with his other hand as though the arm was in a sling. It appeared that he couldn't move it. Both of the boys seemed to have taken somewhat of a beating.

Decker was very anxious to take a closer look at the men on the ground but he also didn't like to get any distance between him and that broken rifle still in John's hands.

Finally John seemed to break out of his trance or mood, or whatever it was and said, "Who are these men?"

"They are law officers," Decker replied.

"The hell they are! That one over there was up here fighting with us earlier tonight. He ain't no law man," John said scornfully.

"Well I don't know about all of 'em," said Decker, "but that one over there is Deputy Sheriff Lange because I know him."

"There's a dead one over there," John said, pointing.

"Well, who did that?" asked Decker.

John said, "I did; but for Christ sake put that flashlight out. Baker's been out there in the brush shooting at us."

"That's not so," Decker said. "Baker hasn't even got a gun. He came running up to my place when the shooting started down here and asked me for a gun but I wouldn't give him one."

As the three men stood there, Decker continued to steal glances at the men on the ground while he held John under careful surveillance. He was anxious to break this off so that he could determine whether or not anything could be done for the wounded men.

"Go on Up Home"

"I've got to notify the officers," Decker said. "You fellas go on up home and stay there 'till morning when the officers come. Don't try to leave 'cause they'll get you anyway. You can't get away; they'll track you down and get you sooner or later."

"Yea," Coke said, "I hear they lynch people who kill officers in this county."

"No they won't lynch you if you give up," Decker replied, "but they sure as hell will if you try to run away. The sheriff will protect you, but not if he has to run you down. Now I'm goin' up to my place and get the car so I can get to a phone. You fellas go on up home like I said."

With that, Decker turned away and started walking toward the walk-log without looking back. He figured that the boys wouldn't make a decision as to what they should do until he got out of there and could talk it over a little bit. He hoped that by the time he got back down there they would have cleared out so he could be of some help to the wounded men.

When Decker arrived back at his place he went over to Bob Lanning's cabin and told him to get the car out. He briefly outlined the situation for him and explained that they would go back to the camp in a few minutes after which they would be going down the creek to Judge Rainey's place to phone the Sheriff's Office.

As the two men were getting into the car, Baker came out of Lanning's cabin. He was still highly agitated. "What shall I do?" Baker asked.

"Go on home where you belong," Decker replied.

"Give me a gun. I don't want to take any chances on meeting those Brites out there," he said.

"No. Just go on home. John and Coke are gone by now," Decker explained as Baker started down toward the walk-log.

When Decker saw that Baker's route would take him right through the camp he figured the last thing he needed now was to have Baker in his condition stumbling through there.

"No, not that way," he shouted. "Go upstream a little ways and get on that trail that goes over to the Government Trail. Don't go down through the camp."

Baker turned and went the other way. When he was out of sight, Lanning started up the car and they headed down to the place where they had to ford the creek. After crossing, they pulled up near the Brite's old Ford and stopped.

The brothers were gone. This was Decker's first chance to really look the situation over in detail. The two men got out of the car. It was an eerie feeling for them, standing there in the still of the night where there had been so much tragic activity just a short while before. Everything seemed so very still except for the low groans of one or more of the men on the ground.

In the headlights of the car lay Martin Lange on his back in the center of the road, still making those same low guttural wheezing sounds that Decker had heard before. But now they were coming slower and lower in tone. The two men went over to him and they were aghast at what they saw.

His face was a mass of spattered blood, torn flesh and mangled bone. There were two bullet holes between his eyes and one below his nostril. Most of his entire upper jaw had been blown away. His head was cocked a little sideways as it lay on the ground and Decker could see a gaping hole blown out of the back of it where a bullet had obviously emerged. One thigh was a mass of seeping blood where another bullet had apparently found its mark.

Decker knew enough to realize that the man was still alive because he had a faint pulse and the blood was still oozing; he continued to make those moaning gurgling sounds. But Decker was unable to get any response from him; Lange was completely unconscious.

"My God," Decker said in a quiet voice, "this is a dying man. We can't do anything for him. I doubt if he would want to live anyway in the condition he's in." Decker raised up from a kneeling position, shook his head as though to shake off the gruesome sight he had been observing, and without saying another word, signaled to Bob Lanning to go on to the next man.

Like Dangerous Dan McGrew, the character in Robert Service's famous poem, Joe Clark was literally "pitched on his head and pumped full of lead." He was there by the side of the creek about fifteen feet north of where Lange lay. Clark was down on his knees and leaning over forward so that his head was on the ground, sort of like a position of praying. His coat was thrown forward over his head and his shoulder holster was hanging loose almost to the ground with his pistol still in it. Across his back lay the broken wooden remainder of the gun that John had in his hands when Decker previously arrived in the camp. He had been shot in the back. He was dead.

Captain Seaborn was lying on his back near the old Ford car just a few paces from where he had last let go of Coke when he threw him down on the bed during the fight. He was alive. He was also making those little moaning sounds and his body was twitching to some extent. Seaborn's face had literally been bashed in by a mighty blow from some blunt object. There had been massive bleeding that was still seeping through an apparent bullet wound that had entered near his left armpit. Decker again tried to get a response from Captain Seaborn but he too was totally unconscious.

"It's no use, Bob. We'll soon have three dead men in this camp," said Decker. "Let's get cracking on down the road to Rainey's place and report this. We'll have to move Deputy Lange's body out of the road in order to get through."

Just as the two men were heading over toward Lange, suddenly they heard a sound behind them. They both whirled around and here came Charley Baker crashing through the woods, running down the hill toward them as fast as he could.

"The boys are up on the hill!" Baker shouted.

"How do you know?," responded Decker.

"I was on the little trail up there and just as I got almost to the Government Trail I saw a match strike not ten feet in front of me and then a flashlight came on. I turned around and ran into the brush. I heard Coke say, 'That's Baker; get the son of a bitch!' I came straight down here."

"Damn it, Charley," Decker said, "will you ever get yourself back down to your house? The Brites were on the Government Trail headed on up to their place and you must have blundered into them. If they followed you down we would most surely have heard from them by now."

Baker was obviously completely shaken and disorganized by now; a nervous wreck.

"What shall I do?" he wailed.

Decker toned his voice down a bit and quietly said, "Mr. Baker, just go right on down the trail through your two gates and lock yourself into your house. The Brites have gone home and they'll do you no harm. We are going down now to Rainey's place and report what has happened here. You'll be alright."

Baker briskly moved out down the trail that he knew so well. When he went in the house he immediately loaded his rifle and sat by the window the rest of the night.

Lanning and Decker went on with their task. They gently lifted up Martin Lange and carefully moved him out of the road. They climbed into the car and headed out, down the twisting dusty six miles of mountain road that probably had never before seen so much late night traffic. They were two couriers in the night bearing the news that would be a great shock to the immediate communities involved. But beyond that, the news was destined to raise some seemingly impossible questions that would impact the whole State of California, and much of the nation as well. All of this notwithstanding, the news also was destined to unleash a series of events still to come that would literally test the fiber of the nation's judicial system and dramatically affect the very nature and character of the American people's attitudes toward law enforcement.

Down the Mountain to Spread the News

When Decker and Lanning arrived at their destination, Mrs. Rainey was able to get right through to the Sheriff's Office in Yreka. Deputy Sheriff Eddie Mathews was on the line; the same deputy who had been Acting Sheriff in the Johnson case and had made that wild dash from Dunsmuir to Yreka in a vain effort to intercept Johnson's lynchers. Mrs. Rainey did all the talking as Decker told her what to say. Mathews informed her that he would round up some more deputies and they would be on their way immediately; he said that he would stop at Rainey's for more instructions on the exact location of the trouble. Decker and Lanning then started back up the road followed by Judge Rainey and Joe La Plant. Mr. La Plant had been doing some work on Rainey's place and had been staying with them for some time. Baker was at his self appointed post at the window and watched the two cars go by.

When the four men arrived back at the camp, Seaborn was dead but there was no change in Martin Lange. Decker and Lanning took the car on up to the house where Decker began preparing a huge pot of coffee; he figured he would be having plenty of company before this night was over. Rainey and La Plant stayed at the scene to await the arrival of the officers.

After taking the phone call from Mrs. Rainey, Deputy Mathews called Sheriff Chandler at home and told him all he knew of the situation.

Chandler said, "While I get dressed, please call Dr. Schlappi and tell him to get right over to my house. I want to get him on board and leave immediately. It is doubtful from what you tell me, but there may be a possibility of saving someone's life down there. Even if we're too late for that, we need him down there to make a preliminary examination of the bodies. Also call Frank Bills and see if you can get an ambulance rolling. Then round up everyone you can and head down there too. I'll meet you at the scene."

Mathews quickly took care of the instructions from Sheriff Chandler and then called Deputy Sheriff L. L. Fortna. He was able to also recruit the two Yreka City night officers, Gilbert Rhodes and Frank Fullerton. These officers all reported to the county jail in just a few minutes. The four of them took off in Mathew's car at high speed. There was soon to be a veritable parade of traffic up the old Horse Creek road.

After checking in at Rainey's house, Mathews and his passengers navigated the twisting dirt road on up to Baker's place where they found Sheriff Chandler and Dr. Schlappl talking with Charley Baker; they were standing there next to Martin Lange's empty car.

When Mathews pulled up, Chandler said, "Good. We're all here. We'll go up together. Mr. Baker has told me how to get there."

As the officers started up the trail on foot, Baker called after them, "I'll be along in a few minutes. I want to come up there and look for my hat."

When Decker heard voices in the camp, he returned to the scene and made himself known; he offered any help that he could give. Judge Rainey and Joe La Plant, of course, were already there.

Dr. Roy Schlappi immediately conducted superficial examinations of the three victims. All of them were now dead.

Sheriff Chandler took immediate and complete charge. He called everyone present around him and instructed them to start out in the center of the camp and fan out in all directions, working every inch of the site in an effort to find any and all pieces of evidence that may turn up.

He announced, "If and when any of you find a weapon, sing out and we'll all gather round and witness an inspection of it to determine if it has been fired and if so, how many shots."

As the men went to work they soon found a pistol lying a foot or two from Captain Seaborn's head. It was mashed into the sandy soil as if it had been stepped on. It wasn't covered with any sand or soil but it was impressed into the surface to the depth of the thickness of the gun. Everyone gathered around as the sheriff had instructed; one of the deputies handed it to Chandler.

"Now gentlemen," Chandler said, "I want you all to observe this pistol which is known by all of us to have been Martin Lange's."

As he swung the cylinder open he said, "You can all see that the cylinder contains five live rounds of ammunition. One chamber is empty. It contains neither a live round nor a spent shell. We all know that this is the way that Martin always carried his gun, with the empty chamber under the hammer. I am now inspecting the barrel and determining that this pistol has not been fired. I want you all to look at it and verify this. And remember it."

The men all followed Chandler's instructions and agreed with his findings.

Immediately, Deputy Joe Clark's gun was found still in its holster on Clark's body. This gun, a 38 caliber Smith and Wesson revolver with a five inch barrel, blued color with walnut checkered handle, was also well known to all the officers. All six chambers contained live ammunition. The gun had not been fired.

As the group worked the area they kept bringing things over to Chandler. Clark's billy, the "tap" which Coke had felt; Lange's billy that had come apart when Coke had lunged for it; the wooden rifle stock from the broken gun that Decker had found John holding, retrieved from the fallen Clark's back; Seaborn's US Navy flashlight that he had struck Coke with in his efforts to get him off of Lange; Seaborn's unlighted Coleman lantern; Lange's handcuffs that he was never able to put on John. All these things and many more were picked up and meticulously accounted for.

Charley Baker found the empty wine bottle that one of the boys had thrown at him and Seaborn in their first encounter with the Brites the previous day. And next to it, he even found his hat.

Down the Road Rolled the Hearse

Deputy Coroner Frank Bills arrived at the scene in a Studebaker hearse driven by Walt Bower. All the men gathered around to quietly and carefully assist with the loading of the three bodies into the hearse. Sheriff Chandler turned over much of the evidence collected thus far to Mr. Bills, with instructions to deliver it back to the Sheriff's Office. Dr. Schlappi got in the hearse and they pulled out.

Down the road rolled the hearse. Inside, the body of Martin Lange, a farm boy who had become a deputy sheriff but wanted to get into something else in a "couple of years," was still wearing his badge, "Siskiyou Deputy #1." There was the body of Deputy Joe Clark, a kind and decent man who had agreed to come along, although it was not really in his line of duty; he had just wanted to be helpful. Here was Captain Fred Seaborn, leaving for the last time these beloved mountains where he had come to hunt with his old friend for so many years. He had lived a life of success and prestige, having served in the last war, but here he had come up against a culture that was beyond his comprehension; one with which he simply could not cope. All through the affair he had attempted to set things "right" by his standards but this battle he lost in the end.

The men continued to search further throughout the area as a few more things of interest were picked up. Chandler was really just killing time, waiting for daylight. About 4:30, when full visibility was available, he called everyone to the center of the area.

"We will now go up the trail to the Brite home and see if the brothers are there. I want each of you to be on alert lookout at all times; we don't know what lies ahead for us. Be on your guard."

Chandler then turned to Decker and asked, "Would you go along with us and show us the way?"

"I'd rather not," Decker responded.

Like the answer that Baker gave to Seaborn's question concerning "Who's car is that?" Chandler's instructions fast became just as controversial. Even Decker's answer to Chandler's question became part of the controversy.

There soon developed a faction which claimed that instead of saying "Be on your guard," Chandler had said, "If you see them, shoot and shoot to kill."

Decker claimed that the latter is what Chandler had said and having heard this, he refused to go up the hill with them. Chandler vehemently denied ever saying it and all the deputies backed him up on this. But later, Judge Rainey, under a blistering cross examination, very reluctantly confirmed Decker's version of what was said.

Upon Decker's refusal to go, Chandler said, "Well boys, come on, we'll go."

Up the Trail to the Brite Cabin

Up that steep rugged trail the five of them went, Chandler in the lead, followed by deputies Mathews, Fortna, Fullerton and Rhodes. It was tough going all the way. When they spotted the cabin, Chandler signaled for a stop and they ducked down in the brush to have a conference. But Ma Brite had already seen them; she came out on the porch and waved them in.

As soon as they were within speaking distance, Chandler asked her if the boys were here.

"No," she said, "they've gone. I've been expectin' you. You ain't in no danger here. Keep your hands off your guns and come right on in the house."

The men entered and Chandler introduced himself and informed her that they would make a search of the house. Mr. Brite emerged from one of the back rooms but said nothing.

"Mrs. Brite," Chandler said, "it would save us a lot of time looking if you would tell us whether or not they were carrying any guns with them when they got here last night."

"Yes they was," she said, "I'll git it for you."

She went into another room and brought out the remains of the broken 30/30 rifle, the stock of which was then on its way to Yreka in the evidence box aboard the hearse. The barrel was covered with dried blood. Without a word, she handed it to the sheriff and he handed it to Lloyd Fortna. Fortna pumped six live cartridges out of the magazine; the chamber was empty.

"Are the boys armed now, Mrs. Brite?" Chandler asked.

"Lord, I guess so. At least there ain't a single gun left now in this house," she said.

In a rather stern voice, Chandler asked, "Where are the boys, Mrs. Brite?"

"Them boys is far from here by now. They come in here in the dark early this morning all beat up in torn clothes and blood all over them. Coke has somethin' wrong with his arm and he can scarce use it. They're plumb scared of lynchers. They's afraid you can't or won't pertect 'em from lynchers. They loaded up with grub and headed fer the hills. You'll nar' catch them boys until you can guarantee pertection. Then they'll come in on their own."

All in the group later admitted that this was an impressive speech by the old lady. They all agreed that she was "some woman." Chandler thought to himself that this lady is going to have to be dealt with before they will ever get another look at "them boys."

The sheriff told her that they would now search the premises and then they would leave. He advised her that it is his duty to organize a posse and they would be back later today to commence combing the woods in order to find her sons. With this, she just kind of threw one hand up a little and stoically nodded.

When they all got back down to Baker's house, Chandler asked Mrs. Baker for a pair of scissors. He had given the blanket from the Brite's old makeshift bed roll to Charley earlier and told him to keep it for him. He now had Baker get it and Chandler snipped two large squares of material from it. This he wanted for scent for the dogs he intended to use in the manhunt that was to follow.

Let the Manhunt Begin

The whole group then departed for Yreka to make the necessary arrangements to commence the greatest manhunt ever conducted in the State of California; a manhunt that was faced with the task of fine-tooth combing some of the most rugged mountains and ravines on the North American continent; a hunt that would eventually involve law enforcement people in two states. The quarry was two young men, presumably fully armed, thoroughly experienced in mountaineering and wilderness survival, running scared and undoubtedly of the opinion they had everything to lose if captured. They were men who had now committed murder and if cornered, most surely would not hesitate to kill again.

A newspaper photo of a group of possemen heading out from headquarters at Horse Creek Camp to look for John and Coke. (Siskiyou County Sheriff's Department)

Aged Deputy, Woman Control Yreka Jail

YREKA (Siskiyou County), Aug. 31. The shooting of three men at Horse Creek by two half-breed Indians Saturday night left the sheriff's office here temporarily in the charge of an aged undersheriff and a woman.

Mrs. Mabel Passburg, the county jail matron for the last year, virtually took charge of the county jail when Sheriff W. G. Chandler and his staff of deputies led bands of posses into the hills in search of the killers of Deputy Sheriffs Martin Lange and Joe Clark of Yreka and Fred Seaborn, captain of the port at Vallejo.

Matron is Unperturbed

Until she was appointed a year ago Mrs. Passburg had never seen the inside of a jail. She is gray-haired, smiling, modest and unperturbed by the swirl of events around her.

"Some of the prisoners in the county jail are terrified at the prospect of them bringing those killers [John and Coke Brite who are sought for the triple slaying at Horse Creek] in here," she said. "They can hardly talk."

"We have a Negro prisoner who is so scared he actually looks pale. Another is making a great show of bravado, just to cover his fear."

Waits for Developments

When asked if she chanced to be in charge of the jail if the brothers were brought in and the jail surrounded by a mob intent on lynching them, what she would do, she said:

"There is not much one could do. At least I wouldn't be afraid to face them."

B.J. Neilon is the Undersheriff who has been left to carry on with Mrs. Passburg. He has grown gray in the county service and is unable to go into the hills on anything so rigorous as the present manhunt. But with the rush of queries and constant stream of visitors and the prisoners to handle, he has his hands full.

124

5

The Brite Brothers:
Manhunt!

It was still early that Sunday morning August 30,1936 when the sheriff and his men passed through Horse Creek on their return to Yreka. There had not yet been an official announcement of the shocking middle-of-the-night happenings, but news has a mysterious way of traveling in the mountain communities. As the authorities went by, there was already a considerable crowd gathered at the Horse Creek Store.

As the sheriff's group arrived at the courthouse in Yreka, a large gathering was there also. Word had gone out via those unseen mountain conduits. The loved ones left by the fallen officers had by now heard the worst; the friends of the victims had come to the courthouse to verify the electrifying news. Neighbor had told neighbor.

The Sunday early services of the three Yreka churches had let out and many of these people came across the street to see what the excitement was at the courthouse. It is safe to surmise that the telephone operators that had been directing the "heavy" traffic of calls during the night, both within Yreka and between Horse Creek and Yreka, had most certainly been passing on the news to friends and callers. Reporters from both of Yreka's weekly newspapers were on hand at the courthouse.

The feeling among the crowd that morning was at first surprise and shock; then sympathy for the murdered officers and their families; then anger. Anger over how this little community, this quiet remote county, could have such a series of tragic events. First the Hall case, then the Johnson case, and now this one. Four peace officers killed along with two civilians plus a lynching in a three year period; this had to be stopped. There was plenty of

---

(left) The Brite brothers' story was covered by newspapers all over the country and every possible angle of that story was exploited by the newspapermen. Apparently it seemed newsworthy that a woman, along with a man past his prime, were able to "hold down the fort," so to speak, at the jail with most of the officers out on the manhunt.

talk about another lynching that morning, but talk in a frustrated vein; the killers were far from accessible at the moment.

As soon as Chandler made it through the crowd into his office he went very carefully over the facts of all of the night's events with his duty officer. He instructed him to give out any and all parts of the information to anyone that wanted to know. But he admonished him to "give only the facts; give no opinions whatsoever; only the facts."

The sheriff then called all of his deputies who were on the premises into his office where he laid out his plans for the coming manhunt that he had worked out in his mind during the ride in from Horse Creek. Orders were given, ideas were exchanged and his officers went out on their errands. Nobody mentioned anything about getting some sleep. Then Chandler latched the office door; his calm voice could be faintly heard through the wall as he talked on the telephone for more than an hour.

As the morning wore on, the crowd in the courtyard continued to grow. But official activity in and about the Sheriff's Office was building even faster. All of the department personnel had been arriving. Possemen answering calls from the deputies and from Sheriff Chandler himself began arriving. Two blood hounds were brought in by their owner from his home in the mountains nearby. District Attorney Davis came in for a briefing from the sheriff. Cars were coming in and going out. Men were arriving carrying their own rifles, taking the deputy's oath and leaving in posse groups. The dogs, with the owner and two of the deputies who had been at the scene such a short time ago, left with another group. It was a time of sorrow for the community but the excitement of the moment was now building with a great momentum of its own.

Court Reporter Ralph McMurry and his wife were attending the 11:00 o'clock service at the Episcopal Church as usual. They had heard about the tragic event before leaving home that morning and had seen the crowd in the courtyard as they entered the church across the street. When they came out, they saw that the crowd was even larger but it was against the Court Reporter's principles to intrude until he was called. He thought it best that they go on home because he knew the phone would be ringing in connection with the event before this day was over. But their youngest son was there in the crowd. He was a high school freshman by this time and was more inquisitive now than ever before, if that was possible.

In the 1930s in Siskiyou County there were several newspapers, all weeklies, two of which were published in Yreka, the *Siskiyou News* and the *Yreka Journal*. These papers stayed with mostly local news but they did subscribe to the wire services. The national news from the services was not of too great importance locally though, because there were three metropolitan daily newspapers available; the *San Francisco Examiner*, the *San Francisco Chronicle* and the *Sacramento Bee*. These three papers came to the county every day for sale on newsstands and home delivery.

At that time, as it still is today, each of these three metropolitan dailies had a very distinct character or personality. The *Examiner* was the more sensational and flamboyant in its news treatment; the *Chronicle* was more conservative and dignified, while the *Bee* was sort of "countrified" and "small townish" even though it was a metropolitan paper.

The news of the weekend's events in Siskiyou County reached these three papers on Sunday. The two previous murder cases involving police officers and a lynching had been rather cursorily covered by the three metropolitan papers. But those cases had planted a very subtle seed in the heads of the news gathering management of those papers. This seed was labeled "Siskiyou County - Lynching County." When news of the current murders broke, these papers smelled "lynch." All three forthwith dispatched complete reporting crews including photographers via private aircraft.

Here Come the Newsmen

On Monday morning the word was out in Yreka that the *Examiner* reporting crew would arrive at the local airport around noon, with the other two papers following close behind. Many Yreka citizens were on hand at the

Although this photo is of an air show at Siskiyou County Airport near Montague during this same time period, the crowd gathered for the arrival of three planes carrying reporters from the big city probably looked like this. (Siskiyou County Museum)

127

airport to watch the planes come in; among them was Court Reporter Mc-Murry's inquisitive youngest son.

True to its reputation as the sensational and flamboyant paper, the *Examiner* won the race for first arrival on the scene. As per its image, the plane was the very latest cabin model Beechcraft biplane. The lower wing was mounted farther forward than the upper wing which gave it a very speedy and classy look. When the reporters emerged from it, they were all quite young wearing slacks and pull-over sweaters, no ties of course; an accurate manifestation of the "gung ho" reputation of the *Examiner*.

In the middle of the afternoon the *Chronicle* crew arrived in an airplane that most certainly expressed the image of that paper. Its aircraft was a large two engine monoplane that looked more like one of the commercial air liners of the day. When the *Chronicle* crew came out, they were mostly middle aged men, all wearing suits and ties, obviously responsible and conservative in nature; a very accurate portrayal of the character of that paper.

Now it was the turn of the crew from the *Bee* to arrive; but it seemed they were never going to come. As the daylight was just beginning to give way after many of the Yrekans had left the field, a tiny spec in the southern sky was finally spotted. As it slowly neared, it was obvious that it was moving at a speed not much faster than a good runner could travel. It turned out to be the most outrageous looking airplane that had ever come this way.

It was an old radial engine biplane upon which everything on it appeared to have been broken at one time or another and had simply been nailed or wired back together. It did have a closed cabin but that was the extent of the amenities of the contraption. It could best be described as resembling one of those planes used by Eddie Ricketyback Air Lines featured in the famous *Little Abner* comic strip.*

When the reporters were finally able to bang and pry the door open they came out in the entirely expectable format of the *Bee*. They were all skinny fellows of varying ages, wearing suits with unbuttoned open vests but no ties. Each was wearing a hat that was pushed back on his head with a card stuck in the band upon which was printed the word "PRESS;" a true portrayal of that paper's image.

As soon as each of these groups of reporters were on the ground they immediately set about questioning members of the crowd at the airport. In every case the thrust of these questions was identical:

Little Abner was a comic strip about a fictional clan of hillbillies by Al Capp that ran in newspapers from 1939 to 1977. One of the recurring characters was WWI ace Eddie Ricketyback, pilot for the decrepit Trans-Dogpatch Airlines.

The search for the Brites was headquartered at Horse Creek Camp, comprised of the store, the post office and a handful of cabins. The road across the bridge led up the edge of the valley and beyond into the mountains to the shooting site and the trailhead to the Brite family cabin. (Livingston Collection)

"Have they caught the Brite brothers yet?"

"Is there any talk of lynching?"

At the first meeting of the *Chronicle* reporters with Sheriff Chandler, the use of the company owned airplane was offered to help in the manhunt. Chandler turned them down on this with the explanation that an air search of the densely timbered mountains was not effective. He told them that he might accept the offer at a later time.

As the week rolled on, the tension and excitement in Yreka was growing at a frenzied pace. Mayor Al Herzog released the following statement:

"I will if necessary, in my official capacity, call out the militia if the threat of lynching is rumored in the event the Brite boys are captured and placed in the jail in Yreka."

When California Governor Frank Merriam was informed of the Yreka mayor's statement, he issued one of his own:

"There must be no more lynchings in California; I will take whatever action is necessary to enforce the law."

In Parker & Messner's Barber Shop, former District Attorney Charley Johnson was heard to remark, "After those two statements, I'm certain that if there is anyone left that hasn't considered a lynching, they will now be sure to get the idea."

The Wednesday issue of the *Yreka Journal* seemed to capture the feeling and excitement of the situation in the lead article as follows:

NO TRACE OF BRITE BROTHERS

POSSIBILITY OF CAPTURE LESSENS AS BRITE BOYS ENTRENCH IN WILDERNESS

THEORY OF PARENTS THAT BROTHERS WOULD GIVE THEMSELVES UP TO JACKSON COUNTY OREGON POLICE DISPROVED BY FRIENDS

Brothers Believed Now Firmly Entrenched in Wilderness Fastness Near Base of Mt. Sterling

Possible Winter Refuge Known

Hope of capture of the two Brite brothers, murderers of Joe Clark, Martin Lange, both of Yreka and Captain Fred Seaborn of Vallejo, waned today as search for the killers continued in the wilderness of the Siskiyou Mountains in the vicinity of Mt. Sterling. According to members of the posse, continued search is useless in the mountain fastness, as both boys, expert mountaineers, have by now, no doubt, entrenched themselves in the most remote section. Well versed in the terrain in which they are hiding, search could be continued for months without results if the Brite brothers could acquire additional food, is the belief of many residents of the sector.

Bold killers now, the danger of search increases as they continue to evade the law and become more desperate as days pass. It is the belief of Oregon State Troopers guarding mountain passes in the Applegate that the Brite boys will never be captured alive, but will, if cornered, shoot it out to the last.

Search to date by the members of nine posses has led officers to believe that for the first day the boys collected what supplies they could in remote cabins and circled the mountain ridges to throw off searching parties. In the days following, firmly entrenched by additional ammunition and a 30-30 rifle stolen from the Ward cabin, the boys sought refuge in one of the cabins near the base of Mt. Sterling.

Fred Combest, an old time resident of Jacksonville, Oregon and a miner, this morning, in an interview with Associated Press reporters, told of a mine at Mt. Sterling known as the Scheming Guishang Claim which he believes will be the headquarters of the boys if winter settles down and they evade capture. Combest stated that the boys have worked the mine and are well acquainted with the intricate tunnel work and entrances which would provide shelter in the event of siege.

The theory that the Brite brothers would turn themselves over to police of Jackson County was scoffed at by former friends of the boys who live in the vicinity of Jacksonville, the former home of the Brites. These former friends of both Coke and John state that at the present time they know of no one in Oregon, with the possible exception of a John Wolf, living on Mt. Sterling, who might aid the two. It was first stated by the parents of the boys, Mr. and Mrs. A. J. Brite, who live on the upper reaches of Horse Creek that the sons would undoubtedly turn themselves over to police of Jackson County to prevent the possibility of lynching in Siskiyou.

Dead End Leads and Reward Money

The rumors of sightings of the fugitives began pouring in. The Sheriff's Office was receiving information from all over the west. Each of these messages had to be checked out and investigated by the Sheriff's Department and decisions made as to whether or not to pursue it. One of the most logical "sightings" that seemed worthwhile to follow up came in from Rockport, Mendocino County, on the coast.

Constable P. A. Stenberg of nearby Fort Bragg relayed the information to Yreka that the Brite brothers had been seen at an idle lumber mill near Rockport. Jack Ross, the caretaker had sent word to the constable that two rough-dressed men had appeared at his place seeking food. According to the caretaker, one of the men who had a heavy growth of beard answered the description of one of the Brite brothers. After checking with Yreka, Constable Stenberg sent men to Rockport to check it out but nothing ever came of it.

Each morning at the jail a fairly sizeable crowd gathered to watch the various posses receive instructions and head out. Much to the chagrin of

Sheriff Chandler, District Attorney Davis organized his own posse. Each morning this group was duly dispatched with oratorical encouragement from the district attorney.

On Thursday the Siskiyou County Board of Supervisors in a special meeting announced the posting of a reward of $500 each for the capture, dead or alive, of the Brite brothers. Sheriff Chandler thereupon requested Governor Merriam to match this action with a similar amount.

Deer hunting season was now open. In addition to the organized posses, the woods were literally filled with gun toting men who would like nothing better than rounding out a deer hunt with a couple of additional shots that could be worth $1,000 or more. At this time of year the talk in the beer joints and the barber shops was traditionally about deer hunting. But this year it all contained this new and exciting embellishment of the manhunt.

In those days it was legal for a county supervisor to form a posse and more than one of them did. Supervisor Bill Davidson of the Scott Valley district had a small posse of his own. They were acting on some information that one of the Brites had been seen in the vicinity of the eastern slope of Gazelle Mountain. As they were beating the brush in this general area they looked up and saw a man coming down the mountain on a well worn trail carrying a full pack. The possemen hid in the brush as the "fugitive" walked right into the trap. The man was terrified. The Supervisor kept demanding his name but the captive didn't seem to understand what was wanted. There seemed to be a slight problem here; the man was apparently feigning a lack of ability to speak English. About all he was able to shout were two words, "Soy Yang."

One of the possemen said, "He sure as hell ain't no 'Chinaman.' He's just pulling our leg. I've seen that John Brite once and I'm practically sure we got him now."

The posse brought him in. To the county jail? No; to a roadhouse, the 99 Ranch, on the highway near Weed. As soon as they brought him in and got the beer flowing, the word went out and the inevitable crowd started to form. Now there was talk in earnest about "getting a rope." Finally some of the more responsible individuals present gained control of the situation.

"I saw Mrs. Chester Barton in Yreka early this morning," one of the men said. "She and her husband run the Horse Creek Store; I've heard she is very well acquainted with the Brites. Let's call Yreka and see if she could be brought here to identify this fellow once and for all."

Telephone calls were made as the angry crowd continued to grow. Sure enough, Mrs. Barton was located and she agreed to come to the 99 Ranch.

In about forty-five minutes Mrs. Barton arrived. She was ushered through the crowd and into the barroom to confront the cowering fellow being held against the wall still muttering those strange words, "Soy Yang."

"That's John Brite"

Before speaking a word, she hesitated and looked the man over very thoroughly. After what seemed like endless minutes she raised her arm pointing to the "suspect" and said, "That's John Brite."

Several of the men inside the bar slowly began to move toward the door to make preparations for what everyone knew was coming next.

Mrs. Barton continued talking to the man. "Come on John, own up to who you are. Your mother will be ashamed of you if you act this way. You know me and I know you."

But the man was by now nearly out of his senses with fear. He too began to realize what was coming next.

Before anyone realized it, there was another man suddenly in the room. Sheriff Chandler had gotten wind of the strange messages that had been floating around Yreka. He had seen John Brite before and knew exactly what he looked like. He feared the worst and dug out as fast as he could go.

As Chandler came in, a hush fell over the room. Some of the men felt relieved while others were disappointed. He walked right over to the man against the wall, took one look, and said, "That man doesn't look anything like John Brite; or Coke Brite either."

When some of the others objected to Chandler by telling him that Mrs. Barton had identified the man as John Brite, Chandler went straight to her and very courteously informed her that it was not the man she thought.

Mrs. Barton looked him over again and agreed with the sheriff this time. She went again to the man and apologized profusely as he was being released.

His name later was found to be John Soyang, a native of Finland who spoke practically no English. He had been prospecting in the Gazelle Mountain area. He had heard nothing prior to this time about the murder at Horse Creek or that there was a huge manhunt underway in the mountains. John Soyang had come very close to a mistaken "rendezvous with destiny."

Governor Merriam Speaks Up

And the fever kept building.

Governor Merriam, upon hearing unofficially of Sheriff Chandler's request for the state to match the county rewards, issued another statement:

> Any official request for posting of state reward for the capture of the Brite Brothers will be given consideration, but as yet none has been received.
>
> I am unalterably opposed to lynching as a method of punishment or as a means of teaching a lesson. In the first place, California cannot advance without proper regard for processes of law and order. California courts are established for the purpose of protecting the individual when he needs it, as well as punishing him when he deserves it. For this reason justice prevails only under a system of efficient courts. In the second place, those who engage in lynching activities cannot be sure they are punishing the right man. Lack of evidence at hand and lack of time to investigate might easily result in execution of a wrong person. Mob violence should always be discouraged, even to the extent of prosecution.

Out there among all the frenzy there were also men of good will and sober judgment. One was Court Reporter Ralph McMurry. In answer to a question from his son he said, "No one can disagree with the position of all these people such as the governor and the mayor who are uttering these stirring disclaimers against lynching. But not one of them is actually addressing the real problem. The problem in the first place is the judicial system's frequent inability to deliver absolutely true justice. In the second place, the problem is with the system's total failure to deliver any kind of justice in a timely fashion."

The rumors were still coming in. Chandler had two big posses working around the Blue Ledge Mine near the Oregon border. Sheriff Lowe of Klamath Falls had a detachment of Oregon Police on a "hot trail that may soon lead to the taking of these desperados." The Brite cabin on Horse Creek was under constant surveillance but there was no indication that the brothers had returned or that the parents had any communication with them. Two men were reported to have been seen in the deep wilderness near Mt. Sterling but a follow up on this one came to nothing.

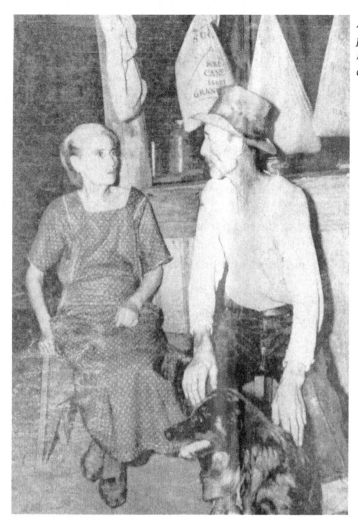

A newspaper photo of Ma and Pa Brite in their cabin.

Ma and Pa Brite were seen in Yreka from time to time; they seemed to be conferring with one or two different lawyers. Whenever they were recognized it generated a small crowd in which could be found some who cursed them and others who showed considerable sympathy. On a promise from Associated Press that they would give it wide circulation, Ma Brite wrote out an appeal to her sons that said, "For God's sake, come home to mother and dad. The sheriff has promised a square deal." The parents' pictures appeared in the papers nationwide as well as the local publications.

B. F. Decker was not very well known in Yreka. But since the murder his role as "first on the scene" had brought him considerable notoriety. He began appearing in town on numerous occasions during the manhunt. He was probably the person in the whole county who was the most closely acquainted with the Brite brothers. When he was in town he always frequented the various local bars where he was constantly expounding all he knew of the case before very willing listeners. In hearing his side of the case it became obvious that his sympathies were with the brothers. It was repeated around town that Decker claimed "those officers got everything they deserved." While this kind of talk didn't do much for Decker's standing in the community, it did create a counterpoint within the constant discussions about the case.

Former District Attorney Johnson, who was noted for his wit was heard to remark, "My friend Decker seems to have caused a sensation around town with his remarks about the case; at least it is a relief to know that there is one resident of the county that would be opposed to lynching the Brite brothers."

Fugitive Murderer Caught – But Not a Brite

And then in the middle of all this upheaval that was keeping Chandler on the go, a most bizarre event occurred. At first it made Chandler furious, but then in retrospect amused him to some extent.

Robert Miller Barr, Clyde Johnson's accomplice in the murder of Dunsmuir Chief of Police Jack Daw the year before [Chapter 3], was arrested in Los Angeles.

He had been detained in connection with a series of burglaries in Southern California and his "wanted" status in Siskiyou County had been uncovered. This meant that he had to be returned to Yreka which would require the detachment of two deputies for at least three days. Under the circumstances, Chandler was in no position to arrange this. After considerable negotiations with the Southern California authorities who were fully aware of Chandler's problems at the time due to the extensive newspaper coverage, they finally consented to deliver the defendant to Yreka.

When Barr was safely ensconced in the Siskiyou County Jail, the story of his activities since the shooting in Dunsmuir was what disturbed Chandler. After he interviewed Barr in his cell, the sheriff was furious.

He called a press conference and told the reporters, "Robert Barr fled the scene of the shooting that night one year ago on foot through the brush in the Sacramento River Canyon. He was able to flag a ride on the highway very quickly and was able to make a clean getaway from the immediate area. He made his way to Portland and Klamath Falls and some other Oregon towns, sleeping and hiding in the woods and brush for nine days after the shooting. He then was able to hitchhike to Lake Tahoe."

With his voice beginning to rise, Chandler went on, "And what do you think he did in Lake Tahoe? He was in the movies! He got a job as an extra in the movie, *Rose Marie*, which was being filmed there. He was in numerous scenes in the picture. And by golly he was using his true name, Robert Barr, when he was hired. All this at the same time that his picture and name were on every post office wall in America, and while there was a highly publicized manhunt on for him!"

After the reporters left the press conference and Chandler had cooled down a bit, he began to chuckle about it and said to one of the deputies, "You know, that son of gun had a lot of guts; stupid, yes, but a lot of guts."

On the Tuesday after the shooting, Joe Clark's funeral was held and Martin Lange's was the next day. There was a very large turnout of local citizens for each one. Afterwards there were the usual quiet conversations among small groups of people discussing the tragedy of the situation. But as before at the funeral of Chief of Police Daw in Dunsmuir, the old subject of a potential lynching reared its head. This was not a mob that would call for action; there were no actual provocateurs involved. The subject had been discussed so much in the previous few days that by now it had become commonplace conversational fare. At these two occasions this talk seemed to consist mainly of polite quiet discussions among friends as to whether this person or another felt that a lynching would actually take place.

At 7:00 o'clock in the evening of the day of the Lange funeral, the inquest was held in Yreka. As might be expected, there was a large crowd in attendance.

The purpose of an inquest under California law is primarily to determine if possible the cause of death of a deceased person. Its purpose is not to find or accuse murderers even though the verdict of an inquisition jury may state that a deceased person was killed by so and so, but the naming of the killer is not the primary purpose. The inquest is to determine the facts involved in the death of a person and if the facts include a murder, the verdict often so states. This concept must be kept in mind in view of the strange twist that this case was about to take; a twist, the first subtle indications of which were manifested during the inquest.

By law an inquest is conducted by the county coroner but the district attorney is allowed to be present and also question the witnesses if he so desires. The law recognizes that if some obvious facts are present that indicate a felony, it is very useful for the district attorney to have his chance at questioning witnesses, thus gaining as much information as possible concerning a case in which it is obvious he will soon be very much involved. From this point of view, it has become customary for the coroner and the district attorney to cooperate very closely in cases where a serious crime most likely has been committed.

The manner in which an inquest is conducted is very similar to that of a trial. One of the major differences, however, is in the rules of what testimony is allowed. In the case of the inquest, the law is not nearly as restrictive as it is for a trial. Hearsay and even a narration of the thoughts that were in the witnesses' heads are entirely admissible. Of course there is no judge to act as a "referee" to see that the rules are observed as is the case in a trial.

Inquest Held; Suspects Still at Large

Coroner Felix J. Kunz conducted the inquest before nine jurors plus Court Reporter McMurry and District Attorney James G. Davis. Just four witnesses were called. The first was Frank Bills, the mortician who had taken the hearse to the scene of the shooting. His testimony was very short and consisted only of the names of the individuals whose bodies he found there.

The second witness was Dr. Roy Schlappi whose testimony was very lengthy. He minutely described the various wounds he found in the victims and then continued on through the results of the autopsies that he and the county physician, Dr. Albert Newton, had performed the following day. As always where doctors give testimony in a case such as this, it consisted of endless technical descriptions in surgeon's vernacular. They described the various wounds together with giving opinions on the trajectories that the bullets followed inside the bodies. All of this was as usual very difficult for laymen to understand. Inasmuch as this evidence was ultimately destined to become a factor in subsequent public opinion concerning the case, it can be interpreted here in more common language as follows:

Dr. Schlappi stated that at the time that he arrived at the scene, Martin Lange had been dead approximately two hours. He said that the head was very badly mutilated by three gunshot wounds. At the later autopsy the next day he and Dr. Newton found a cut on the right ear, a jagged lacerated wound in the forehead, two bullet wounds between the eyes and one below the left eye. They also observed what was thought to be still another bullet wound in the nostril. There was one wound of exit in the back of the head. Lange's body also had a bullet wound in the left thigh that had shattered the large bone in the left leg.

Dr. Schlappi went on to state that in the body of Joe Clark they found just one bullet wound. It had entered the back just to the left of the spine, totally shattering the right lung, touching the tip of the heart and emerging at the right arm pit; he had been instantly killed.

Captain Seaborn, according to the autopsy report, had a compound fracture of the skull over the right eyebrow penetrating into the brain. This wound was caused by a blow from something other than a bullet as no exit wound in the head was discovered nor any ballistic fragments found in the brain. Two bullets were found to have entered the left armpit, both coursing downward severing the large vessels of the right lung and fragments of which penetrated both kidneys.

When Coroner Kunz asked the doctor if any powder burns were found on the bodies, he replied, "There were powder marks from the effect of only one bullet on Martin Lange, that being the one beneath the right eye. There were powder marks on first examination of Joe Clark; powder had burned his shirt. None were found on Captain Seaborn."

The next witness called was Charley Baker, the only survivor and eye witness of the events that led to the deaths of the victims. Contrary to nearly everyone's first impression, Charley Baker turned out to be a literally magnificent witness.

Coroner Kunz started out with the usual questions for leading into the pertinent testimony. Baker's responses were quick, sharp and to the point. Then as Kunz's questions led Baker into the events of the shooting, the answers became longer and longer, more detailed and more vivid. Here was a simple man who was hard of hearing and could scarcely read or write, but he was now demonstrating an amazing ability to remember and describe the events in a clear and concise manner. As he went on describing what had happened, event after event, action after action, Kunz was finding it unnecessary to even ask more questions. He just let Baker go on and on with his story. Baker's grammar, of course, left something to be desired but his eloquence and confidence out weighed any other considerations. It was truly an amazing performance.

Baker's Story

Baker told of the altercation that he had with Coke Brite at his front gate, how Coke had cursed him in front of his wife and the fight that ensued.

Coroner Kunz interrupted here to ask, "When was this, Mr. Baker?"

Charley replied, "Well, I disremember exactly when it was, but it was a good month ago anyhow."

He told about Seaborn coming and how they went out to search for the horse. This narration included all the conversations between himself and Seaborn. He vividly described the battle that the two of them got in with the Brite brothers. He told everything in strict sequence, never hesitating, never faltering. Then he related in minute detail the events of the shooting itself, leaving out nothing right up until he ran from the scene half way across the walk log and jumped into the creek "to keep that log 'tween me and whoever was shootin' at me." The transcript of the inquest shows that in 297 lines of testimony, nearly ten pages, Kunz only asked him nine questions, two of which were the opening ones of "What is your full name?" and "Where do you reside?"

Then Coroner Kunz sat down after motioning to District Attorney Davis.

In an actual trial of a defendant charged with a crime, it often happens that a cross-examining lawyer will take the defendant, or even a witness, back over the exact same territory that has just been covered. There are other reasons for this, but generally it is done in an effort to trip up the defendant or witness in order to show that he has bias or is lying, or in the case of a witness, that he is the one that is guilty of the crime. Whatever his motive was, this was exactly what District Attorney Davis attempted to do with Charley Baker.

He started in all over again where Charley had originally commenced with a description of the first altercation with Coke Brite. The district attorney's tone of voice was somewhat mocking and accusatory. When Baker told him he had hit Coke with part of the rose bush trellis and he had wanted to have Coke arrested but Chester Barton had talked him out of it, Davis asked, "You were going to have him arrested because you struck him with a club?"

When Baker described the fight that he and Seaborn had with the Brites by the creek the evening of the shooting, Davis persisted in insinuating that Baker had uttered something other than that to which he had just testified in answer to the same question from Coroner Kunz. This very well may have been the beginning of the rationale of that faction that came to believe that Baker's reply to Seaborn had been fifteen words instead of the famous ten. This developed as follows:

Q. On that Saturday afternoon, you say that you and Captain Seaborn came to a little creek; just came to Horse Creek just below Decker's house?

A. Yes sir, we did.

Q. You say that Captain Seaborn wanted to have a drink?

A. Yes sir, he did.

Q. You say that Captain Seaborn asked you who owned the automobile parked there?

A. He did.

Q. What was your answer to that question?

Baker's answer was the famous controversial ten words, "It belongs to the Brite boys up on the hill."

Q. It belongs to the Brite boys up on the hill?

A. Yes sir.

Q. Did you say anything more than that right there?

A. I did not.

Q. Awhile ago, you testified that Captain Seaborn said, "If we had said anything that offended you, we are sorry for it."

A. I did.

Q. What did Captain Seaborn mean when he said, "If we have said anything that offended you, we will apologize?"

A. While Coke was cursing us and calling us sons-of-bitches, Mr. Seaborn made the remark, he says, "If we have said anything that offended you boys, we are sorry for it."

Q. Captain Seaborn was with you, wasn't he?

A. Yes sir.

Q. When he was with you when he said "If we have said anything that offended you," by "we," he meant you and him?

A. He did.

Q. Well, what had actually been said?

A. We hadn't said anything. I didn't even know they was there.

Q. Not knowing they were there, did you say anything?

A. I did not.

Finding Baker unflappable on this point, Davis led him through the details of the fight and on to Seaborn and Charley's visit with Justice of the Peace Rainey in order to get the warrant. His line of questioning seemed to be an effort to belittle the witness for not cosigning the warrant.

Q. Had Captain Seaborn been struck with the fist?

A. He had been struck with the fist several times.

Q. Do you remember talking to me the other day on Horse Creek, Mr. Baker?

A. Sir?

Q. Do you remember when I questioned you?

A. Yes, I remember when you questioned me.

Q. At that time and place when I asked you about this, why didn't you tell me that you had been struck with a club?

A. I think I did.

Q. Now, Captain Seaborn had only been struck with the fist, you say?

A. Yes sir.

Q. Later on, when you got this warrant from Mr. Rainey, that is, when Captain Seaborn got the warrant and filed a complaint.

A. Yes sir.

Q. Captain Seaborn filed a complaint, didn't he?

A. He did.

Q. Do you know what kind of a complaint he filed?

A. Yes, I think I do. I don't know whether I can repeat it or not, but anyhow it was an assault and battery; assault and battery, deadly weapon and intent to kill.

Q. Assault and battery, deadly weapon and intent to kill?

A. Yes, swore he would kill.

Q. And he swore to that?

A. Yes sir.

Q. And he swore to that in the face of the fact that he had only been struck by the man with his fist?

A. Yes.

Q. You were the man that was actually hit with the club?

Q. Yes, that read "we." If I ain't mistaken, it read "we" because we discussed it there when Mr. Rainey was writing it out. Mr. Seaborn swore they would kill us both, and they struck Mr. Baker with a club.

Q. But nevertheless, in the face of that, he swore to a complaint to all of those charges that you describe, and you didn't sign anything, is that right?

A. No, sir, I didn't sign anything.

Davis then worked his way into the actual shooting itself. It was here that his questioning of Baker seemed to be implying that perhaps Baker was the provocative cause of the shooting.

It went like this:

Q. All right. Then, the man that is lying in the bed, Officer Lange would be on the left hand side of the man that is lying in the bed?

A. Yes, that was it.

Q. Now, Officer Lange said, "We are officers?"

A. Yes sir.

Q. Did he then make the statement, "You are under arrest"?

A. "You are under arrest."

Q. Still these boys were under the covers?

A. Yes sir.

Q. Then, what did Lange do next?

(No answer)

Q. Now, where did Mr. Clark stay, in front of you?

A. Yes sir, right in front of me. Officer Lange walked up there when he says, "Hello boys!" He just made another step and Clark stepped right in here [pointing to the site drawing that Davis had prepared] between me and Lange. And he says, "We are officers; you are under arrest." Mr. Clark reached over and pulled the blanket out.

Q. Did he reach over with his right hand or his left hand?

A. I don't know. He had the search light in one hand. He pulled the blanket back. He jerked the blanket right off of their face.

Q. He jerked the blanket right off of their faces?

A. Yes sir.

Q. Did they try to grab for the covers in any way?

A. Well, I won't say that they did; don't know.

Q. Well, just after that, the next thing that happened? Who went into action next?

A. Mr. Lange reached over and hit John with the billy.

Q. That is your story. Mr. Lange reached over and hit which one, John or Coke?

A. Coke. John raised his head up. He was cursing. He told Mr. Clark, "There was no son-of-a-bitch of an officer could arrest us."

Q. All right. Now, after Officer Lange struck this blow, struck the man who was lying in the bed, what did Officer Clark do?

A. Coke then raised up like and Clark reached over.

Q. Officer Clark then struck Coke?

A. Coke?

Q. Coke.

A. Yes sir.

Q. What did he hit him with?

A. Hit him with a billy, or blackjack, or something of the kind.

Q. You were how many feet of where those officers were doing this?

A. Well, I was anywhere from two to three feet.

Q. Anywhere from two to three feet. Where was Mr. Seaborn?

A. Seaborn was standing right behind me, looking over my shoulder.

Q. You saw Officer Lange strike?

A. Yes sir.

Q. You saw Officer Clark strike?

A. Yes sir.

Q. Did you see Officer Lange strike a second blow?

A. Yes sir.

Q. And a third blow?

A. He had a handcuff then.

Q. He then tried to get the handcuff on him, is that right?

A. Yes sir.

Q. What was Officer Clark doing all of that time?

A. He was trying to make Coke behave.

Q. What method was he using to make Coke behave?

A. Hitting him with the billy two or three times.

Q. Hitting him with the billy?

A. Yes sir.

Q. What were you doing, standing there?

A. I was standing there looking on.

Q. You were standing there looking on. Did you say anything?

A. I don't remember whether I did or not. I don't think I did.

Q. Did you make this statement to Mr. Lange: "Pour it to the son-of-a-bitch, that's the bastard that hit me!"

A. No sir, I did not.

Q. You didn't? You didn't make any statement like that at all?

A. I did not.

Q. You didn't try to help either one of those officers, did you?

A. I didn't have nothing to help them with.

Q. You didn't? Did you have two hands?

A. Yes sir.

Q. Did you have two feet? Did you?

A. Yes sir.

Q. Are you the same man that knocked Coke down some time before with a club?

A. I didn't take a hand in it.

Q. You got the officers up there, didn't you?

A. No sir, I didn't have them officers up there. I taken them up there, but I did not swear out a warrant.

Q. But you went down, you and Seaborn swore out a warrant?

A. I did.

Q. You told those officers those men were killers on the way up there, didn't you?

A. I did.

Q. Didn't you?

A. I didn't swear out no warrant for them. I went with them because they asked me to.

On and on it went; every detail was gone over again even though Baker had already told about it. In the following exchange Davis insinuated that Baker was a coward and that he could have prevented the shooting even after the melee was under way:

A. When Coke made a grab for the gun and pulled the gun out.

Q. Did you see him do that?

A. I seen him do it.

Q. You saw him when he pulled the gun out?

A. Yes sir.

Q. He was about three or four feet from you, was he?

A. Yes, he was about eight feet.

Q. He was about eight feet?

A. Yes.

Q. You saw him when he reached for that gun?

A. I saw him when he reached for the gun and when he pulled the gun out.

Q. And what did you do?

A. I hollered to the boys, "He has gone for a gun!"

Q. You didn't do a thing, Mr. Baker, to stop that man with that gun?

The last witness to be called was B. F. Decker. Coroner Kunz didn't question him at all but turned him right over to District Attorney Davis.

The district attorney went through all of Decker's story in as much detail as he had with Baker but this time the subtle antagonistic attitude was missing. Decker, too, was a very good witness and made an extremely credible presentation.

During the questioning of Decker, one of the jurors interrupted the District Attorney by saying, "This is a Coroner's Inquest, not a trial. Let's get this through."

Mr. Davis replied, "I know, but we want to get the details on this."

"Let's let the witness testify," the juror spoke back, "that is all there is to it. We want to know who killed who."

Later on, the same juror broke in again, "We are not here to listen to what he knows about that."

Davis said, "What is your name?"

"Johnson is my name, from Fort Jones. We want to know how the men got killed. That is cross-examination. We are interested in how those folks got killed."

"So am I," Davis responded.

The juror got the last shot, "Well, then let's get it over with."

First Degree, Second Degree, Manslaughter

District Attorney Davis' attitude and manner of handling himself throughout the inquest was the first indication of the new twist that was coming into the case. A few of the people in the audience sensed this. There was considerable whispering and hopeless glances passed back and forth between some of those in attendance. It was appearing that he was slowly coming to the conclusion that the murdered officers in the case did not handle themselves properly in attempting to arrest the Brite brothers.

It appeared to many that possibly the "D. A." was not going to charge the Brites with first degree murder if and when they were captured. This thought was just a little ripple at this point but in the next few days and weeks it was to become a tidal wave that would have such an effect that events would actually be changed by the nature of the idea.

The concept that this was not a "first degree" case assumed a scenario as follows:

The officers went in the dead of night into a mountain camp where two suspects were sound asleep in bed after having consumed a considerable amount of wine. The suspects previously that day had a fight with two men near their camp and when they retired they prepared themselves for another fight in the event the two previous assailants returned to the camp. The officers failed to adequately identify themselves; they pounced on the suspects and tried by brute force and beating to subdue the two men. The two men, upon being awakened and not knowing that the latest attackers were police officers thought that they were in jeopardy of great bodily harm from their previous assailants. They consequently, and probably justifiably, resorted to the use of their previously prepared firearms to defend themselves.

Among the public, there were very few defenders of this scenario. But could the district attorney be one of them?

As the days went on during the excitement of the manhunt, Sheriff Chandler and his crew were, of course, the center of public interest. But District Attorney Davis was also very much in evidence. He was frequently questioned by the press and was not averse to discussing the case with various friends and often even with strangers. Some people, in talking with him, were absolutely amazed at the things he was saying about the case. Recapitulations of these conversations were passed around throughout the community with more and more people beginning to realize that the district attorney had in fact become a disciple of the "manslaughter" or "second degree" faction, admittedly, even by him, a very unpopular view. Some people began referring to this attitude as the "Decker theory," inasmuch as it was Decker who was the first person involved to imply that the officers were the ones who were at fault and were in fact the cause of the shooting.

It is interesting that Decker had become associated with this line of thinking because few people understood that he may very well have been the instigator of Davis's preoccupation of the rationale. Many people wondered how on earth Davis had come up with his idea in the first place. A careful analysis of the events by a few people did in fact find a connection between Decker and Davis which could explain Davis' motivation.

It must be born in mind that the inquest was held only three days after the actual shooting. This lack of intervening time precluded any sinister plot to sway the district attorney or anything like that. It must be remembered that there were only three live people on this earth who were eye witnesses of what happened at Horse Creek on that fateful night; the two Brite brothers and Charley Baker. During the inquest, three days after the shooting, Davis asked Baker if he had shouted during the fight, "Pour it to the son-of-a-bitch, that's the bastard that hit me!"

Who could have told Davis that this is what had been said? Not the Brite brothers for obvious reasons; and surely not Charley Baker. That leaves only one other person who could speak with enough authority for Davis to believe it had been said; B. F. Decker.

Although B. F. Decker was not at the scene, Decker is the only man on this earth that talked to the Brite brothers immediately after the shooting. If they told Decker this, there had to be more conversation with the Brites at the scene than Decker had testified to at the inquest. On top of this fact, it must be remembered that Decker's sympathies were with the Brites as evidenced by the various statements he was making in Yreka.

Some who scoffed at this analysis of the genesis of Davis' information point out that Ma and Pa Brite also talked to the boys the night of the murder. It is very doubtful though, that Davis talked to either of the parents during the three day period, but it is known that he interviewed Decker during that time. The truth of all this will never be known for sure, but there is no doubt that the subject was a major factor in determining some of the coming events.

The *Yreka Journal* edition of Saturday morning, three days after the inquest, was the first more or less widespread "public" hint at what was coming in the process of transforming Davis into almost as much of a controversial figure in the case as the Brite brothers themselves. It came in the form of an editorial as follows:

> Is it a matter of publicity our District Attorney is seeking in his handling of the Brite murder case? It certainly is not to his own glory to pursue the unethical tactics he has followed to date. From the moment the District Attorney took up the chase of the Brite boys, a job for the Sheriff's Office, certainly not that of an attorney, the case in his hands has been like a feather in the wind. [The editorial is here referring to Davis' act of forming and administering the actions of his own posse, for which the Journal at the time had praised him.] First the rush of the posse in the wild wooded wilderness of the Siskiyous at the headwaters of Horse Creek with only a slight chance of capture if the boys could be located. Regardless, we thought that efforts of the District Attorney in directing the various posse activities in the hills, most noteworthy, and spoke words of praise for a man who would spend endless hours at the phone and short wave radio in an attempt to capture the two men responsible for the most dastardly crime Siskiyou has known in years.
>
> Metropolitan press representatives rushed here by air to cover a story that for a time pushed world news to the inside pages. This evidently turned the head of our District Attorney. Soon, in every paper the length and breadth of the land appeared a story that dumfounded even the most hardened: "The District Attorney of Siskiyou County would promise only manslaughter

charges if the two Brite boys would only give themselves up." This was followed by even more sensational developments that made the Brite case the most notorious in years. Siskiyou citizens, enraged by the murder of two of the county's most beloved peace officers and a well known Vallejo man could not believe that such statements had been made to the press by a man representing the people. Yet as story followed story they could believe nothing else.

Wednesday evening at the inquest held for the three murdered men our District Attorney again showed his hand by his cross-examination of Charles Baker, only eye witness to the triple shooting. The story of the events of the evening prior to the murders as related by Baker may have lacked the eloquence of a college graduate, but nevertheless every citizen in attendance at the inquest was most visibly impressed by the simple story as it poured forth from his lips. Then the cross examination of Baker by Davis in an attempt to find some loophole in his straight forward story, became so unethical that he was finally stopped by one of the jurymen who had the nerve to rise to his feet and call a halt.

How long is this comedy in the District Attorney's office to go on? With the talk of lynching in the air, does the District Attorney think that he is helping any by his actions? After his statements in the lynch case of Clyde Johnson, his attempts to bring to justice those responsible, what end can he gain by placing gasoline on an already roaring fire of public indignation?

Perhaps District Attorney Davis' statement to the press was given without forethought. If so, he has only to withdraw his former declaration of manslaughter in favor of the more serious charge of murder.

There is no question that this editorial was an accurate reflection of the general attitude of the public. But its release seemed to give some aura of respectability to this attitude that by now was running rampant. Even though it was only one editor's opinion, it seemed to make it almost "official" that the district attorney was carrying on in a manner that was contrary to most everyone's perception of what he should be doing. But from all outward appearances, District Attorney Davis didn't seem to notice. He didn't make a response to the editorial; he gave no hint in private conversations that he might withdraw any of his earlier declarations. He did slack off to some extent in his efforts to actively participate in the manhunt, but on balance, he remained silent and withdrawn.

Where Are the "Boys?"

The manhunt continued. It was hard and exhausting work for Chandler and his men but they carried on. Checking this rumor, running down that "sighting," all to no avail. They kept at it day and night. A week, two weeks went by and they stayed with it. Publicity had ameliorated to some extent as the non-local media thinned out. Davis seemed to be causing no more problems. It seemed the whole community was quietly resting in the "eye of the storm," knowing full well that the other side of the great whirlwind would soon engulf them.

But for Davis there were other forces quietly at work building up his own little "mini-whirlwind" which was soon poised to strike. And strike it did on the front page of the *Journal* on September 16th:

DISTRICT ATTORNEY RECALL PETITION CIRCULATED

DAVIS MAKES NO STATEMENT ON CHARGES

DISTRICT ATTORNEY CHARGED WITH MISCONDUCT DURING TERM OF OFFICE IN PETITION BEING CIRCULATED THROUGHOUT SISKIYOU TODAY

Charles Johnson, former District Attorney and Louis Lorenzen, Mt. Shasta Attorney, Ready to Run for Office if Davis is Ousted

Petitions asking for the recall of James Davis, District Attorney, were being circulated today all throughout Siskiyou and according to sponsors of the movement, enough signatures for the recall will be placed on the petitions within the next forty-eight hours.

The conduct of the District Attorney during the past two weeks on the Brite case has speeded action on the recall movement, sponsors state.

Grounds for the recall, as set forth in the petitions being sent out today were as follows:

"That said James Davis, said District Attorney of Siskiyou County is unfit and incompetent to hold the high office of District Attorney as shown by the following acts on his part."

The petition went on in legal vernacular to recite a long list of offenses allegedly committed by Davis such as exposing the county to law suit by arresting two material witnesses in a previous case and holding them in jail without probable cause until after the defendant was tried and acquitted.

It charged that the district attorney spends "the greater part of his time in civil practice to the neglect of public business." The petition further stated that Davis "has absented himself from his office during long periods without leaving in charge any qualified deputy." [It failed to mention that he had no deputy.] It claimed that "he has represented clients in civil actions, refusing to allow the prosecution of his said clients or to have a warrant issued for their arrest on a criminal charge."

The very end of the petition finally got to the point of what it was really all about. This item said that "in the recent killing of two peace officers in this county and of a civilian, he has attempted to make a public showing of the incident and has made statements that have disqualified him from prosecuting the case, making it necessary for the California Attorney General to take charge of the prosecution and investigation, and which has shown the entire county up in an unfavorable light to the citizens of the whole state."

Former District Attorney Johnson had been deposed from office by the relatively unknown Davis just two years earlier by a mere 344 votes and it was known that Johnson still was smarting from it. When the dry and witty Johnson was chided by some of his friends about his possible part in the recall petition he got off another of his quotable replies.

"No," he said, "there is no conspiracy or ill feeling against Mr. Davis in this matter. When you see a cat up in a tree and a dog on the ground barking at it, it is just a natural state of affairs. The dog really has no ill feelings toward the cat; it is just his nature that makes him do that. Well, this thing now is just the same way except that in this case it is known as 'politics.' But don't worry too much about it, because actually the dog almost never catches the cat."

Davis' apparent silence concerning the charges in the recall petition turned out to be a myth. This was due to the spaces between publication days for the two Yreka papers. Contrary to what the *Journal* had intimated in the article about the petition, it had actually been floating around for more than a week. Davis had seen it early on and had immediately begun composing an answer. Of course he was busy with both the Brite case and the Barr case and it was difficult to carefully research and compose the answers to such a series of charges in spite of its importance to him. By the time he had it ready it was late Wednesday morning, September 16th, which made it impossible to have it in the *Journal* until the issue of Saturday, the 19th. Consequently it had appeared that he was not answering the accusations when in fact he was very busy working on it in every spare minute he could find.

When the statement was finally in print, it consisted of more than three full newspaper columns and it was carried in full in both the Yreka papers. The *Journal's* headline for it was:

DAVIS CHARGES MALICIOUS FALSEHOOD IN RECALL

JAMES DAVIS STRIKES BACK AT ACCUSERS

District Attorney Presents Inside Story on Many Discussed Issues in Present Recall Movement

Davis Defends his Stand in Brite Case, Blaming Mob Hysteria for Misunderstanding of His Actions

After these headlines, the article was a verbatim quote of the entire paper prepared by Davis. In most people's opinion the answer was somewhat of a "block buster;" not for what he said about his attitudes on the Brite case, but for how he answered all of the long list of items in the first part of the accusation.

He recited each of these items one by one and followed up with a detailed description of the true facts of each incident as he saw them. On the approximately seven "non-Brite case" items it was definitely seven to zero in Davis' favor.

For example, in the item that accused him of illegally holding two material witnesses in jail until the end of the trial of the defendant and thereby exposing the county to a potential law suit, his explanation was a classic. This case was a "carry over" murder charge after a mistrial during the term of Davis' predecessor, Charley Johnson. He recited the entire case in detail step by step in clear and concise logic leaving no doubt that the case had been handled very well. He then topped it off with the following:

> In this case the most important single piece of evidence con-
> sisted of a handkerchief which plainly showed it had been used
> to wipe a bloody knife. It had been taken from the defendant's
> pocket, and the last trace of it we could get from the former
> Sheriff's Office was that it had been delivered to the district at-
> torney. This piece of evidence was not in the office and was never
> turned over to me, but mysteriously disappeared.
>
> There was no trial brief or office file left of this case by my
> predecessor; there was not in this office, a trial brief or office file
> of the notorious Hall murder case, with all its attendant impor-
> tance and in fact; there was not, in this office, when I came into
> it, a single office file of any case which had been put through the
> process of handling, covering the entire period of my predeces-
> sor. I had no means of knowing that anything had ever been
> handled in this office since the incumbency of Superior Court
> Judge Luttrell, who was a former district attorney.

Upon reading this, some of the men who had previously kidded former District Attorney Johnson slyly told him that he "better get his dog away from that cat that's up the tree because that cat bites back."

When Davis completed his list of explanations and counterattacks concerning the smaller items he then addressed the subject of the Brite case, which of course was the meat of the whole idea of the recall. Regretfully this was anticlimactic for the reasons explained in his answer:

> My accuser knows that People versus Coke and John Brite
> is a "pending" case. What I know of this case I cannot publicly
> discuss even if my neck and political future are at stake. It is my
> clear duty to protect the State's case. Here, again, the facts before
> me and the law govern my steps. I am here to act as necessary
> in the cardinal interest of justice. I felt the full shock of this ter-
> rible tragedy. Both Officers Lange and Clark were close friends
> who worked side by side with me in the interest of the law. Of-
> ficer Clark and his family have been intimate, helping friends to
> me since boyhood. Officer Lange and his family have been my
> friends since my return home in 1934. In 1918, Hemy Lange,

brother of Officer Lange, and I left Yreka for the war together.

On the day of the tragedy I interviewed Mr. Baker and Mr. Decker in a private room at the Barton Store at Horse Creek. I interviewed both men in the presence of each other. I heard Mr. Baker and Mr. Decker testify before the Coroner and I questioned them in the light of my previous conference with them. The public did not know this.

The district attorney closed his paper with a courageous and challenging stroke:

> I have done my duty. If, in doing the right, as I saw the right, I must cast either my neck or my political future in the die, I cannot let political expediency or death outweigh my principle. If the political hounds who are barking on my trail can hoodwink sterling Siskiyou citizens into believing their false charges, I'll take my medicine without a whimper. BUT THEY CAN'T DO IT!"

Davis' response to the recall movement seemed to temporarily throw a damper over that subject for the time being. Then a new matter surfaced that very fleetingly caught the public's interest.

Barr's Return to Siskiyou County

Robert Miller Barr, Johnson's fugitive accomplice in the murder of Police Chief Jack Daw [Chapter 3], had been previously charged with murder and taken to Folsom Prison to await trial. On October 10th, 1936 Barr was returned to the Siskiyou County Superior Court for trial. Yreka attorney Albert Tebbe had been appointed counsel for the defendant; he appeared in court with his client but refused to serve for the reason that Barr was determined to plead guilty. Then, attorney James M. Allen was brought into court and asked if he would accept an appointment as attorney for Barr. He said he would if Barr would agree to do as he instructed.

There followed a private meeting between Allen and Barr in another room. Then another meeting between Allen and Tebbe was held which was followed by still another between Allen and District Attorney Davis. When court was finally reopened about 4:00 o'clock, Attorney Allen appeared with Barr, who thereupon pled guilty with the consent of his attorney.

Allen then introduced but one witness, Barr himself. Barr said that he had met Johnson at different times during the few months that preceded the fatal affair, having first become acquainted in jail at Santa Rosa where the two were serving time for a misdemeanor. He said Johnson continually wanted him to pull something. He said that Johnson was on to some kind of secret method of making slot machines payoff. When they left Santa Rosa, Barr agreed to give it a try but the plan failed to produce any money. After that they eventually found themselves in Dunsmuir where Johnson said they could pull off an easy holdup in a little place called Castella. After the holdup they stole the car to make their getaway and that is when the trouble really started. After abandoning the car in North Dunsmuir and walking south on the highway they were stopped by those police officers. Barr said he saw Johnson immediately get ready for battle and that he heard one of the men in the car say, "Get your hand away from that belt, Buddy." Barr said that he then took to his heels without even taking out his gun, which immediately fell out of his pocket. He heard the shots going off as he went over the bank into the brush; he said he never did have any intention whatsoever of using that gun. He said that after the robbery in Castella, there had been no prearranged plan between the two of them.

In the closing arguments, both the prosecution and the defense stipulated to the facts as related by the defendant and agreed that they were asking for a sentence of life imprisonment rather than execution inasmuch as Barr had not used the gun during the murder nor was it his intention to do so.

Judge C. J. Luttrell accommodated everyone in their request. Robert Miller Barr was sentenced to San Quinten Prison for life.

Fruitless Manhunt Drags On

Chandler was getting very tired; worse than that, he was becoming discouraged. This frustrating manhunt had been going on now for more than two weeks. It seemed to him that his men had covered every square inch of that endless mass of mountains, rivers and streams in ever widening circles. In all of that time after chasing down hundreds of clues, ideas and angles, to this date he had not one hard indication as to the whereabouts of those two fugitives. The woods were full of deer hunters, some of whom didn't know for sure whether they were after deer or men. Every trail up there must have been traversed a half dozen times over by various people with one thing in mind: "find those boys and get that reward." There were plenty of ideas offered, but nobody had anything of concrete value.

Who should finally reappear in the midst of the Brite brother manhunt but Robert Barr, the cohort of Clyde Johnson who had been lynched in Yreka a year earlier. Barr was delivered to Siskiyou County Jail from southern California where he had been living openly and even had a small part in a movie. [See Chapter 3.] (Siskiyou County Sheriff's Department)

Just five days earlier, Chandler had beefed up his posses and expanded the search area into a still wider area. He tried as hard as humanly possible to keep the Brite cabin under constant surveillance but this was proving impossible. It was pitch black up there on that mining property at night and anyone who knew his way could get in and out of there easily without detection. Mrs. Brite was constantly showing up in Yreka, yet his crew only detected her comings and goings about half the time.

Chandler was also worried about the safety of Charley Baker. Baker, against the advice of the Sheriff's Office and his friends, was adamant about staying at home in his isolated cabin only a quarter of a mile from where the shooting had taken place. If the Brites were still in the area and happened to think of it, it would be a simple project to sneak in there and eliminate the State's star witness against them in one easy shot.

On Wednesday, September 16th, Chandler had been very busy when Henry Pallage, the man he considered the best of the posse men, had contacted him. He had tried to get in touch with Pallage the day before but the phone to Horse Creek seemed to be out. He had finally reached Chester Barton at the Horse Creek store and asked him to watch for Pallage and tell him to contact the Sheriff's Office; he wanted to get an up to date report from Pallage.

The assignment that Pallage had been working on since the day after the murder represented the best chance of a breakthrough that was left to Chandler. But even though it was the "best" chance, Chandler had little faith in it because it had been going on so long without any really appreciable results. Then on this day, Pallage had finally come into Yreka but Chandler was so busy, he felt he could put it off a day before hearing what the posse man had to say. He had consequently told Pallage to go on home and get a good night's sleep and that he would be in touch with him in a day or two.

Chandler had only a nodding acquaintance with Henry Pallage prior to his appearance in this case. He had noticed Pallage around the Sheriff's Office from time to time and had a few short conversations with him. It appeared that Pallage had an amateur interest in law enforcement and was taken to hanging around and talking with the deputies. In his brief contacts with him, Chandler had felt that he was an intelligent fellow and he knew him to be thoroughly "woods-wise" and an experienced mountaineer.

Mr. and Mrs. Pallage lived in a cabin on Big Humbug, in the mountains just west of Yreka. When the initial call for possemen had gone out in the Brite case, Pallage had been one of the first to respond. Because of Chandler's high regard for him, he had placed him in charge of radio communications. It was Pallage's assignment to man the radio transmitter and receiver from a point centrally located in the mountains of the search area. Pallage seemed to take to this assignment with a considerable degree of satisfaction. His activities at his post very soon expanded into a situation that in the beginning seemed to have some possibility of bearing meaningful achievement. But as so much time had now gone by with very little progress in what Pallage was attempting to do, Chandler was beginning to lose heart in the project.

Pallage's Part

The activity into which Pallage had worked himself is best described in his own words in a written report that he ultimately made. It reads generally as follows:

I worked on the Brite case starting Sunday, August 30th. My first day on the case I took a Forest Service radio and went up on Dry Lake Mountain and set up on the high road just above Ward's cow camp cabin. I was there all day and night and the posses were making contact to and from my position as they moved back and forth to Dry Lake Lookout, Donnamore and Sterling Mountain. Early in the morning on the 31st, I was ordered down to the Horse Creek posse headquarters camp from where I left to go up to the Brite home. I was a member of a posse that day headed by Mr. Chandler. I set up my radio in the Brite yard and from that position I looked around into the high spots that showed up very plainly from there. I figured out four places where the Brite boys might be hiding. So that night I talked with Mr. Chandler about it and asked him if he would let me check out the places I had spotted from the Brite yard. He said "fine" and told me to take what men I wanted. I took two men the first day and checked out two of the four places without finding any sign. I also found no sign in the third place.

Then on September 3rd, with four possemen and myself, I was going up to the last place I had spotted when two newspaper men from San Francisco came to me and said they had permission to come along. I told them the situation and said they must not tell anyone what we might find because we did not want anything to leak out that would hinder our manhunt. I was sure we were in what we called a "hot spot." We had no sooner left the area of the Brite home when we came across a faint little trail upon which we started moving up the mountain. About a half mile from the house I picked up a fresh footprint track coming down the mountain to the trail. We backtracked it on up the mountain; it soon became obvious that the track was leading us to the fourth place that I had spotted from the Brite's yard.

It was a very fresh track and I told my men to watch very closely for any movement in the woods and brush. I told them not to shoot unless someone fired at one of us and then to return only a volley in the general direction it came from. My reason for telling them not to shoot to kill was because there was too much danger of hurting some innocent person; and there was another reason I didn't mention.

During this assignment I had become quite friendly with the parents of the Brite boys, especially Mrs. Brite. On the previous day I had a long talk with them. I told them that I would not shoot their boys down. I told them that by all means, the boys should come in and stand trial. Mrs. Brite seemed to agree with what I was saying but she was scared to death that the lynchers would get the boys if they did this. Finally she asked me to "swear an oath before God" that I would not shoot down her boys and that I would protect them from mob violence with my life if need be. I swore this oath in the presence of both of them and from that time on they had confidence in me.

We followed the tracks until we came close to the top of the mountain into a fir thicket. The track was very fresh then, maybe less than five minutes old. Suddenly I saw a movement like someone running fast through the thicket. A few seconds later one of my men saw a movement beyond the trees and I went through the thicket on the track and came to where I had seen the movement first.

From there on the tracks were from a man running. The tracks went to the left and joined another track and they both ran fast together. On top of the mountain the tracks went to a place where the grass showed a blanket or quilt had been. It had been picked up and the tracks went down around into what we called the lower thicket. There was still dust in the air when we came to the place where the tracks were going down to the lower thicket. It was late and would soon begin to get dark so we went back and looked the place over good. There were five places for lookouts with paths running between them and the track we followed up the hill led to all of them. We were sure we had found out where the Brite boys had been holed up. The Brite home could be seen very plainly from one of the lookouts.

That night after returning to Horse Creek Camp, I told all of this to Mr. Chandler. We talked it over and I said I was sure I could help him on the case as much as any person could. I was very confidant that I had a good start. Mr. Chandler agreed and gave the order that all posse men in that vicinity were to be moved out and I was to go up to talk to Mr. and Mrs. Brite the next day.

When I got to the house the next day there was no one there and so I started up the trail again where we had found the tracks. After going up quite a ways, I heard a noise. Then I saw Mrs. Brite; she had her hands cupped up to her face and was calling, "Boys; oh Boys; Boys."

I was very close behind a little curve in the trail so I just came walking on as though I did not know she was there. She was very startled when she saw me. We greeted each other and she asked me if I had heard a noise. I told her that I hadn't but that it may have been a deer running down the mountain. She appeared to feel very much eased then, no doubt thinking I had not heard her call to the boys. I had a long talk with her and told her to tell the boys to come in; I said everything that I could to induce her to see it that way. I left her there and went on back down the hill.

About four hours later I returned to the Brite home. Mrs. Brite came running to meet me, smiling, she said, 'I am happy now, I feel better than I have for a long time.'

Then she put her hands on my shoulders and said, "You took an oath to protect my boys; you said you wouldn't shoot them down and now I know you won't." That made me feel sure that she had made contact with the boys since I had seen her a few hours before and that they had told her what had happened. I could have shot one of them I am sure. I have made many more difficult shots hunting deer. I felt more confident than ever now.

From then on my job was to stay at Horse Creek nights and go to the Brite home during the days. Mr. Chandler would go up there with me sometimes and other times Deputy Rhodes would come along. When no one was there to go with me, I would go alone. For many hours on many different days I spent my time with Mr. and Mrs. Brite talking and discussing the boys' case, always urging them to get the boys to give themselves up.

Mr. Brite told me one day that the boys would probably give up soon and that I was to be the one to take them in. That made me feel very happy because I had grown to like these people very much, The last day that Mr. Chandler was there with me, Mr. Brite told him that if the boys came in, he wanted him to know that Pallage was to take them in. Mr. Chandler smiled and said, "That will be fine; that is just what we want and that is why Pallage is here."

It was Thursday morning, September 17th. Chandler had been to District Attorney Davis' office concerning some business in connection with the Brite case as well as the Barr case. As he emerged from Davis' office he passed Court Reporter Ralph McMurry's office which was the next one down the hall. He almost went in there for a visit but he heard the court reporter's typewriter clattering away so thought it best not to disturb him; he went on down the stairs. Back in his own office he sat in his chair and began to turn over the facts in the Brite case in his mind as he had a hundred times before. Searching for an idea, a little crevice in his brain so to speak, where there might be something that had been overlooked; had he rejected so many suggestions that perhaps one or more might have been worth a follow up? Had he failed to see an obvious clue that had been right in front of him?

Chandler's window looked out on the narrow space between the Courthouse proper and his office, which was connected to the jail. As he was thinking he happened to be absent mindedly looking in the direction across the courtyard that he had just traversed in order to get to his office. Suddenly the swinging door of the courthouse burst open and District Attorney Davis emerged into the courtyard, and District Attorney Davis was moving fast! Almost breaking into a run, Davis made a beeline for his car and took off with the gravel flying from beneath his tires.

"Now that's odd," thought Chandler, "it's been less than five minutes since I was in his office and he seemed totally relaxed and said nothing about being wanted somewhere else. Now what's he up to?"

Davis' activities and attitudes had all seemed odd to Chandler lately so he just shook it off and went back to his analytical introspection of his two nemeses, the Brite brothers. But Davis' unannounced hasty exit from the building kept intruding on his thoughts.

"I think I'll go back up there and have a talk with my old friend, Ralph McMurry," Chandler said to himself, "he knows Davis very well and I've been wanting to discuss some other angles in this case with him anyway. Besides, maybe he can cheer me up."

In the election year of 1934 Sheriff Andy Calkins had been in office for sixteen years. He had been a popular sheriff having weathered four elections without defeat but his health was then beginning to fail. As soon as he announced that he would not run again, there developed a veritable stampede of potential candidates to succeed him. Siskiyou County, like the whole country, was then in the depths of the Great Depression and jobs were scarce. One way to find work was to seek public office.

By the time five of the ultimate total of seven candidates had filed for the office, some of the more serious minded civic leaders in the county began to become a little concerned over the caliber of the aspirants for the job. Consequently, a group of approximately six men met together very informally to assess the situation. The concern of the group was that even though the five announced candidates were all good and honorable men, there was, with one exception, no one on the list who had any law enforcement experience. In addition to this there was no one at all on the list who had any law enforcement "training."

A consensus was reached that the members of the group should attempt to find a county resident who had some experience and training for the job and see if they couldn't convince him to file for the office. Their thinking was that even though Calkins had been a popular and effective sheriff, the times had changed to the extent that the job now required a more formally prepared person. Court Reporter Ralph McMurry was a member of the group.

In the course of the discussions held by the group, the name of W. G. "Chan" Chandler kept surfacing. Chandler was a resident of Dunsmuir in the southern end of the county. He was well-known everywhere but most especially in Yreka, the county seat; this was due to the fact that his duties as Special Agent for the Southern Pacific Railroad Company often required his presence at the courthouse.

In 1934 he was forty-eight years of age and had been in the employ of Southern Pacific for sixteen years. His position as Special Agent was high up the ladder in the private investigation and law enforcement department of the railroad company. His duties in that position had consisted of both criminal and civil investigations, which had brought him in contact with the sheriffs of Oregon and northern California as well as practically all the municipal police on the coast. His work had also brought him experience in dealing with the various branches of the federal government including Postal Inspectors and Postal Special Agents, as well as Department of Justice Secret Service Agents.

In addition to these impeccable experience and training qualifications, Chandler was known to be a highly respected person in the south Siskiyou area. He was a local civic leader in Dunsmuir where people often sought his help and counsel. He was happily married and had a fine family. His honesty was beyond question. All in all, he seemed to stack up head and shoulders above anyone else that had been mentioned.

The ad hoc committee, upon being appraised of all these facts about Chandler, unanimously agreed to go to Dunsmuir as an unofficial delegation in order to recruit him as a candidate for sheriff. Chandler was pleased and honored when the proposal was put to him. After two or three more meetings he agreed and duly filed for the office.

This was quite a remarkable thing for a candidate to be asked to run by such a sterling group. It is well known that the usual scenario of the more typical candidate is to go through the entire campaign claiming that "many people have asked me to run" when the plain fact was that no one had ever even suggested it.

Still another candidate filed after Chandler, which brought the primary election slate to a total of seven. When the vote was in, Chandler had led the field, but as predicted, it had been impossible to get a majority with that many people running. He had to run it off with the candidate who had polled second in the Primary race, Stuart Taylor, the current undersheriff. In the following General Election, Chandler was the winner by the very small margin of 238 votes.

So W. G. Chandler had become Siskiyou County Sheriff and the various members of the ad hoc committee were pleased and satisfied. Chandler himself was very happy with the outcome. He had labored hard and seriously over the advisability of quitting his exceptionally fine position with the Southern Pacific Company in exchange for a political career. Now it seemed to have been a wise choice and he was convinced that the experience he would gain in the new position would enhance his career in the long run. He arranged to rent a fine big Victorian home on the main residential street in Yreka and moved his family in during the Christmas break in the school year. The future looked bright indeed.

A Chat with "Chan"

Ralph McMurry lived only two blocks from the courthouse and always walked to work. In fact, he also walked to and from home every day for lunch. This September morning he had been thinking of Chandler as he walked to work. He knew that Chandler was very busy with the manhunt these days and that he had a lot of pressure on him. He saw him frequently, however, mostly just passing and nodding around the courthouse, and also when they were both involved in something official in connection with a case. But the two of them had not talked together to any great extent for some time. In seeing him lately though, McMurry felt that Chandler looked tired and drawn and for the last week he had the appearance of a defeated man. This concerned the court reporter; Chandler was a good friend and he was searching his mind for something that he could say or do in order to ease his friend's burden.

Later that morning, Ralph McMurry heard his door open; when he looked up, there was Chandler coming into his office. Chandler had an "old friends" smile on his face but the flash thought that crossed McMurry's mind was that he looked especially gaunt this morning.

"Come on in, Chan," said McMurry, "I was just thinking about you. I was thinking it was time we had a good visit. How's it going, anyway?"

"Ralph, you just say the word if you're too busy to spend some time with me and I'll get right on out of here," responded Chandler. "But if you can spare the time, I'd like to bounce some chatter off your brain in the hopes that you might be able to help me."

"Chan, sit down right there and stretch those long legs of yours out so you can put your feet up in that other chair," replied McMurry. "You might not believe this but I really was just thinking about some way that I could approach you so that we could have a talk. You know, you don't look very well Chan; you've been walking around with kind of a hang-dog look as if you're carrying the whole world on your shoulders. I think I know what's bothering you and I hope that I can say or do something that might ease your burden. So go right ahead and try me."

Chandler sat down and stretched out as McMurry had suggested. He then leaned back and cast a long look out of the upper portion of the high window of the old 1800s courthouse; he seemed to be studying a big billowing cloud. After a very long pause he appeared to come out of his reverie and began to talk. At least the first sentence was said with a smile.

"I have problems, big problems, and Ralph, I half blame them on you and that committee of yours that came down there to Dunsmuir and talked me into running for sheriff."

Both men were smiling now; McMurry said nothing as Chandler went on:

"By golly, Ralph, I must be the unluckiest cuss that's ever been elected sheriff in any county anywhere. Everything looked great when I was sworn in; the future looked unlimited. But I hardly got the sheriff's seat warm before things started going wrong.

"Of course you recall the Gilmore case. That poor young fellow lost his life, shot by one of my deputies in my presence. It was a life-threatening situation and we both felt it was either him or us. I don't think that the event would have caused any stir at all except for the fact he was a local man. I realize that makes a difference. Consequently we took a lot of criticism. I felt that was OK; I was willing to take that criticism because I understood what motivated it. The public never did know how much I actually grieved for that young man."

The court reporter could see that Chandler was in a mood to unburden himself. McMurry felt the best thing he could do was remain silent until an opportunity arose for a mutual exchange. Chandler was going on:

"Then barely six months into my term, along comes the 'famous' Johnson case. There I was; sick in bed trying to recoup from surgery. A police officer in my former home town is murdered and while I'm still flat on my back, we lose the prisoner to the lynchers. Now I'm not criticizing my deputies in any way. I think both Lange and especially Mathews did all they could under the circumstances."

Chandler was just going along, on and on in a very calm voice. McMurry was hearing a very articulate and intelligent individual recite a series of extremely troublesome events that had obviously threatened the man's peace of mind both at the time as well as now. Of course McMurry knew what was coming next but he still withheld comment out of deference to the mood of his friend. Chandler went on in somewhat of a lighter tone.

"Now we come to the momentous second year of the great Chandler administration and here we go again. This time two of my own deputies are murdered, plus a civilian; probably the bloodiest murder case in the history of the county. And I might also add that those two deputies were two of my closest friends. Because we've already had one lynching, the lynchers are out in full cry again. Only they are as frustrated as I am because we have mounted the greatest manhunt probably in the history of the state and we just can't lay our hands on the fugitives. And Ralph, all these foul-ups are taking place in the full glare of national newspaper publicity.

"Now that sounds like a pile of problems, doesn't it? Well, I'll tell you, Ralph, that is one pile of problems alright; but incredible as it may seem, we now have an even bigger problem right on top of the whole heap."

Chandler finally paused for a second or two and a slow smile came over his face. Then he jerked himself back into a more sober mood and continued.

"I think you know the problem I have in mind because I know he is a friend of yours, Ralph. That in fact is why I'm here. Tell me if you can, what in damnation is that goofy district attorney of ours up to?"

Even though this was expressed in the form of a direct question, McMurry still gauged the situation as not yet calling for a comment. He just responded with a grin and Chandler resumed his soliloquy.

"Anyone taking lesson #1 in Law Enforcement knows that the district attorney is supposed to help, not hinder. To this day, he hasn't done one thing to help and everything that he has done, has hindered, not helped. As soon as the news was out, he organized that so-called posse of his and then proceeded to make a fool of himself right down there in the courtyard below that window there. I'm referring to those morning "musters" that he conducted with that gang as he dispatched them off into the mountains to catch those criminals.

"He stood there like a drill sergeant and made them the most outlandish speeches you ever heard as he sent them forth into the fray. And all that took place right outside my office window and in full view of the reporters from the local and national press. And then after getting together with that fellow Decker and also possibly Mrs. Brite, he shows up at the inquest and lights into our star witness as if he was the cause of the murder instead of the sought-after fugitives."

The sheriff was really sailing now. The court reporter continued to hold back and let him ramble on.

"And now here is the latest performance of his. You may know that in view of all this lynch talk I have made arrangements through California Attorney General Webb to take the Brite brothers to Folsom Prison for safe keeping as soon as they are booked, when and if we capture them. Not over a half hour ago I went to Davis' office in order to tell him about this and to discuss some matters with him concerning the Barr case. As I entered his office, there sat Mrs. A. J. Brite. I asked her again, like I had so many times before, about the whereabouts of the boys. We had been dickering with her and Mr. Brite for some days recently in an attempt to get her assistance in getting the boys to surrender because we are now convinced that they are hiding out in the mountains not far from home.

"She was evasive to my question and said she knew nothing of their whereabouts. I told her that the boys could not escape and that our officers were closing in little by little and that it would be only a matter of a few days until they were captured.

"She said she wondered what would happen to them if they were taken and I told her that they would be charged with murder but that the results would be up to a jury. Even to this she gave no apparent concern. By that time I was seated and she asked Davis if I was going to remain there. I told her I was not if it was to her displeasure. I then got up and went back downstairs and over to my office. I'll tell you, Ralph, my construction of how she acted is that she was saying to herself, 'I don't need to make any deals with this evil man because District Attorney Davis is going to see that no harm ever comes to my boys.'

"A few minutes later, under the hopeful assumption that she was probably gone from there, I returned to Davis' office and just as I entered I bumped into her face to face as she was coming out. She brushed right past me in a huff without saying anything or ever acknowledging my presence."

There was a slight lull as Chandler caught his breath. McMurry's thoughts now were that this plot was certainly thickening. But it appeared that Chandler wanted to go on some more so the court reporter said nothing.

"So I went on in to get my business taken care of with Davis. I was in there at least a half hour and he seemed perfectly relaxed and normal. He made no effort to bring the meeting to a close and made no comment concerning Mrs. Brite. When finished, I went on back to my office. And then by golly you can't imagine what happened next. I looked out my window not five minutes after leaving Davis' office, and out the door of the courthouse he came like a shot, jumped in his car and took off in a cloud of dust and gravel. I have the eerie feeling that something big is about to break in this case but I can't think what it is. Whatever it is, it feels like the sheriff of Siskiyou County is being left behind in the action.

"But Ralph, maybe it's nothing. Maybe that wild dash out of the building is just something personal with Davis and has nothing to do with the case. But notwithstanding, what on earth is that fellow up to? I swear to God on the Holy Bible, that fellow is not going to charge those murderers with "first degree" when the time comes. And I also know that as soon as we're able to get them he's going to make some deal with them for something far less than the charges he should hit them with. And I further guarantee you, Ralph, that when he does that, his career is going down the drain because the people of this county are in no mood to stand for it. And lastly, Ralph, my career will probably be sucked right down with him. So that is why I'm here talking to you. What is the man thinking? How can he conclude that what he is doing is in his interest or in the interest of justice?"

With that, Chandler stopped abruptly. There was a long silence.

All through Chandler's long dissertation Ralph McMurry had listened patiently. He was now able to feel in his heart the tremendous disappointments and frustrations that had descended upon his old friend. The job of court reporter was one that called for a passive role in the scheme of things, to be an observer rather than a participant in the great and sometimes petty matters that pass through the courts. But McMurry now felt himself drawn into the rush of the immediate sequence of events as if he himself had now become one of the players rather than the "reporter." He knew that he must say something to ease the burdens carried by his friend, but he also realized that there was a lack of options available to Chandler. He felt the man was doing all he could; he felt that only "events" now could ease these burdens, not "talk." But the nature of the situation at hand now required talk, and McMurry was ready.

"Chan, I want you to know that to a very great extent I have been fully aware of each and every one of the problems you have so eloquently described. I know the pressures you're under. As I mentioned to you, I've been watching for the right time to have a chat with you in order to see if I couldn't be of some help. So now we're here, just the two of us, so I'll take a stab at it.

"First, let's talk about Davis. You remarked when you came in here that he is a friend of mine. You're right, he is. But not only that, I also admire him very much."

With that, Chandler sort of jerked up into a more alert position in the chair as if the statement actually startled him, which it had. But the innate courtesy of the two men precluded that he say anything at the moment. He relaxed again as if signaling to McMurry to proceed.

"I thought that would get your attention, Chan. But before we get excited over that statement let's see if we can't figure out what kind of a person our friend Mr. Davis is and what really makes him tick. Did you know that Davis is part Indian? I don't know how much but I think at least half. Unfortunately, Indians in general do not have the best of things in our so-called white society. I don't propose to go into a long analysis of the shabby treatment that a whole race of people has received from the white man for the last 400 years. But just look around Siskiyou County, for example. How many Indians do you see in positions of trust and leadership within our white society? Very, very few. They have been shut out from these avenues so long that it seldom even occurs to them that they could participate.

"But Jimmy Davis is the exception; a little Indian boy that grows up with an ambition to become a part of the very society that generally denies a place for him and his peers. But he is able to accomplish that. It is no mean task to come up against these odds, to get an education and eventually become an accepted lawyer in the white man's world. And then to go on to hold the respected position of a District Attorney; I'll tell you, Chan, that is a mighty achievement, and for that I respect and admire him."

Chandler made no indication as to how this was striking him with the exception of a little nod that either indicated approval or just encouragement for Ralph to go on.

"I see, Chan, that didn't stir you up too badly. So prepare yourself for another shock. I also admire him for his actions as a result of his belief that the Brite brothers are guilty of something less than first degree murder."

Chandler sat bolt upright with a look of total consternation. He appeared frozen in that position. Obviously he could not believe what he was now hearing.

"Relax, Chan," said McMurry, "I sort of tricked you on that one but hear me out. Let me explain my position. Let me ease your mind on it to this extent. I agree with you 100% that Davis' position is dead wrong. Let's look some more at who Mr. Davis really is and at what makes him tick. We both know that he is not dumb, nor is he 'goofy,' as I've heard someone around here term it. He is an intelligent person. I know this from my personal acquaintance with him. But in addition to that, anyone must come to the same conclusion when you consider his heritage and lack of opportunities in the light of the position in life that he has achieved. The man is not stupid, not dumb; he is merely wrong. That's all, just wrong; it's that simple. Even the wisest men are sometimes wrong and in my opinion and in yours, this is one of those times for James G. Davis."

With this development in the conversation, Chandler relaxed to some extent and even slightly nodded his head in affirmation a time or two.

"Davis, honestly, and I mean to emphasize the word 'honestly,' believes that your officers did not adequately identify themselves as they went into the Brite's camp to arrest them. He honestly believes that the actions of your officers were such that a fair assumption could be made by the Brite's that they were being attacked by the same parties with whom they had previously had a fight earlier in the evening. He believes that the Brites came out of that bedroll in the belief that they were then fighting in self-defense, an act that is not a first degree felony.

"Now Chan, I don't know how or where he got the facts that have led him to believe this. There is not a shred of evidence that has come out so far that indicates this. In fact, the physical evidence at the scene indicates just the opposite. Perhaps either Decker or Mrs. Brite was able to convince him of it. I just can't account for it though. I can't believe that Davis could be swayed that easy. But wherever he got it, is not material to this discussion. We know he believes that way. We both agree that he is dead wrong. So how come I say I admire him?

"You mentioned awhile ago that it is likely that Davis' career will 'go down the drain' if he persists in this view. I agree that that is very likely. But look at his position. He is the district attorney of this county which requires him, as it does for you, to take an oath. As the district attorney and as a practicing lawyer he is an 'officer of the court.' He is bound by all this to see that justice is done. From a practical point of view, that means 'justice' as he perceives it. This is the only way it can be. He can consult with anyone he wants in an effort to aid him in determining what is the proper justice in this case or that; he even has the California Attorney General and all his staff available to him for consultation. But in the end, he must decide the degree of justice that he will attempt to enforce, and this is accomplished by the charge he decides to bring in any given case.

"Apparently in this case he has decided that the charge should be some thing other than first degree murder. I think that he is thoroughly and fully aware that his career hangs in the balance. Already there is a recall petition being circulated against him; the newspapers are all editorially criticizing him.

"But that man takes his oath of office seriously. He means to stand by what he believes even if his career goes 'down the drain.' This is why I admire him. Not because I think he is wrong or right. That's not the issue. He is too smart to not know the consequences for him in the position he is taking. I admire him because he feels that his duty comes first regardless of what happens to him; in other words he stands on 'principle.' And Chan, we could use a lot more of that in our society today, most especially from elected officials."

Chandler's face now bore a countenance that defied McMurry's ability to analyze. The court reporter had no inclination whatsoever as to whether his friend was mad, merely disappointed, or maybe agreeable.

Chandler cautiously brought his knees up in order to disengage his feet from the chair and stood up. He slowly turned toward the door and started walking. Not even for an instant could McMurry believe that he was "walking out." This would be unthinkable in view of the background and personalities of the two men. These men, both born in the 1880s, were products of the Victorian era, both reared in households that held courtesy and consideration between mankind in high esteem. No, McMurry concluded, Chandler was just gathering his thoughts about him in order to form a response to these theories which heretofore he had not considered.

There was a long table in the office which the court reporter used to collate the trial transcripts when he finished typing them, sometimes in as many as five carbon copies. Chandler walked along the length of this table and continued right on around it and came back to the chair where he had been sitting. As he sat down he appeared to be more relaxed but with a very serious look.

"Ralph," he said, "I apologize to you for all those derogatory things I said about Davis. I simply had not thought this thing through. I have been so immersed in the details and problems of this case that I haven't been able to see 'the forest but for the trees.' As always, you have been able to calmly put it into an understandable and probably correct framework. I intend to also apologize to Jimmy Davis himself. In dealing with him the past few weeks, I have at all times made an effort to conceal my antagonism from him but I fear now that my feelings were so strong that he must have picked them up in someway. Therefore I will attempt to set things straight."

"You owe no apology to me, Chan," McMurry replied, "I'm just happy that you agree. I know that this is heavy stuff and it takes a real man to say what you just did."

But the court reporter realized that all this merely eased one of his friend's major problems; it did nothing about Chandler's concerns over his career and the foreboding thoughts that he was having over something big being about to break in the case.

"Chan, what we have discussed so far still leaves your other more important problem unresolved. I am referring to your concern over your own career and its relationship with what happens in this case. I must agree with you without qualification, your tenure in office as sheriff has been buffeted with the worst string of luck possible. I agree that the Sheriff's Office must bring this case to a satisfactory conclusion very soon or the repercussions upon you personally will be unbearable. In saying this, I want to emphasize the word, "satisfactory" when speaking of the conclusion.

"From your point of view, this means that you must capture these two fugitives; not some bounty hunter; not some adventurous deer hunter; not some other police agency; you, your office, your men, must be the apprehenders. And included in that 'satisfactory conclusion,' must be the protection of the fugitives from the lynchers, and all without anyone getting hurt. Chan, this is one tall order, but there is no doubt in my mind that you can pull it off."

Chandler seemed very calm now. Hopefully thinking of Henry Pallage's project he said, "Ralph, on this one I feel better and have some hopes that it will be alright. As I intimated earlier when I was telling you about my 'visit' with Mrs. Brite in Davis' office, I think that we are very close now. Without bothering you with the details, we have every indication that those boys are not far from Horse Creek and the whole thing will be over in a very short time."

Then with a smile Chandler said, "That of course is on the assumption that there is nothing to my gut feeling that something weird is about to happen in this case."

Both men were smiling now as Chandler got up to leave. As they said goodby and the sheriff went out the door, the court reporter was thinking of how sure and certain he himself had sounded in expounding all these thoughts. Yet he really was not all that sure of anything. He knew full well that all this was a matter of how certain human beings were going to react, and that specie seldom reacts as expected. McMurry looked at his watch; it was exactly noon, time to walk home for lunch.

Surrender!

Exactly twenty-four hours after Chandler left McMurry's office, an event was taking place that confirmed Chandler's foreboding. The news of it reverberated throughout the state as well as the nation. The consequences immediately came under the most intensive debate from the smallest group discussing the case in the Horse Creek Store to the inner chambers of the office of the Governor of California, and it was Topic #1 with practically everyone else in between. It dashed all of Chandler's new-found confidence in one fell swoop; his world came crashing down in pieces all around him.

Chandler had received only the slightest inkling of the news before it hit the streets. His disaster struck at 8:00 o'clock Saturday morning when his home phone rang. It was Folsom Prison Warden C. A. Larken.

Yreka Journal headlines, Saturday Morning, September 19, 1936:

KILLERS SURRENDER TO DAVIS

DISTRICT ATTORNEY TAKES JOHN & COKE BRITE FOR SAFE KEEPING

Sheriff's Office Here Not Notified of Surrender of Brite Brothers Until Early This Morning

Mother of Brite Brothers Carries Message of Terms of Surrender

The Brites and James Davis went to bed immediately after Mr. Davis turned the brothers over to the Warden at Folsom. Davis quoted the brothers as being unwilling to talk for publication, and Davis himself forbade interviews. Before filing charges Davis said he would consult Attorney General Webb.

John and Coke Brite are in Folsom Prison! Word was received here this morning early that James Davis and Dr. Earl Harris had arrived at Folsom Prison with the two boys accused with the murder of Martin Lange, Joe Clark and Fred Seaborn. According to Mrs. James Davis, the boys surrendered yesterday about noon to the District Attorney and Harris, and the four left immediately by back roads for Folsom. The boys arrived at Folsom Prison at eight o'clock this morning.

Chandler was of course besieged by the press. In spite of his emotional turmoil, he kept a stiff upper lip and remained very cool under the barrage of questions. He was able to add nothing to the story beyond what was known already.

As the news filtered through the general community in Yreka and the surrounding areas, there were two distinct and literally audible reactions. The loudest came from the "pro lynchers" who vented their wrath in disappointment upon being deprived of their "prey." The other group, which was by far in the majority, heaved a collective sigh of relief in the realization that justice "under the law" was intact and could now be exercised. It seemed as though there were no "in-betweeners," no "hedgers." It seemed that everyone was either for absolute law and order or for "citizens" reprisal with no shades of grey in the middle. Talk, talk and more talk; for two days the constant talk and discussion held sway in the coffee shops, on the streets and in every conceivable encounter between two or more people.

And then a strange thing seemed to take place. As if on a given signal, all this busy discussion and exchange of opinion seemed to cease. It just stopped, as if the community was exhausted with the subject and wanted a rest. People seemed to shrug it off and resume their customary and normal less vociferous existence. The metropolitan press immediately left the area, thereby greatly contributing to this aura of silence. The excitement was over and there was nothing more that could be said. And strangely enough, it stayed that way.

When the news of the arrest of the Brite brothers had initially broken, District Attorney Davis had declined to make any official statement concerning the episode. But after a few days passed, he began to loosen up to some extent and reveal the facts surrounding the negotiations that led to the event.

The brothers had surrendered to Davis and his friend, Dr. Edward Earl Harris, a Yreka dentist, at noon Saturday, September 18th, 19 days after the fateful shooting. All through the manhunt, Davis had been convinced that the Brite brothers were actually never far from home and that their mother, Mrs. A. J. Brite must be in touch with them. For the past nine or ten days Davis had been in frequent but irregular contact with Mrs. Brite. During each of these encounters he had constantly urged her to attempt to arrange for the boys to give themselves up into his custody.

Davis said that Mrs. Brite, during these conversations, slowly began to learn and understand many of the intricacies of the criminal laws in which her sons had become enmeshed. When she finally realized that it would be impossible for anyone in authority to promise her anything that could lead to the boys' escape from a charge of murder, she began to openly show some interest in an arrangement that would be limited to only a guarantee of protection from a potential lynching. But Davis was frank to admit that it was his feeling that she was a long ways yet from agreeing to any such compromise. Because of this feeling, Davis was very much surprised to see her come walking into his office unannounced and without a prior appointment on the morning of September 17th. At this point, it appeared to Davis that she had finally "come around" and was apparently eager to acquiesce in what he had been trying to convince her of all along. He again proposed the plan of his receiving their surrender under his assurances that he would immediately transport the boys to Folsom Prison where they could be lodged out of reach of harm. He assured her that arrangements with the warden at Folsom were already in existence. The deal was struck and Mrs. Brite produced the boys, unarmed as agreed, at a point near the Brite home on Horse Creek.

Davis, in hopeful anticipation of coming events had enlisted the help of his close friend, Dr. Ed Harris who owned a two door Ford sedan that Davis had deemed the proper vehicle to use in the surrender operation. The final arrangements had in fact been made at that meeting in his office with Mrs. Brite that had been interrupted by Chandler's visit on Thursday the 17th. Chandler had been 100% correct in his fears that something big was coming down when he witnessed Davis' hasty exit from the courthouse about 11:00 o'clock that morning. Davis was hurrying to make the necessary final preparations with Harris in which the surrender and transportation of the defendants involved a trip of several hundred miles over unpaved back roads from Horse Creek to Folsom, near Sacramento.

At the surrender there was no one on either side of the transaction that was armed. The brothers were put in the back seat without any handcuffs or other restraints whatsoever. Davis and Harris rode in the front seat. Davis had brought a large heavy blanket and instructed the boys to hunch down and put the blanket over them whenever he gave the signal. The boys were of course under the blanket when they went through Horse Creek. Instead of turning east at Horse Creek to follow the Klamath upstream on the familiar road toward Yreka, they turned west and traveled down the great gorge in which the Klamath flowed toward the ocean. Along they went, down that crazy twisting course of the Klamath. Through the little hamlets along the river; Hamburg, Seiad Valley, Happy Camp; all these little places where people now lived that had once held a place in the history of the region as a roaring gold miners camp in the not too distant past. And at each one of them on signal the Brite boys ducked under the blanket.

In the 1930s, this road was a narrow dusty unpaved semi-improved wagon trail carved out of the almost perpendicular walls of the Klamath Canyon. It was quite a thrill meeting an oncoming car or truck on one of the many blind curves, with the river below appearing as a tiny silver ribbon straight down.

Close Call!

Whenever someone met another vehicle on these back roads it usually involved a stop by one or both in order to squeeze by, especially if a curve was involved. In fact, if it was someone you knew, both cars would automatically stop to visit a spell.

Just as the foursome rounded a curve some miles below Happy Camp, they saw a familiar car coming along in their direction. Davis gave the signal to get under the blanket and told the Brites to be especially quiet because he was going to stop. In the oncoming car was Captain George Daily, head of the Siskiyou County detachment of the California Highway Patrol, and a friend of both Davis and Harris. Both cars stopped. The two men greeted Daily and joshed around a bit with him. Daily, knowing that Davis had spent much of his youth in this downriver country and in fact still had kin about, didn't bother to ask where they were going. After passing a few pleasantries, the two cars continued on in their opposite directions.

Thirty-eight years later in Yreka, Court Reporter McMurry's youngest son asked a long retired Captain Daily what he would have done if he had known that the Brite brothers were under that blanket.

Without hesitation Daily replied, "I would have pulled my gun and arrested all four of them."

The four men in the Ford kept going, twisting and turning, nearly always in sight of the ever present river. They went through Clear Creek, Somes Bar, Orleans Bar, all sites of great gold strikes in the 1850s and 60s. On they went through Weitchpec, where the Trinity River flows into the Klamath, then on through Hoopa and Willow Creek, all old Indian settlements. Once the road reached the coast, it was easier going as they turned onto Highway 101. At Calpella they turned east, passing by Clear Lake and working their way to Williams on Highway 99, where they headed south again into Sacramento and the additional short distance to Folsom. They had traveled nearly 380 miles, much of it on unpaved roads, without a single incident. They had departed Horse Creek at noon on the 18th and arrived at Folsom at 8:00 p.m. on the 19th. All four of them immediately went to bed at Folsom.

Behind Bars At Last

The Brite brothers, wanted for a triple murder, were at last behind bars. As Davis went to sleep, his thoughts were that the brothers were at last safely behind bars.

So for the time being at least, Davis was now the man of the hour. But little did he know how close he had come to losing his moment of glory. The remainder of Henry Pallage's report tells this story as follows:

On Tuesday, September 15th I went to the Brite home the last time. Joe Clyburn was with me this day when Mr. Brite said very plainly that the boys were going to give up and that he wanted me to stay at their place for a few days and not go back to Horse Creek Camp at night. I told him that I would do that very gladly, but I would need to go back to the Camp to get some things and also run over to my home in the Big Humbug and get what I needed. I assured him that I would be back and stay with them.

I went to the camp that evening and ate supper after which I went on over to my home and got the things I wanted. I came back that same evening to the camp and slept there.

The next morning, Wednesday, the 16th, I had all my things together in my car and was just going to leave for the Brite home to stay. Chester Barton suddenly came out of his store and said, "Pallage, you are wanted in the Sheriff's Office in Yreka; they told me yesterday to tell you to come in. They said they couldn't get you on the phone. I came home late last night so I am telling you now."

I said, "I just can't go now; I'll call them on the phone and tell them."

But I couldn't get Yreka [on the phone] after trying several times. Mrs. Barton said she was sure the phone was out of order. So I drove to Yreka and Mr. Chandler was not in. After I waited for him until after noon he finally came in with some other people.

As he came in he saw me and said, "Mr. Pallage, I am glad to see you but I am too busy to go over things with you now. I need a day or two to think the situation over and then I will let you know what plans we will make. Go on home and get a good night's sleep; you deserve it and I am sure we can put it off one or two days."

I went on home and did some cleaning up and did a few things. We heard nothing from Mr. Chandler in the next two days. In the evening of the 18th my wife and I talked things over and we decided that it was too critical to wait any longer. We planned that if we didn't hear from the sheriff the first thing the next morning that I would go on up to the Brite's as they had wanted me to and stay there with them. The next morning, September 19th, just as I was leaving for the Brite's home, word came through that the Brite brothers were in Folsom prison.

About a week after the Brites had been deposited at Folsom, Henry Pallage bumped into Mrs. Brite at the Horse Creek Store. They greeted each other effusively as Mrs. Brite explained to him what had happened after he had left the Brite's home. Pallage in turn explained what had happened to him since he last saw her. He finally asked her if she would be willing to give him a written statement about his part in what had happened. To this she very graciously agreed. It was Pallage's idea that it would be best if they could get an outside witness; to this she willingly agreed. The two of them thereupon drove to Yreka and located Pallage's friend, Don Avery. Mr. Avery was a prominent Yreka businessman who later became a long time member of the Siskiyou County Board of Supervisors.

Mrs. Brite dictated the statement as Avery wrote it. When it was complete and had been read back to Mrs. Brite she signed it. It reads as follows:

When the boys come in Wednesday night between eight and nine o'clock, we talked it over. They said we've come in to surrender. We told them Mr. Pallage was down at Horse Creek, that he was a deputy sheriff and that we trusted him. So we decided and I advised them. I said I'll go down to Decker's in the morning and ride with them to Horse Creek and get Mr. Pallage. They agreed to do this. We told them how nice he'd been to us and that he had taken an oath to protect them and take them to Folsom Prison.

The back side of Mrs. Brite's note explaining her agreement with Pallage. It was dictated to and written by Don Avery in Yreka and signed by Mrs. Brite. Pallage would use it in an attempt to claim part of the reward for the capture of John and Coke.

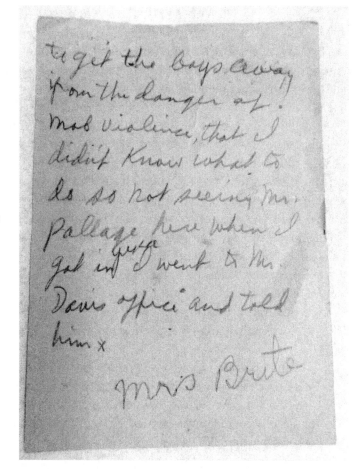

Instead of going to Horse Creek, I phoned to Horse Creek from Rainey's for Mr. Pallage. I planned to have him go back with me and get the boys. They told me then that Mr. Pallage had gone to Yreka the day before. The phone was bad so Rainey brought me on into Yreka. I was so nervous and excited because I wanted to get the boys away from the danger of mob violence that I didn't know what to do. So not seeing Mr. Pallage here when I got in Yreka, I went to Mr. Davis' office and told him.

The statement is signed in very labored and scrawling handwriting, "Mrs Brite."

Who Will the Lawyers Be?

Two days after the Brites had been ensconced in Folsom Prison, their defense attorney surfaced. It is not known how on earth this had been arranged but it was none other than Horace F. Frye, a very prominent and competent defense lawyer in Sacramento. On the day after the incarceration at Folsom, Frye was interviewing the Brites at the prison. The general assumption by the public as to how this arrangement could have been made was that during the long ride to Folsom, the subject must have come up between the Brites and Davis. It was felt that Davis himself surely had made the arrangements by phone the next day after their arrival at Folsom. As Folsom is but a few minutes from Sacramento, Frye must have immediately responded.

In another two days, Attorney Frye appeared in Yreka and announced to the press that he had visited the defendants at Folsom as well as their parents in Yreka. He stated he was very happy that he had been chosen as the defense counsel in the case.

At a preliminary hearing held in Folsom Prison a few days later, John Brite's account of the killing was given as follows:

> The first thing I knew, two men were on each side beating me. I didn't know who they were. They beat me so bad that my head hurt me for two or three days afterwards. I couldn't rest or sleep. I couldn't even put my hat on. They kept on beating me and I hollered to Coke, "My God, can't you help me?" Coke didn't answer. One of the men said, "Grab his arms and I'll fix him." They beat me until I don't remember what happened until I came to my senses walking in the corn patch near our house.
>
> When I first came to, I thought me and Coke had trouble between ourselves. I asked him what he did to me. He said, "I didn't do nothing to you."
>
> I said, "I'm sick. So let's lie down and go to bed."
>
> Coke replied, "We can't go to bed. There's three dead men down at the camp."
>
> I asked him who had killed them and he said he didn't know.

On September 26th the *Yreka Journal* published the following piece that had come in on the Associated Press wire:

ACTION OF DAVIS IS LAUDED BY
S. F. BAR ASSOCIATION

A. W. BROUILETT LAUDS ACTIONS OF
DISTRICT ATTORNEY OF SISKIYOU
IN PREVENTING POSSIBLE LYNCHING

SAN FRANCISCO. Special (AP)—The City Bar Association today lauded District Attorney James Davis of Yreka for his action in avoiding the possible lynching of John and Coke Brite, accused of the slaying of two officers and a vacationer in a mountain gun battle several weeks ago.

A. W. Brouilett, President of the San Francisco Association wrote about Davis, "He had in this instance vindicated that priceless heritage which is that every person is entitled to trial by jury of his peers.

The release of this endorsement by the San Francisco Bar Association seemed to have little effect upon the attitudes of Davis' critics. It was generally looked upon as "just another attempt by the 'city slickers' to stick their noses in where they were not wanted."

The collective community calm continued to hold, but with a new angle. The avowed lynchers had definitely retreated in total defeat. One would be hard put to locate anyone now who would even own up to having carried that banner in the past. But there were those in the winning "law and order" side of the equation that were slowly becoming concerned over a new consideration. In their minds there was a question that Davis may have, by his actions in making promises to the defendants' mother, legally disqualified himself from further handling the prosecution.

This was a hard question for a serious person to face. In one sense, Davis, by getting the fugitives to surrender and then taking them out of reach of the lynchers, was a hero to the serious law and order advocates. But this was not to say that they as a group supported the idea that the case called for anything other than a "first degree" murder charge. This same group in fact stood nearly unanimous against the "lesser degree" attitudes that Davis had previously indicated by his words and actions.

Davis, of course, was fully aware of the feelings of the majority of the community that first degree charges should be brought. At one time he actually publicly declared that he would charge the Brite brothers with first degree murder. But after a few days of this sort of "no confidence" feeling becoming more evident, he announced that he would turn the whole case over to the California Attorney General and ask that the case be prosecuted by that office and staff.

On October 3rd, Davis returned to Yreka from a lengthy conference with Attorney General Webb in San Francisco. Upon his arrival home, he went directly to the two local newspapers with his statement and a letter from Webb. The *Yreka Journal* story appeared in that day's issue:

WEBB NOT TO PROSECUTE IN BRITE TRIAL

WEBB TELLS DISTRICT ATTORNEY TO PROCEED WITH THE TRIAL OF THE BRITE BROTHERS AS HE IS NOT DISQUALIFIED

Davis States, "I Will Do My Duty In Face of Everything"

In an interview today, James Davis, District Attorney, stated that he will positively prosecute the Brite brothers on charges of murder if they stand trial in Siskiyou County. "I will do my duty in the face of everything," he declared this morning. "Attorney General Webb has clearly outlined the path and I will follow his instructions to the letter," he further stated.

Davis has just returned from San Francisco, where he went in person to request that the Attorney General take over the prosecution. Webb refused on the ground that "Davis was not legally or otherwise disqualified to represent the people in the further prosecution of this case."

His letter to Davis follows:

You have asked if you should proceed in the case of People vs. John Brite and Coke Brite, who are charged by complaint with the crime of murder committed in Siskiyou County.

In reply, I may say to you that I feel quite familiar with all the facts involved in that case. An investigator from this office, prior to the apprehension of the Brite brothers, spent some days in Siskiyou County and I have a full report from that official of the facts as ascertained by him.

I have before me a transcript of the testimony taken at the coroner's inquest, and a copy of the statement made by the defendants at Folsom prison. In addition, I am familiar with what you did in obtaining the surrender of the Brites and of your action in placing them in custody in Folsom prison.

From all of these facts it appears clearly that you are not legally or otherwise disqualified to represent The People in the further prosecution of this case. There is no fact or circumstance indicating that your further duty will not be well and faithfully performed.

I am quite aware that your action in this matter has met with the disapproval of some residents of Siskiyou County, and it is unfortunate that there are in that county people who are disappointed because of your performance of official duty.

You promised the Brites, in the event of their surrender, that they would be protected against threatened local violence and safely delivered into the custody of the law, and you assured them of a fair and impartial trail. Relying upon these promises, the Brites surrendered to you and thus far you have furnished them the protection promised and may be relied upon to perform your full duty hereafter to them and to the People of the State.

Your entire action has been in strict accord with official duty, and with due regard to public welfare.

I need not speculate upon what might have occurred in Siskiyou County if these defendants had fallen into the hands of some persons, for the declared intentions of some of the residents of that county left no doubt of what would have occurred in that event.

You are entitled to the commendation of all law abiding citizens whether residing in Siskiyou County or elsewhere, and a public official cannot expect the commendation of the lawless residents.

As to the course to be pursued, may I suggest that though you have a complaint charging murder pending, upon which, if the prosecution proceeds, the holding of a preliminary examination in Siskiyou County before a committing magistrate will be necessary, at which the presence of the defendants will be required. This course may be avoided.

You have informed me that you have in Siskiyou County a grand jury already impaneled, and it occurs to me that you should request the judge of your Superior Court to call a session of that grand jury to whom this case will be submitted under fitting instructions of the court; that you should present to that grand jury all pertinent evidence bearing upon the case, and if an indictment is found, that the defendants be brought to trial upon that indictment.

I have been informed by the attorney for the defendants that a motion for a change of place of trial will be made upon the ground that the defendants cannot be afforded a fair and impartial trial in that county. That motion will, of course, be submitted to the judge of the Superior Court and by him determined. If the motion should be made and granted, the case will be transferred for trial to another county selected by the judge. If denied the case will be tried in Siskiyou County.

May I add that your action, in the event of such motion being presented, will depend upon the showing made and upon your knowledge of the local conditions. If from all of the facts you are satisfied that the defendants can have in that county a fair and impartial trial you should resist the motion, but if you are not satisfied that they can there have a fair and impartial trial the law would not justify your opposing the motion.

Should questions hereafter arise upon which you would desire the advice of this office, be assured that we are ready to furnish you every aid.

With entire confidence that your action hereafter as heretofore will be taken in entire accord with the law and that the interest of the People on the one hand, and the defendants on the other, will be at all times safeguarded, I remain.

Very truly yours,
U. S. Webb
Attorney General

Davis' release of the Attorney General's letter along with his own announcement to reporters that he intended to follow Webb's scenario definitely seemed to be an assurance to the public that Davis was in charge. But the letter, long as it was, did nothing to relieve the public concern over what the actual charge against the Brites was to be. If Davis had finally come around to actually bring the charge as first degree murder, there was nothing in Webb's letter or the district attorney's newspaper statement to indicate it. But strange as it may seem, there seemed to be no general public uproar; the mood of silence was still in effect.

During this hiatus of public calm the machinery of the case itself had been going on. On October 14th, Superior Court Judge C. J. Luttrell released to the *Yreka Journal* notice that he would empanel a Grand Jury about November 1st.

By the morning of the 4th, the grand jury empaneling was complete and the first order of business was Davis' presentation of the Brite case. As per the California law, grand jury proceedings are secret; therefore the outcome of this would not be known until the jury's findings were presented to the Superior Court. Normally this would be a matter of a few days but in this case, the grand jury made it short and quick.

Baker and Decker both testified along with Dr. Schlappe and Deputy Coroner Frank Bills. It was over in one day and the Grand Jury was ready to report to the court the next morning.

On the morning of the 5th, court was convened and the Grand Jury presented three separate indictments against John and Coke Brite. Each of the indictments was identical except for the names of the victims. The first one read as follows:

> The Grand Jury of the County of Siskiyou, State of California, hereby accuses John H. Brite and Coke Brite of a felony, to-wit: Murder, in that on or about the 30th day of August, 1936, in the County of Siskiyou, State of California, they, the said defendants did willfully, unlawfully and feloniously, and with malice aforethought, murder one Martin Lange, a human being.
>
> That at the time of the commission of the offense hereinbefore set forth, said defendants were armed with a deadly weapon to wit: a rifle.
>
> That at the time of the commission of the offense hereinbefore set forth in this indictment, said defendants, John H. Brite and Coke Brite, were in the Superior Court of the State of Arizona, in and for the County of Coconino, convicted of the crime of burglary, a felony, and the judgment of said court was,

on or about the 22nd day of December, 1935, pronounced and rendered, and said defendants served a term of imprisonment therefore in the State Prison at Florence, Arizona.

Judge Luttrell set the date for arraignment of the two defendants for the following Monday, November 9th, 1936. He further instructed the sheriff to have the Brite brothers brought to Yreka and be ready for trial.

While the above steps in the judicial process were mainly routine and of little importance, they were given wide publicity by the media. The public seemed to understand that this was only the "preliminary" and the "main event" was yet to follow. The people remained very calm and almost disinterested. But underneath the surface of public awareness, some new forces were beginning to stir. This was apparently a movement by the local leaders within and on the fringes of the governmental and judicial establishment. There was a total lack of publicity of any nature concerning what was going on; no "news leak" of any kind; no pompous speeches on the courthouse steps; just total silence.

But some people knew. Some, because they were participants and others because they were in the legal machinery and had to know in order to execute what was going on. But it was there and it was moving, and nobody was talking.

Davis had returned from San Francisco to Yreka bearing Attorney General Webb's letter on September 2nd and released it along with his statement on the 3rd. But not until thirty-seven days later, on November 9th, did the first hint surface as to what had been going on out of sight of public awareness. The "hint" arrived in the most unexpected place that could be imagined.

At the end of their most recent regular meeting, the Siskiyou County Board of Supervisors had scheduled a special meeting for 10:00 a.m., November 9th, which coincidentally was also the time for commencing the Brite brothers' arraignment. As this action by the Board of Supervisors was a frequent one and totally routine, it had aroused little notice from the public and none at all from the press. Actually, at the same moment that the Supervisors were meeting, the courtroom in the same building was jammed to overflowing as the arraignment was getting under way.

Davis Out, Allen In

Without any preliminaries whatsoever, the chairman of the Board of Supervisors gaveled the meeting of the five members to order. He immediately recognized one of the supervisors who moved that the appointment of Yreka attorney James M. Allen as Special Prosecutor in the Brite case be approved. A second to the motion was duly made and it was carried unanimously. Another motion was also made and carried to the effect that Yreka attorney Joseph P. Correa was thereby appointed temporary Assistant District Attorney in order to represent Davis in the Brite case as well as to assist Special Prosecutor Allen. A short further discussion was held relating to the compensation to be paid the two attorneys, after which the meeting was quickly adjourned.

There were no reporters present to run for the door. There wasn't anyone present to dash into the corridors with the news of the astounding development. District Attorney Davis himself was out of sight; he was busy at the arraignment.

So, District Attorney James Davis was now out of the case. This had all developed entirely behind the scenes without so much as even one "leak" as to what was under way. This development was the new prime subject of discussion throughout the county. Every coffee shop; every barber shop; anywhere two or more people gathered, this new twist was topic #1. How was this planned and executed? Had Davis agreed to it; or maybe he had suggested it himself? Nobody that could have been involved had anything to say.

The news media asked Sheriff Chandler for a comment on the matter.

"I have no comment," he replied.

The *Siskiyou News* reporter questioned Charley Johnson about the matter. As might be expected, his reply, given in his usual good natured and witty manner, contained nothing that threw any light on the question.

Johnson said, "No, I was not involved officially. Yes, I had some definite ideas on the subject. No, I was not asked for my ideas because I am sure everyone involved already knew them anyway. As for the mechanics of how it was accomplished, yes, I know how it was done because the law contains provisions for anyone to be disqualified or to disqualify himself if he has a conflict in a particular case. You can ask any competent lawyer to explain this, but be prepared to get a bill from him later."

Court Reporter Ralph McMurry's youngest son asked his father what had happened.

His answer was, "I can't talk about it. Someday, after a long time, I may be able to discuss it."

Undaunted, the boy asked his mother the same question.

Mrs. McMurry was a remarkably intelligent woman. She was born and raised in San Francisco and was graduated from the University of California at Berkeley in 1907. This was a considerable feat in itself as in those days there were very few women that attended college at all. She became a teacher of English, German and Latin. She was teaching in Redding, California when she met and married Ralph McMurry.

The question from her third son gave Mrs. McMurry some pause. She sensed that it was a fair question from a boy who was exhibiting considerable interest in all of these matters.

She replied, "I heard you ask your father that question and I heard what he said. It is the same with me. You must realize that married people share confidences but in doing so it goes without saying that these confidences are never revealed by either of them. In this matter about which you asked, you must understand Daddy's position. There were of course several people involved in this development of the case; all of them were talking back and forth, making this and that arrangement and generally trying to agree on what actions to take while at all times considering the implications of what they were doing. The nature of your father's position places him right in the middle of all of these conversations, plans and negotiations.

"The position he has, however, is not as a participant, but more or less like a traffic officer or guide. He is secretary to both the judge and the district attorney. He has a legal connection with the Board of Supervisors. He is well known and trusted by the entire law enforcement and legal establishment in this county. It is therefore just a natural development that even though he is not a policy maker or one of the major players, he is automatically sort of in on everything that goes up or down. Most certainly as this system operates, many of the major participants frequently seek his advice and counsel. So therefore, if the subject at hand is a confidential one, this confidence is respected by all the participants. No one of them need warn the other or even mention that it is confidential; that goes without saying. It is just naturally respected by these men of good will and honest character.

"When your father says that he may be able to tell you after a long time, it is because time usually tends to release the confidentiality of this type of thing. As the actions taken here in this particular matter bear the fruit of an event such as the changing of prosecutors in the case, the event of course becomes public knowledge. Later, through time and happenstance, the facts that led to the publicly known event slowly come out. Your father means that he cannot reveal any of it until this has taken place."

The boy considered and understood his mother's answer to his question. By the time he thought about asking his father again, many years later, it was too late.

Notwithstanding the rigid silence in the matter maintained by the participants, a consensus was generally achieved by the public as to how this development was managed. There was but one publicly observable bit of evidence as to what might be taking place during the period leading up to the action by the county Board of Supervisors. This was an obvious unusual high degree of traffic in and out of the offices of the local law firm of Allen and McNamara. This traffic consisted of many of the prominent "leaders and shakers" in the community.

It was also interesting to note that during this period, "Ma Brite" herself had been a visitor in that office on more than one occasion. As former District Attorney Johnson had indicated in his statement, there were several resident attorneys who were not participants in any way who gladly lent their expertise to the coffee and barber shop discussions as to what the legal requirements were in order to change prosecutors in certain circumstances. This was all there was available to go on for reaching a public conclusion; the rational went something like this:

James M. Allen was by far and away the leading attorney in Siskiyou County. At the time, he was also the incumbent State Senator, representing Siskiyou and Del Norte Counties in the California State Legislature. It was also known that as a result of his position in the state government, he was a personal friend of California Attorney General Webb. Many leaders and concerned citizens in the community began to individually, and collectively as all the talk went on, come to the realization that something here had to be done. Their concern was that District Attorney Davis, right or wrong, no longer had the support and confidence of the people. They felt that no matter the outcome of the case, the general public would never be satisfied that justice had prevailed. These men probably felt that by this time, even Davis himself was probably seeking a graceful way out and might be amenable to the idea of his withdrawing from the case. If a change in prosecutors could be accomplished, Senator Allen was the immediate and logical person to enlist in such a project.

This conclusion was based upon three obvious facts known throughout the community:

1. Allen, being a lawyer, would surely know the legal procedures for accomplishing the change.

2. Allen, being the Senator, would have the contacts in Sacramento, the State Capital, for enlisting any help at that end that might be required.

3. Allen, having been a former District Attorney and currently the acknowledged leading local practicing lawyer, obviously had the respect and backing from the entire community. He most surely would be the wisest choice to take over the prosecution in the event a change was to be made.

So the thoughts and conclusions of the community leaders began to surface out loud within this group. Approaches to Allen were made and the procedure began to roll. Allen, of course, was of a like mind with the others in the group. His only requirement if he took the case was that he take it "without prior conditions" and that he be "in sole charge of its conduct."

When the time came to face Davis with the idea, it was anticlimactic. Davis was an intelligent man and it was no surprise to him to be approached at last by these citizens whom he respected. He understood very well that he had become a "problem" in the case rather than a "solver" and that in the interests of the public good, it would be better if he withdrew. It is not known to this day whether or not Davis received this development with relief or bitterness, but he was man enough to take it. He agreed to withdraw and the deed was done.

6

The Brite Brothers: The Trial

As per the judge's instructions, Sheriff Chandler had retrieved the two defendants from Folsom Prison and deposited them in the Siskiyou County Jail. There was absolutely no excitement generated by this event and Chandler had them in the courtroom on schedule for their arraignment on November the 9th.

An Anguished Mother

The arraignment itself was little more than routine except for one minor incident. The judge quietly called the court to order and asked the defendants to rise for the reading of the indictments. At this point, Mrs. Brite suddenly burst into the room and, rushing through the rail gate, stood between her two boys with her arms around them. Luttrell sternly admonished her to withdraw from inside the rail and she immediately complied by taking a seat directly behind the defendants, but on the public side of the rail.

The Brites readily admitted to the facts as contained in the indictment concerning their difficulties with the law in Arizona, after which they both pled not guilty to the current murder charges.

Judge Luttrell then set November 30th, 1936 for the coming trial. But Defense Attorney Frye then reminded the judge that he had filed a motion for a change of location for the trial. The judge withdrew his order setting the date and instead set the change of venue hearing for Tuesday, November 10th, the next day.

At the Change of Venue hearing, James G. Davis appeared in a very buoyant mood. As per prior arrangement with the judge, he announced James M. Allen, who was present, had been appointed Special Prosecutor in the case and that he, Davis, had selected attorney Joseph P. Correia of Yreka to represent him as his deputy in the trial. It should be mentioned here that fifty years later, a still active Joe Correia explained that Davis' announcement to the effect that he was "his representative" was news to him. Correia said that it was his understanding that he was to assist Allen in the prosecution and that all of the negotiations prior to his taking the job were conducted by Allen.

Attorney Frye then announced that he had selected Yreka attorney J. Everett Barr as his counselor.

Judge Luttrell duly accepted all of these various nominations and the cast was now complete for the coming trial.

Frye halfheartedly submitted but two affidavits supporting his contention that the defendants "could not get justice in Siskiyou County due to the prejudice" against them and because of the prominence of two of the three victims in the case.

Allen was ready. He submitted affidavits from fifteen prominent citizens from all over the county, including those from Sheriff Chandler and District Attorney Davis. All of them declared that a fair and impartial trial would be given the Brite brothers if kept in Siskiyou County.

Allen then stated, "It has never been necessary to call for a change in venue because we have in Siskiyou County a fair minded and impartial people who are law abiding. They believe that any person charged with a crime should let the law take its course by means of a fair and impartial trial. The metropolitan papers have given an exaggerated impression of the feeling in this county against these defendants. Such feeling did not and does not now exist. The impression was given that Siskiyou County was after the blood of these men; this is false. These Brite men will be fully protected and given a fair trial. We owe it to the citizens and society to have the trial here. A change of venue is unwarranted."

It had been "no contest;" score one for the prosecution. Luttrell adjourned the court for lunch after which he denied the motion and reset the trial date for November 30th. From the bench he stated, "The defendants will be given a fair and impartial trial."

By 10:00 a.m., Monday, November 30th, the Siskiyou County Courthouse in Yreka was filled to overflowing with spectators. Milling about the hallways were one hundred citizens that had been called for the jury panel. The judge, the court reporter, the clerk, the bailiff, the sheriff, and last but not least, the defendants, were all in place. Allen and Correia were present at the prosecutor's table and J. E. Barr was accounted for at the defense station. But Horace J. Frye was nowhere to be seen. He was flat on his back in a sick bed in Sacramento.

As soon as Judge Luttrell called the court to order, W. R. Houston, a Sacramento associate of Frye's, made his presence known. He informed the court of Frye's circumstance and presented a physician's certificate verifying the situation. He moved for a two week postponement of the trial.

Allen addressed the court and sustained the motion by stating that under the circumstances he would not oppose it. He went on to say that this is a very important case in which Mr. Frye had taken an interest in its very earliest stages. He said that everyone, the bench and both sides, desired a fair and impartial trial and that he therefore recommended the granting of the motion.

The judge thereupon granted a one week postponement, setting the date for December 7th. He stated that due to the importance of the trial it must commence as soon as possible. He remarked that in the event that Mr. Frye would still be unable to respond at that time, his assistant, Attorney J. Everett Barr could carry on in his place.

J. E. Barr, who was at the time a very young man who had been in the community only a very short time, gulped.

Court was recessed for the week.

The Trial Finally Begins

The following week at the appointed time the same cast, but this time including Frye, was present on both sides of the rail. J. E. Barr breathed a sigh of relief. The trial immediately got under way with the arduous task of examining the members of the jury panel in an effort to form a trial jury. It had been predicted by all involved that this stage would be a rigorous one due to the great sensitivity and notoriety of the case.

After two days of this, the *Yreka Journal* came out on Wednesday with its usual colorful but accurate account of the proceedings which read in part as follows:

SELECTION OF JURY
PROVES LENGTHY TASK

Defendants Apparently Taking Small
Interest in Trial Proceedings

A list of 100 jurors is slowly being examined in the effort to secure an impartial jury to try John and Coke Brite. 29 of the jurors were excused for various causes and those examined up to date, about 25 more, may be excused and others also, before the case really starts.

The fact that many do not believe in capital punishment or are friends of the slain officers, or neighbors of the Brites on Horse Creek, or have already formed an opinion in the case, is playing havoc with the present venire [a panel of prospective jurors] and another one may be called before the case can actually get under way."

Horace Frye, attorney for the Brites, is very stern in his demands of every prospective juror as to whether or not he believes in the right of self-defense.

Special Prosecutor Allen stated that the State of California is depending on the jury to see that justice is meted out for the slain officers killed in the act of discharging their duty.

The Brite men apparently give little heed to the procedure of the case. Their mother sits between them inside the court rail. Mrs. Irene Lange, widow of Deputy Sheriff Martin Lange, also sits inside the court rail and listens attentively to every step of the court.

Mrs. Fred Seaborn and Mrs. John Seaborn, widow and mother of Fred Seaborn, came in from Vallejo to attend the trial.

The courtroom is crowded and the trial may be a long drawn out one lasting for two weeks or more."

But the jury selection proceedings went faster than the *Journal* had predicted. The process required only Monday afternoon, all day Tuesday and Wednesday morning. The preliminaries were now over and the trial could begin in earnest.

Standing Room Only in the Courtroom

That afternoon, all involved were present including the jury. Every spectator seat was occupied while additional people were allowed to stand in the side aisles. A great tension filled the air. But this soon waned as it always does even in the most exciting trials. The public does not generally realize that the early periods of most every trial consist of routine formal proceedings, more or less "housekeeping" matters that must legally be covered.

After the formal reading of the indictment by the Clerk of the Court, the first of these routine items was the almost universal request by the prosecution that the witnesses to be called by the defendants be barred from the courtroom while the trial is proceeding. The purpose of this is of course that the one side does not want the other side's witnesses to hear the testimony of his witnesses for fear that they will be influenced by what they hear. This request was granted and executed for both sides and the room was cleared of the witnesses. Now many of the spectators standing in the aisles slipped into the vacated seats.

The prosecution then proceeded with the examination of his witnesses. The lead off one was Albert Parrott, the Siskiyou County Surveyor, who had made a large detailed map of the scene of the crime. Prosecutor Allen went to great lengths and considerable time in getting the surveyor to explain every little detail of it, including the exact distances involved thereon.

Allen next called John "Snappy" Goodrich, a local professional photographer who had been retained to make detailed photographs of the crime scene. He was questioned in the minutest detail concerning each and every one of the photos. Then Mr. Arthur O'Connor, a local civil engineer was put on the stand. He had been retained to make a detailed three dimensional model of the scene to the same scale as Parrott's map. This also was very thoroughly explained through questioning by the prosecutor.

Cardboard figures representing the three victims used during the trial, presumably in conjunction with the 3D model of the crime scene.

All of these witnesses were the usual lineup by the prosecution to present a picture of the scene of the alleged crimes. This is, as in all cases of this nature, for the use of the judge, the jury, and even the defense, in order that all will be thoroughly familiar with the physical layout in which much of the coming testimony will be presented. No excitement here; just endless, somewhat boring detail, but very necessary nonetheless.

Next came witness Ann Spangle, an x-ray nurse. She was shown and identified a long series of x-ray pictures of the victims' bodies. Miss Spangle's testimony was a preliminary to the appearance of the main witness for the day, Dr. Roy Schlappi.

Here again was a long, sometimes gruesome, examination of all of the wounds in the three victims inspected at the scene on Horse Creek and as further studied in the subsequent autopsies. But, as usual in such situations, the opinions were expressed in the unemotional and dry technical terms and phrases of the medical profession. Altogether, Dr. Schlappi's testimony including cross examination by the defense the next day consumed several hours, which subsequently required twenty-five pages of trial transcript.

The next day, Thursday, December 10th, during the preliminaries involved with getting Dr. Schlappi back on the stand, Attorney J. Everett Barr broke into the proceedings.

Two Meals a Day

"Before further testimony is taken," he said, "I wish to ask the court for an order that these men be fed at regular hours. They weren't fed for fifteen hours the other day, from noon until nine o'clock this morning."

Judge Luttrell replied, "Well, take that up with the sheriff. That is his business."

Barr added, "I think it is very much the business of the court."

"No, no," replied the judge, "take it up with the sheriff. That is between you and him."

That was all there was to it. Fifty years later, the jailer, Deputy Sheriff Ed Mathews was asked about this matter. This was the same Ed Mathews who had figured so prominently in the Johnson case. As always, his memory of the matter was vivid and precise.

Mathews said, "I remember it very well. I was not in the courtroom at the time but I was very surprised when I heard about it. I was feeding those two prisoners on the very same schedule as the rest of the inmates; two meals a day. Due to the trial, the timing for those two men might have been a little off from the rest but they received the same food and number of meals as anyone. My own opinion is that it was strictly a lawyer's maneuver to get some recognition in the trial because traditionally the defense is more or less always in the background relative to the prosecution in the early parts of any case."

After Schlappi's testimony was completed, Special Prosecutor Allen brought on two witnesses from the State Bureau of Criminal Identification and Investigation who were asked technical questions about their findings regarding the guns and ammunition in the case.

Sheriff Chandler was then introduced to the proceedings for the purpose of identifying a long list of exhibits, most of which had been picked up at the site of the shooting the night and morning after it happened.

Allen's purpose in putting the sheriff on the stand at this time was merely routine in order to get the exhibits identified and entered as evidence. It was his intention that this appearance of the sheriff was to be only for that purpose and that he would recall him when they were into the real crux of the case.

But Horace F. Frye crossed up Allen on this one. Frye took the opportunity of Chandler's presence on the stand to finally come to life with a blistering cross examination that was entirely expected by Allen, but not at this early stage of the trial. What happened next went a long way toward revealing the kind of a defense Frye was going to present in the Brite brothers' behalf.

In order to understand what is involved here, a clarification of a rule of law should be pointed out. The rules of the game are that under cross-examination, the witness can only be asked questions relative to what had been discussed by the other side during direct examination.

As Allen was finishing up with this first appearance of Chandler he was entering into evidence a pistol holster that the sheriff had identified as having been picked up by him off the defendants' bed the morning of the shooting.

After the court had marked and accepted the holster into evidence, Allen said, "I am going to recall this witness for further direct examination later on, and I want to withdraw him now."

Mr. Frye then broke in, saying, "I would like to cross examine at this time, Your Honor."

Defense Attorney Goes on the Offense

Allen was astounded by this but he let it pass; the judge allowed it by advising Frye to proceed.

The following portions of the trial transcript give the best account of what then transpired:

Q. Mr. Chandler, you stated you received the barrel of the rifle from Mr. and Mrs. Brite on the morning of August 30th?

[Note: It should be recalled that a broken rifle stock was found lying across the back of the body of Joe Clark. Mr. Frye is here referring to the barrel of that rifle that Chandler had obtained from Mr. and Mrs. Brite at their cabin.]

A. That is correct.

Q. About what time?

A. Just about one hour after daylight.

No, I don't think it was that long. Just the time it would have taken us to walk from the scene of the alleged killing to the Brite home and that was about the first thing I asked them for. It was either one or the other of them that walked in the house and brought it out. Mr. Brite, I am quite sure brought the portion of the rifle out.

Q. Now who went with you to the Brite home?

A. There was Deputy Sheriff Ed Mathews, L. L. Fortna, two Yreka City Police officers, Gilbert F. Rhodes and Frank Fullerton.

Q. You all went together right up to the cabin where the Brites lived?

A. We did.

Frye now launched into a lengthy detailed cross-examination of Chandler concerning the minutest details of how Chandler had come into possession of each and every one of the exhibits that Allen had submitted as evidence. It was Allen's intention to later get into some of these matters on a much broader scale when he recalled Chandler. But Frye had now "grabbed the ball" and was running with it. There was nothing Allen could do about it as long as Frye's questions remained related to the items that had been submitted in evidence.

Frye very well knew that this group of evidence was actually noncontroversial, but he obviously had something else in mind. As he continued, it very quickly became clear that he was using this vehicle to attempt to belittle the sheriff in order to decrease the jury's confidence in him.

Frye continued:

Q. Now, you say you were looking for Mr. Baker's hat when he picked up this bottle?

Baker had lost his hat in the first battle with the Brites. There are many things in life that are entirely unimportant to a mountain man, but his hat is not one of them. In spite of the harrowing day and catastrophic night Baker had endured, the loss of his hat was greatly on his mind. He had told Chandler about it and asked him to watch for it because he wanted it back. Chandler considered it "evidence" to be retained in the case and was therefore keeping an eye out for it. The hat was ultimately found and placed in evidence but Baker finally got it back after the trial. The bottle was the one that the Brites had thrown at Baker and Seaborn, also in the first battle.

A. Yes.

Q. Well what time was that?

A. Oh, that was just directly before daylight. I remember we were using the flashlight on the morning of the 30th.

Q. Before daylight?

A. Yes, if I remember right.

Q. And did you make this trip down to the road for the express purpose of looking for Mr. Baker's hat?

A. Yes. He said he had lost a hat earlier in the evening when he had that fight at that place, and he wanted to find it.

Q. And who picked up the bottle?

A. Mr. Baker picked up the bottle, if I recall correctly.

Q. Well, do you recall?

A. Yes, I am quite positive.

Q. Do you know now who picked up that bottle?

A. I think Mr. Baker did.

Q. Well, do you know?

A. I would say that he did, yes.

Q. Did you see him pick it up?

A. Yes.

Q. You are sure about that?

A. Positive.

Q. How far was he from you when he picked the bottle up?

A. Right against me; probably not more than a foot or two.

Q. There is no doubt in your mind now as to whether or not he picked up the bottle?

A. No, I don't think so.

Q. You still don't think so?

A. Yes.

The affable former District Attorney Johnson had been sitting in on this session. During the mid-afternoon recess he was heard to remark, "I would certainly hate to be around that fellow Frye if he was searching for a 'full' bottle of wine."

Q. And Seaborn was lying where? [Note: This exchange was involved with the location of a gun that was found.]

A. Mr. Seaborn's head was lying just about...

Mr. Allen [interrupting]: I object to this as not cross-examination. We didn't put in testimony as to where Mr. Seaborn was lying. We intend to go into all of those details later on.

The Court: Well, just for the purpose of showing where the revolver was, I will permit it as it is. Overruled.

On and on, the defense conducted an in-depth, comprehensive inquiry into the smallest detail of each item as to where it was found, by whom and to whom it was handed. Details that obviously had no bearing on the basic issues of the case, but details that came to nearly bringing Chandler to a state of exasperation with Frye's probing into the depth of his memory.

But the defense counsel's ploy did not work. Chandler kept control. He held his temper and was courteous at all times. Throughout, he answered all the questions to the very best of his memory and ability. Those who know and are familiar with these tactics awarded the victory to Chandler.

(right) Evidence shown in the trial included the braided leather head of the "billy," Seaborn's flashlight (note the "USN" engraving), and an envelope holding spent cartridges.

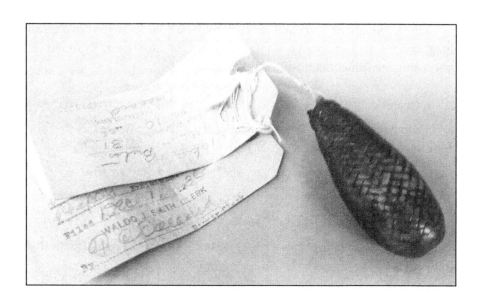

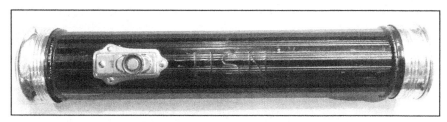

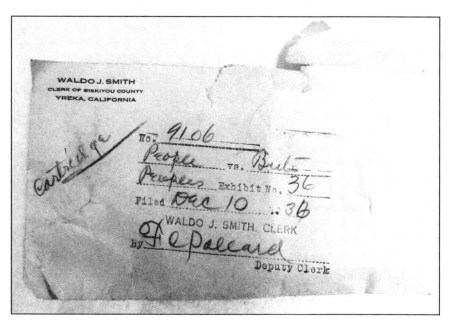

Finally, though, Frye arrived at the point where he had been heading all along. Everything so far had been just the warm up; now came the question concerning the thing that it was really all about.

Q. Mr. Chandler, you have a very great interest in this case, haven't you?

A. Yes, I have an interest in this case as sheriff of this county, the fact that one of my deputies was killed, yes.

Q. As a matter of fact, you have a very special interest, haven't you?

A. I have a very special interest in all such cases, not only this case, but all.

Mr. Frye: I ask that be stricken out as not responsive to the question.

The Court: Yes, I think the answer may go out. He was asked just about this case.

Q. I will ask you now, Mr. Chandler: You have a very special interest in this case, haven't you?

A. I do, yes sir.

Q. Your mind is definitely made up that you want to see these men hanged, don't you?

Mr. Allen: I object to that as not proper cross-examination.

The Court: Just on the question or interest. I will overrule the objection and admit it for the limited purpose of showing interest or lack of interest of the witness.

Mr. Frye: Mr. Reporter, will you read the question?

The Witness: I understand the question.

[The reporter reads the question.]

A. No sir, I only have that interest in mind to see that justice is done.

Q. That is all?

A. That is my answer.

Q. That is your best answer?

A. Yes sir.

Q. Now, when you went up to the Brite cabin that morning, of course, you had a conversation with Mr. and Mrs. Brite?

A. Yes.

Q. With seven men, as I understand it, or seven or eight?

A. No.

Q. How many?

A. Five, including myself.

Q. Five all together. I imagine you were more or less the spokesman for the crowd, were you?

A. I think I was.

Q. Did you tell Mrs. Brite and Mr. Brite there that morning that they were damned liars and that the minute that you saw the defendants you were going to shoot them down like dogs?

Mr. Allen: I object to that as incompetent, irrelevant and immaterial and not proper cross-examination and hearsay.

Mr. Frye: If Your Honor please, it is very important in this case that we show interest, and that is the only purpose this is for.

Mr. Allen: You are attempting to show any conversation of Mr. Chandler or any other witness out of the presence of the defendants as having an entirely out-of-context meaning. It is absolutely hearsay, and the State is not bound by any such statements. It is not cross-examination. The only thing that we brought out from this witness was on this question of where he got the gun, and that is the subject to which you are bound.

The Court: But it did come out on direct examination; some conversation between the sheriff and Mr. and Mrs. Brite about the gun. It is fundamental that where a part of a conversation is had—

Mr. Allen [interrupting]: I didn't ask for any conversation. I asked for no conversation.

It sounds here as if Allen is "sassing" the judge. Even though his choice of words is somewhat unfortunate, that is not his intention. He is attempting to point out that when he introduced the event earlier wherein the officers got the broken gun from Mr. and Mrs. Brite, he had asked at that time for no conversation from them. As a result his contention in this exchange is that Frye is not allowed to ask under cross examination for something such as conversation when none had been produced during direct examination.

Judge Luttrell seemed to understand the correct context as he gave no indication that he was offended in any way.

The Court: I think that the witness testified that he asked them for the rifle there. I will have the record looked up, though.

Mr. Frye: He testified as to the rifle.

The Court: That is my recollection, that he asked them for the rifle, one of them, he thought Mr. Brite.

Mr. Allen: On cross examination, he made that remark, yes.

The Court: No, I think on direct examination.

Mr. Allen: Well, whatever it is.

Mr. Frye: But regardless of that, Your Honor, we have a right to show interest of this witness, as one of the most fundamental points in the case.

Mr. Allen: But you can't show it by hearsay evidence.

Mr. Frye: It is not hearsay evidence.

The Court: Well, what are you offering it for at all; on just the question of interest or by reason of the fact that the witness on direct examination stated that he did have a conversation with Mr. and Mrs. Brite there at that time?

Mr. Frye: On the question of interest of the witness, Your Honor.

The Court: I will admit it for the limited purpose, then, of showing interest or lack of interest of the witness and for no other purpose. Now, lady and gentlemen of the jury, you will understand that when certain things come in for a limited purpose, it is admitted only for that purpose of showing interest or lack of interest of the witness upon the stand, and that only goes as to whether he is telling the truth or not; that is the credibility of the witness, of which the jury are the sole judge.

Mr. Frye: Mr. Reporter, will you please read the question?

[The reporter reads the question.]

A. I positively made no such statement.

Q. You did not?

A. No sir.

Q. Now, Sheriff, of course, you have charge of the defendants and have had since about the 17th of September of this year; 17th or 18th.

A. Something like that.

Q. And they have been in the county jail here under your charge since that time?

A. Yes sir.

Q. Do you know a time about, we will say about September the 20th or thereabouts, when the defendants were in the county jail, that Mr. Lange, the brother of the deceased, was taken into the bars outside of the cell when these defendants were having their dinner, and in the presence of Mr. Mathews, was allowed to chide and ridicule and ask these men how they thought they would feel when they climbed the thirteen steps?

Mr. Allen: I object to that question on the ground it is not cross-examination and I want to assign it as prejudicial error on the part of this counsel and put in here for the sole purpose of prejudicing this jury. It is not cross examination in any manner, shape or form, and I assign it as error.

Mr. Frye: That goes, again, Your Honor, please, to the question of interest of this witness.

The Court: I think it has gone a little far. I think I will sustain that objection. The jury will understand that any question that may be asked and an objection made to the question and the objection sustained, the jury will give no heed or attention to the question. In other words, it is not a part of the testimony in the case. You may proceed.

Q. Mr. Chandler, as sheriff, you have charge of the matter of feeding the prisoners, of course, haven't you?

A. I do.

Q. How many meals are these men given a day now?

A. Two, the same as all other prisoners who are awaiting trial.

Q. For instance, they received their lunch yesterday at noon?

A. I am unable to tell you that.

Q. That is routine, isn't it?

A. When this trial started, I will say this:…

Q. [interrupting] Just answer my question.

A. I can't. I don't know whether they had lunch yesterday or not.

Mr. Allen: If Your Honor please, I think this is all objectionable. There was a certain statement made here in court this morning during my absence and out of my presence where that matter was brought up, and I am going to have that matter investigated. I am going to ask this witness to testify on that.

Mr. Frye: We would be very glad to have it investigated.

The Court: Well, that is a past incident. You may proceed with the examination of the witness.

Q. Then they receive no evening meal at all, do they?

Mr. Allen: I object to this as not proper cross-examination; nothing to do with the issues of the case.

Mr. Frye: The question has been answered.

The Court: The answer may go out until the objection comes in. What is the object of the testimony?

Mr. Frye: To show interest, Your Honor.

The Court: I will permit it simply on the question of interest or lack of interest of the witness and for no other purpose.

Mr. Frye: That is all, Your Honor.

The Court: And the jury will only consider it for that purpose and no other. Overruled. You may answer.

Mr. Frye: Do you remember the question?

A. I do. I can only say that these defendants get their breakfast at 9:00 o'clock in the morning, and I haven't found out yet what time they have chosen to accept their later meal, whether it is at noon or at 5:00 o'clock when they get out of court. They get two meals a day, the same as all prisoners.

Q. Do you know they went from 12:00 o'clock yesterday until 9:00 o'clock this morning without food?

A. I do not.

Q. You do not?

A. No.

"You Can't Unring the Bell'"

An analysis of the foregoing exchanges from Mr. Frye's standpoint is not at all concerned with the actual subject matter of the two arguing lawyers. The whole thing was an attempt to get the jury to perceive Sheriff Chandler as a bumbling nincompoop, forgetful of important facts in connection with the case, undependable as manager of the jail and strictly out to "get" these two defendants at all costs. Mr. Allen of course was very much aware of exactly what was going on and did a fairly admirable job of fending it off.

The calm, sure manner in which Chandler handled the situation probably negated most of what Frye was trying to do as far as the jury was concerned. The testimony in itself had only a very peripheral relationship with the case and undoubtedly would be long forgotten by the members of the jury when it came time to deliberate.

This exchange was also notably replete with the time-worn typical legal arguments over admissibility into evidence. These arguments traditionally revolve around whether or not this statement can remain "in" or must be put "out" of the record. The implication is that if it is "in," it is to be considered by the jury and if it is "out," the jury cannot even mentally consider it in their deliberations.

The plain fact of the matter is that by the time a long case is finally completed, the members of the jury can in no way sort out all of this and remember what is to be considered and what items they heard are to be ignored. In fact the human mind is very poor at anything of this nature. It is like the old saying, "You cannot unring a bell." The lawyers know this, the judge knows this, but these are the rules of the game. It is actually a flaw in the system with which legal scholars have been grappling for years to no avail.

At the same time, flaw or no flaw, these seemingly useless and time-wasting considerations are very carefully handled by both sides in any given case as well as by the judge. This is because they often become critical and even crucial points of consideration should the case go on up to a higher court on appeal.

There was another episode much later in the case that is closely related to some of the testimony already mentioned. It turned out to be a textbook example of why a good lawyer should carefully evaluate and learn everything he can about a witness before attempting to question him under cross-examination. Quite some time later, Mr. Allen had routinely put Deputy Sheriff Eddie Mathews on the stand in order to get his testimony concerning his part in the sheriff's investigations at Horse Creek the night of the shooting. After direct examination, Frye's assistant, J. Everett Barr took over the cross-examination. Mr. Barr was very close to the end of it, when he abruptly changed the subject. It went like this:

Q. Now, Mr. Mathews, isn't it true that you and the rest of the Sheriff's Office have a great interest in this case?

A. I can say it is true in my case. I can't say what the rest of the Sheriff's Office has.

Q. And you were a friend of Mr. Lange?

A. I was a very close friend.

Q. In addition to that, perhaps you and other members of the Sheriff's Office have sort of put yourselves on the spot by seeing what would happen to these fellows, isn't that true?

A. I can't say that I ever have.

Q. You just want to see justice done?

Mr. Allen: What was the question? I didn't hear it.

Mr. Barr: You just want to see justice done?

A. I do.

Q. Always treated these prisoners as you treated the other prisoners?

A. I think they will vouch for that, yes, sir.

Q. Just the usual, customary treatment?

A. I have given them every courtesy that I have extended any of the boys.

Q. Is it usual and customary treatment of the prisoners, Mr. Mathews, to allow people to go into their cells and curse them; is that usual and customary?

A. No, it is not.

Q. Well, isn't it a fact that you allowed Martin Lange's brother to go in and curse the defendants?

Mr. Allen: I object to that as being incompetent, irrelevant and immaterial and not proper cross examination.

The Court: Read the question, Mr. Reporter.

[The reporter reads the question.]

Mr. Allen: And an attempt to go outside the issues of this case for the sole purpose of prejudicing the jury, and nothing else.

Mr. Barr: It is to show bias.

The Court: On the sole question of interest, counsel having pinned it down to the particular individual witness on the stand, I will permit it to be answered yes or no, simply on the question of the interest or lack of interest of the witness, going to his creditability as a witness.

Mr. Correia [Assistant Prosecutor]: I believe the reporter didn't read quite the last question. The question that he read was answered by Mr. Mathews.

He said, "No." The question that the reporter read, I believe was answered "No."

The Court: Did you answer that question, Mr. Mathews?

The Witness: If I didn't, that will be my answer.

The Court: Well, to save time, I will permit the question to be answered again, for the purpose of the record.

Mr. Barr: My last question was....

The Court [interrupting]: Well, let's get the record clear on the matter. The question, Mr. Reporter, that you read to the court a moment ago, do you have an answer for that?

[The reporter reads the question again.]

The Court: You may answer that question that was read, Mr. Mathews.

The Witness: May I have the question again please?

[The reporter reads the question again.]

The Court: You may answer that.

A. I will have to add some explanation to make myself clear in my answer.

The Court: Well, you may answer then explain it.

A. No, I allowed no one to go in and curse them. Yes, there was some remarks passed there, but there was no cursing that I recall.

Mr. Barr: That is all.

Some years later in discussing the case, the then Siskiyou County Superior Court Judge, J. Everett Barr, explained, "I underestimated Eddie Mathews. When Luttrell finally turned him loose to answer, I thought I had him, but it was just the opposite; he had me. It took a minute and a half for me to get my mouth shut after he gave me that answer. The only thing left for me to say after that was, 'That is all.'"

Baker Takes the Stand

Next to be called was none other than Charley Baker, the prosecution's star witness. Since Baker's testimony in the inquest some three months before, he had become the "darling" of the "law and order" faction of the public. The evening of Thursday, December 10th, word had gone out, presumably from Allen's office, that Baker would be put on the stand the next day. Attendance at the trial by the general public had decreased to some extent after the first day. But on the 11th the big crowd returned; the room was overflowing and many were turned away.

This time, under Allen's guidance, Baker's performance as a witness was even more amazing. Allen took him through the scenario step by step in the minutest detail. Baker's memory never faltered as he answered decisively, question after question in his colorful mountain-man vernacular. Gone of course, this time, was the badgering and doubting in the questioning that Baker had weathered in the inquest under the hands of Davis. It was easier for him and an absolute delight to the gallery.

But the badgering was yet to come.

When Allen completed the direct examination, it was Baker's turn to face Horace F. Frye, and this was a different situation. But not so different, really, as Frye's approach was very similar to that of Davis' three months earlier.

Frye started out with Baker at the very beginning, right from the fight at Baker's house and through each step of the way. Just exactly as Allen had done, nearly the identical questions all over again, but with a difference. This time, unlike with Allen, the tone and manner of Frye was accusatory and laced with sarcasm. As was the case with Davis, Frye's implications were that Baker was really the villain here, that it was Baker's words and actions that were the cause of the whole affair. By the manner in which he delivered the questions, Frye was attempting to implant in the minds of the jurors that Baker was a trouble maker, a coward that had orchestrated the whole series of events up to the point that the shooting started.

It appeared at first that here was a battle between a lion and a mouse. Here was Horace F. Frye, a sophisticated metropolitan lawyer of wide repute toying with this mountain man who could barely read or write and was hard of hearing on top of it all.

But it was no contest. Sixty pages of testimony in the trial transcript and it was no contest.

For example, when Frye was taking a run at Baker on the famous "ten words versus fifteen words" controversy, it went like this:

Q. Isn't it a fact, Mr. Baker, that when you got down there, Mr. Seaborn asked, "Whose car is that, Baker?"

By this time, these various "strange lawyer fellows" through their admonishments to him in prior joustings had driven the lesson home that he was to answer only the question, nothing but the question, and even then in its narrowest interpretation.

A. No sir, he did not.

At this answer, Frye was somewhat taken aback inasmuch as this same day, Baker had testified the other way.

Q. He did not?

A. He did not, when he walked down there.

In a very narrow sense, the above answer was technically correct. In some exasperation mixed with frustration, Frye came back with, "When did he ask you that?"

A. After he walked down there and knelt down to get him that drink.

Frye just shook his head a little, and with a smirk on his face took off with this.

Q. And isn't it a fact that you said, "It belongs to those two sons of bitches, the Brite boys, up on the hill?"

A. No sir.

Q. You didn't say that?

A. I did not.

Q. What did Mr. Seaborn say when this thing started? This fracas?

A. He said, "Boys, if we have said anything to hurt your feelings, we are sorry for it."

Q. "If we have said anything to hurt your feelings, we are sorry?"

A. Yes sir.

Q. You don't know why Mr. Seaborn made that statement?

A. Yes sir. Because Mr. Seaborn is a clean-cut man; I never heard him say a swear word in my life, nor would he take a drink. When they came after him fighting, it is plain to me that the only thing that made him say it was that he thought he might have offended somebody.

Q. Did he say anything that could have offended these boys or anyone else?

A. No sir, he did not.

Q. Then he said, "If we have said anything to offend you, we apologize?"

A. "I" or "we"...I don't know exactly what he said. "If we have said or done anything to offend you, we are sorry for it."

Q. You hadn't said anything to offend them?

A. No sir, just what I told you.

Q. You hadn't?

A. I hadn't, no sir.

As Baker was describing Seaborn's and his ensuing fight with the Brites, he demonstrated a mountain man's pure form of logic. It is doubtful that even the most antagonistic lawyer could disagree with it. Frye, through his questions, was trying to get Baker to recant his testimony that John Brite had hit him with a stick. It went like this:

Q. When did you first remember, Mr. Baker, after this little altercation here; when did you first remember that John had a stick and hit you with it?

A. Just as he brought it down on my head.

Enough said.

At nearly the end of Baker's cross examination, he gave a demonstration of how vivid and concise this nearly illiterate mountain man could express himself. He was describing his exit from the scene of the shooting. It came about this way:

Q. You weren't in the war were you?

A. No.

Q. Well, do you think that any of those shots were fired at you?

A. My belief is that they was.

Q. What makes you believe that?

A. Because when I started to run, Coke hollered, "There goes one up the creek, John, kill that son-of-a-bitch!"

Q. Where were you when he said that?

A. I was running up the creek.

Some days after Baker had given his testimony he was introduced to former District Attorney Charley Johnson. In the conversation, Baker referred to his cross-examination as an "odeal." Johnson reported later that he told

Baker, "Don't you worry about that. It was not an "odeal" for you. The person that had been put through the "odeal" was none other than Horace F. Frye."

Day 5 – "Shoot to Kill?"

Baker's testimony was given on the fourth day of the trial, Friday, December 11th. In the 1930s, the idea of Saturday being observed as a day off had not yet come into existence. Accordingly, proceedings continued through a half day on Saturday.

After Baker's appearance, the prosecution called eleven additional witnesses before resting its case on the following Tuesday morning. Frye's cross examination of many of these witnesses had dealt extensively with his efforts to discredit Chandler.

The first of these efforts involved the allegation that Chandler had ordered his deputies to "shoot on sight, and shoot to kill." This was at the time they were leaving the scene to go up the hill to the Brite's cabin. Frye very meticulously bore down on this in questioning Deputies Mathews, Rhodes and Fortna. All of them vehemently denied that Chandler had said it. But when he had Justice of the Peace Rainey on the stand it went like this:

Q. Did you hear the sheriff give instructions or orders to the deputies before they started up the hill?

A. Some.

Q. What did you hear him say?

A. Well, I don't remember all that I did hear.

Q. Well, I will ask you this. Did you hear him tell the deputies to shoot on sight and shoot to kill?

A. It seems like I did.

Q. You did, didn't you?

A. I did.

Q. You heard him say that to the deputies?

A. I think that is the last orders that I heard him give.

Frye's other effort to nail down Chandler did not succeed so well. That was the incident at the Brite's cabin where he implied that Chandler had called Mr. and Mrs. Brite "damned liars" and that "the minute that he saw the defendants he was going to shoot them down like dogs."

On this one, Frye tried three of the four deputies that were there at the cabin at the time without getting corroboration from any of them. Both of these issues were hotly debated by the general public afterward. If in fact such a thing as a public consensus was ever reached, it was probably that in the heat of the terrible tragedy that had taken place, Chandler may have said something like the "order," with his loyal deputies protecting him in the questioning. But in the second matter at the cabin, the public simply could not believe that a gentlemen of Chandler's stature and caliber could be so crude, cruel and impolite to have ever uttered such a thing.

When the prosecution rested its case, Frye then did the standard thing that is almost universal in cases such as this. He advised the judge that he wanted to make a motion out of hearing of the jury. The jury was duly excused and absented from the room. Allen of course knew what was coming.

Mr. Frye said, "If Your Honor please, at this time, I move for a directed verdict of not guilty on the ground that the prosecution has not only failed to produce evidence which, as a matter of law, would be sufficient to convict the defendants beyond a reasonable doubt. The testimony produced by the prosecution has established our right to a directed verdict."

This was followed by the defense's arguments and citations. Mr. Allen responded by advising the judge that it was his intention to reply and argue the motion.

Judge Luttrell interrupted Allen by saying, "Well, it is not necessary. I was going to deny the motion and let the jury decide. The motion for a directed verdict will be denied and it will be passed to the jury."

A 100% predictable outcome of this matter was now in the record and the trial was ready to proceed.

Proceed with the Defense

It was now the turn of the defense to control the proceedings. The audience had been somewhat confused when Allen had rested his case without calling Decker as a witness. It was generally assumed by the public that Decker, having been a friend of the Brites and first on the scene after the killing, would be a key witness. But those in the know of things were not surprised at all. Decker's testimony in the inquest had been much slanted in favor of the defendants. Allen was fully aware of this and didn't want to touch Decker with a ten foot pole in the role of a prosecution witness. He assumed that sooner or later his chance would come to tackle him. He preferred that this be as a hostile witness in the much more adversarial setting of a cross examination of the opponent's witness. Allen and other knowledgeable people had expected Frye to lead off with Decker.

But Frye crossed everyone up. He wanted to take one last shot at discrediting Baker.

The defense opened by calling Orion Maplesden. Maplesden, it will be recalled, was the man that was with Coke Brite the day that the fight with Baker had taken place at Baker's house. Frye had Maplesden recount his view of the fight. Though the description given by the witness was somewhat different from Baker's version, it was substantially the same. Allen disdained to even cross examine.

Frye then called Sam Bratt. The key exchange here was as follows:

Q. How long have you known Mr. Baker?

A. Oh, I must have known him four or five years.

Q. Do you know his general reputation for truth, honesty and integrity down on Horse Creek?

A. Yes sir; part of it.

Q. Is it good or bad?

A. Bad, as far as I know.

Under cross examination by Allen, it went along this way:

Q. Now you had some trouble with Mr. Baker; that is, your goats got in his corn, didn't they?

A. They didn't get in his corn. They got in his field, yes.

Q. You had some trouble with him about that, didn't you?

A. Well, he come down after me about it.

Q. That made you pretty mad, didn't it?

A. It sure did.

Q. That is why you are coming in here and testifying against him, isn't it, because you are mad at him?

This last question was asked by Allen in order to demonstrate that Mr. Bratt's attitude toward Baker stemmed entirely from the altercation that the two men had and not from a general attitude "throughout the community" that Baker's reputation was bad. There were several more questions posed by Allen along this line which provoked objections from the defense. The line eventually led Allen into questions about another episode which was more to the point of relating to a "general" reputation. It was even more interesting as an example of some of the common trials and tribulations faced by people living in the type of isolated mountain community that the Horse Creek area represented. The questions came like this:

Q. Mr. Bratt, when Mr. Baker, when the Forest Service allowed him to fence his place down there where he is living, that made some of the people on the creek kind of mad at him, didn't it?

A. No, not that I know of. After he ran the stock off, the stock always went up Horse Creek to get on the ridge. Every time they come to his place, instead of letting them through to get on the ridge, he would chase them back.

Q. That is what made them mad at him?

A. I suppose the people didn't like it. He said he was going to scatter beef all over the hills.

Q. That is what you meant by "dirty tricks," is that it?

That was to have been Allen's last question but before it could be answered, considerable wrangling between the two sides and the judge broke out; the question was never answered. Frye then stepped back into the fray as follows:

Q. Mr. Bratt, have you ever heard other people down on Horse Creek talk about Mr. Baker's reputation about whether or not he is honest and truthful?

A. They say he ain't truthful.

More arguments ensue:

Q. The judge says you can answer yes or no whether or not you ever heard other people talk about him.

A. Yes, I heard them talk about him.

Q. You have.

A. Yes sir.

Q. What do you mean by scattering beef all over the hill?

More wrangling resulted and the question was never answered.

Frye then called Mathias Lamish as the next witness. Mr. Lamish had lived in the Horse Creek area for more than thirty years and testified that he had known Baker since Baker had come there.

Mr. Frye: Do you know his general reputation in the community for truth, honesty and integrity?

A. Yes.

Q. Is it good or is it bad?

A. Bad.

Mr. Frye: That is all.

Mr. Allen, on cross examination:

Q. Weren't you carrying food to the Brite brothers when they were out in the hills above Horse Creek?

A. No sir.

Q. You didn't go out and visit them?

A. No sir.

Q. Are you sure of that?

A. I am sure of it.

Q. Well, weren't you putting up money for their defense?

A. No sir.

Q. But you have been very much interested in it, haven't you?

A. They are my neighbors.

This last answer of Mr. Lamish was another example of the "code of the mountains." Here we have two people living some distance apart, but living as neighbors, nonetheless. Obviously they did not particularly care for each other. But when asked the question as to whether or not he gave his neighbor food under apparently needy circumstances, he gave an answer that in his world seemed perfectly obvious: "They are my neighbors."

Frye then called Mrs. Dolittle. She testified that she had also been on the ridge for thirty years and that she had known the Bakers since they came there. When asked by the defense counsel about Baker's "general reputation in the community for truth, honesty and integrity," she replied that it was bad.

Allen then jumped right in with the following exchange:

Q. You had some trouble with him about your goats getting in on him?

A. Yes.

Q. You are kind of mad about that.

A. No, I am not mad at him.

Q. Didn't you have trouble with him over it?

A. Yes, I had trouble with him over it.

Q. You are related to Mr. Bratt, aren't you?

A. Yes, I am his sister.

Mr. Allen: That is all.

Again, and for the last time, enough said.

Charley Baker, the poignant, stereotyped "mountain man" had defeated the sophisticated renowned trial lawyer from the "big city." It was not noticed much by Charley himself, but it certainly was by Horace F. Frye.

In spite of the apparent vicious battles that were being waged between the antagonists in the trial in full view of the public, the local people who were involved in the proceedings very quickly became acquainted with Frye. It was obvious to all; the law enforcement people, the judge; the prosecutor and others involved in the judicial machinery; that Frye was actually a very nice and friendly individual. His obvious abilities were recognized as very superior by all. But on top of this, he really was a considerate and kind individual.

In a casual conversation with Court Reporter Ralph McMurry during a recess in the proceedings, Frye remarked, "You know, taking on that Charley Baker was a very humbling experience. I knew his background; I knew he was illiterate. I thought it would be 'duck soup' to break him down. But I learned something about my fellow man in this case and that is to never underestimate an individual. That man is in full control of himself and his surroundings; any 'wise guy' or some 'slick lawyer' like you-know-who, that thinks he can defeat him is badly mistaken and will come to grief in the process."

But now it was time for the semi-final in the case.

"Call B. F. Decker"

Mr. Frye's voice rang out, "Call B. F. Decker."

Decker had lived on Horse Creek for about six years. He was fairly well known in the Horse Creek community but that was about the extent of it. He often came to Yreka, most generally shopping, but he had not developed a wide acquaintance there. People that did know him, perceived him as a friendly enough fellow that was best described as a sort of "take charge" kind of person. His background as a building contractor was an indication of this trait inasmuch as it was the type of vocation that would require him to routinely take the lead in "bossing" his crew of workmen.

He lived very quietly up Horse Creek, tending his garden and conducting a little mining with his partner, Bob Lanning. Nobody else ever really paid much attention to him but he did enjoy some degree of respect.

Then, when the scene of this notorious triple murder case turned out to be practically in his back yard, he was suddenly catapulted into the glare of publicity. The story of his actions and how he handled things immediately after the shooting was more evidence of his "take charge" nature. The publicity about it at first was complimentary in every respect. No one really could fault the way he had handled things at the scene and how he had taken immediate charge of the situation and reported it to the authorities.

In a short time, however, he suddenly found that everyone with whom he came in contact wanted to hear all the details and it appeared that he was enjoying this new status that had been thrust upon him. He then began making numerous trips to Yreka and to a considerable extent, visiting around in the bars where he was immediately recognized. It seemed that he was on a constant campaign to promulgate the facts of the case along with his opinions concerning it. He was apparently relishing every minute of it.

As previously related, the public in Yreka was generally divided into the two groups: the "lynch" faction and the "law and order" faction. Decker was a friend of the Brites and his sympathies were with them. Because of this, he of course did not fit into the "lynch" faction. But the law and order faction stood for a fair trial; that was the extent of it. Beyond that, they were practically unanimous in the feeling that it was a first degree murder case and that the Brites should be hanged. Consequently, there was no place for Decker in this faction either.

So Decker's popularity began to wane in very short order. Even though he soon became perceived as the "killer lover," the public still seemed to enjoy talking and listening to him. Strangely enough, this change in his status didn't dissuade him one bit in his eagerness to expound on the case at any and all times.

Decker had been subpoenaed by Allen as a defense witness. Approximately two weeks before the trial, Decker had met with Allen and his staff at the lawyer's office. Sheriff Chandler was also in attendance. This type of procedure is a common practice in order to go over the forthcoming testimony. It is for the purpose of getting the lawyer up to date and fully informed as to what he can expect from the witness. At the same time, the witness becomes aware of procedures and the nature of the questions that he will be expected to answer.

There was no publicity at all about the meeting, but it soon became obvious that it did not turn out anything like Allen had planned. The first manifestation of this was, of course, the fact that Allen never did call Decker as his witness. What had gone on at the meeting was soon to be more and more revealed by the nature of some of the questions that both Frye and Allen eventually put to Baker.

Decker, as in the inquest, again proved to be an excellent witness. Frye's questions started him out from the time that he heard the dog barking and guns going off in the night. He vividly repeated what he had found at the camp after Baker had come to his house. Decker's demeanor at the scene and the manner in which he described it reinforced his image as a thoroughly capable "take charge" type of individual.

The Decker Theory

Very quickly the questions arrived at the point where Frye intended to develop testimony that would substantiate the so called "Decker Theory," the scenario wherein the officers had not adequately identified themselves. It held that the Brites had fought in self defense under the impression that they were being attacked by the same individuals, plus reinforcements, with whom they had the fight earlier that day.

Frye needed this for two reasons. It was vital to the defense for any chance of an ultimate acquittal, but even more importantly, it was the key to any favorable outcome in the event that an appeal would eventually be made.

Frye's questions had brought Decker to the point where he had just entered the camp after the shooting. Decker was telling how he had first come upon John Brite.

At this point Frye asked him what John said. Both Allen and Correia well knew the avenue down which Frye was now going. Allen jumped in with a vehement objection on the grounds that any conversation was "hearsay" which is not admissible. There followed a long bout of arguing between both sides and the judge until it was finally allowed to "go in."

Mr. Frye: Now, Mr. Decker, I will ask you again, did John say anything else at that time, if you recall?

A. He did.

Q. What did he say?

A. He says, "Who is these people; who are they?" And I told him, I says, "They are officers."

Mr. Correia: Just a moment. What the witness said … [Mr. Allen, with a resigned shrug of his arms and hands, here signaled Correia to let it go.]

Correia changed course with, "Go ahead and put it in."

Mr. Allen: Go ahead and let it all in.

Mr. Frye: Go ahead, Mr. Decker.

A. And he says, "That fellow isn't. I know him; he was up here this evening fighting with us. I know him; he was here fighting before." I says, "Well, these, I think, are officers." And he didn't know they were.

Q. Is that what he said?

A. Yes, he didn't know.

With acquittals and or appeals in mind, Frye later brought Decker to the point where he wanted to show that the defendants had been "beaten up."

Mr. Frye: Now Mr. Decker, when you went in there, what was the condition of John's face and head, if you noticed?

A. Well, the blood was running down over him here, right across here and running down clear over to his chin; dropping, I think.

Q. Were you able to see any cuts or bruises on his head?

A. No, I didn't examine him at all.

Q. Did you see the condition of Coke's head?

A. Yes. On the left side of Coke's head. There was a stream of blood running down here, dropping off on his coat.

Q. Was there anything else peculiar about the way Coke acted at that time. I mean with reference to his physical...

A. [interrupting] Yes, he held his arm like this, and I thought...

Q. The Court [interrupting]: Well, as to what you thought...

Decker was a "fast learner" of court procedures; he had been on the stand through all the previous arguments about admissibility of what was "said" as opposed to testifying about what was "seen." He knew instantly what the judge was starting to tell him so now he interrupted the judge.

A. Well, I saw that he acted as though it was broken. I asked him, and he says, "No, it's not."

Q. Now from your observation of John at that time, Mr. Decker, did he act like a normal man?

More objections and argument. The judge finally ruled for Allen on the point that Frye's last question was "leading" the witness and that is not a legal thing to do. Frye therefore modified the question as follows:

Q. Did you notice anything unusual about John?

A. I did.

Q. What did you notice about him at the time, about his actions that impressed you as being unusual?

A. Well, I had to hold him, because he didn't seem to be normal and he was so much afraid that I asked Coke to take care of him. "I don't want to hit him," I says, "He don't know what he's doing."

Q. Did he impress you as being in a condition of mind that he didn't know what he was doing, is that what you mean?

A. He did.

As Frye's direct examination of Decker continued into the afternoon session, it became an object lesson of what murder trials are really all about. It was a classic demonstration of the defense lawyer's standard game plan: Keep the options open for the unlikely possibility of a not guilty verdict, but above all, keep the record well guarded in the interest of the more possible favorable outcome on appeal. The following testimony is a typical example of this maneuver.

This series of questions also illustrates a weakness in the system itself. It shows how the technicalities of the procedures combined with the constant wrangling of the opposing sides makes a mockery of the jury's role in the matter. The exchange of questions and answers is actually quite limited and covers only two meaningful and relevant bits of evidence. But by the time the lawyers and the judge are finished with it, it has occupied four and a quarter double spaced pages of the trial transcript. It is safe to assume that the jury was unable to sort out which parts of it were to remain "in" and what portions were to be disregarded. The record shows that even the participants were confused at times.

Defense attorney Frye starts it off on one of his favorite subjects, the "viciousness" of Sheriff Chandler. It must also be added that this particular matter had already been gone over at length. In it, Decker is describing the events at the scene of the killing as daylight is coming on.

Mr. Frye: Were you there, Mr. Decker, about daylight on the morning when the officers started up the hill?

A. I was.

Q. Had anything been said to you about going with them?

A. There was.

Q. Who spoke to you about that?

A. Mr. Chandler asked if I would show him the trail up, show him the way.

Q. What was said?

Mr. Allen: We object to that as hearsay.

Mr. Frye: Well, all right.

Q. Did you go up the hill with them?

A. I did not.

Q. Why not?

Mr. Allen: I object to that as incompetent, irrelevant and immaterial.

Mr. Frye: I think it is very material, Your Honor.

Mr. Allen: What difference does it make why this man didn't go up the hill?

Mr. Frye: Well, you know why he didn't go. It does make a difference. I will withdraw the question and put it this way:

Q. Mr. Decker, did you hear Mr. Chandler issue orders, "Shoot on sight and shoot to kill?"

A. I did.

Mr. Allen: I object to that as leading and suggestive.

Mr. Frye: That is an impeaching question, Your Honor.

The Court: I think the foundation should be laid if it is offered for the purpose of impeachment. I will sustain the objection to the question as propounded, if you are offering it for impeachment.

Mr. Frye: Who was there at that time, Mr. Decker, besides yourself and Mr. Chandler?

Mr. Allen: I object to that as incompetent, irrelevant and immaterial.

The Court: Overruled.

Mr. Frye: Who was there?

A. Mr. Lanning and Mr. Mathews and two gentlemen. There was two others, perhaps three; they were all strangers that come up there, but I think it was Mr. Rhodes and one or two others.

Q. Mr. Mathews?

A. Yes.

Q. Mr. Rhodes?

A. Yes.

Q. Do you know Mr. Fortna?

A. Yes, Mr. Fortna.

Q. He was there? Do you know Mr. Fullerton?

A. No.

Q. And this statement…Did Mr. Chandler make a statement about that time?

A. He did.

Q. That was here at this place [pointing to the map]?

A. It was along at the upper end of the little path.

Q. And about what time in the morning?

A. Oh, I suppose the sun was about ready to break; it wasn't shining into the canyon yet, but it was daylight.

Q. Just daylight?

A. Yes, it was daylight.

Q. Now, at that time and place did you hear Mr. Chandler issue orders to these men to "shoot on sight and shoot to kill?"

A. I did.

Mr. Allen: I ask that the answer be stricken out. There is no foundation laid for the question.

The Court: Well, I think the foundation is sufficiently laid.

Mr. Allen: If Your Honor please, you have to lay the foundation by the witness that you are going to impeach, not by the witness that you are impeaching.

The Court: Well, if I remember right, the question was asked of Mr. Chandler.

Mr. Allen: Well, then, we will withdraw it to save time.

The Court: As I recall, the record will show who was present as they started up the hill.

Mr. Allen: I will withdraw the objection.

The Court: Very well, the objection is withdrawn. You may answer.

Mr. Frye: You heard him say that?

A. I did.

Mr. Allen: I object to that as cross examination of your own witness.

The Court: I will sustain the objection.

Mr. Frye: After Mr. Chandler made that statement, what did you do?

A. I refused to go.

Mr. Allen: I object to that as incompetent, irrelevant and immaterial.

The Court: I will sustain the objection.

Mr. Frye: Did you offer assistance to them in case they had trouble up there?

A. I did.

Q. You told them you could get the boys alone?

A. I did.

Mr. Allen: I object to that as incompetent, irrelevant and immaterial and not proper direct examination.

The Court: I will sustain the objection.

The sustaining of Allen's last objection by the judge was the third in a row in favor of the prosecution. As a result, the general audience in the court room was beginning to get the impression that Allen had been awarded the victory in this last series of questions brought on by Frye. As a matter of fact, just the opposite was the case. Frye, of course, wanted to be very sure that he brought out the fact that Decker had offered his help to the arresting officers. He further wanted to get into the record that upon hearing the "threat" made by Chandler in the form of his instructions to his officers, Decker had refused to go along with them to show the way. Frye knew very well that this line of questioning would be objected to by Allen and that the objections would be sustained. But he also knew that the mere asking of the questions was enough to get the matter into the record and there was no way that the opposition or the judge could prevent the jury from hearing it. Of course the jury, or an eventual appeals court judge, was not supposed to consider it. But as the saying goes, once again, "You cannot unring a bell."

That Meeting in Allen's Office

Frye was now ready to proceed with another matter. This was the meeting at Allen's office that had been attended by both Decker and Chandler. As previously mentioned, the public was not aware of what had transpired at the meeting, but it was about to find out.

With Fry's very first question, Allen was aware of what was coming; he was also ready.

It went like this:

Mr. Frye: Now Mr. Decker, you know Mr. Allen?

A. I do.

Q. You know where his office is?

A. I do.

Q. I will ask you if within the past few days, or a couple of weeks, in the presence of Mr. Chandler, in Mr. Allen's office, Mr. Chandler endeavored to force you to change your testimony in this case?

A. He did.

Q. You were subpoenaed here as a witness, weren't you?

A. I was.

Mr. Allen: I object to that as incompetent, irrelevant and immaterial.

The Court: I will overrule the objection.

Mr. Frye: By the prosecution?

A. I was.

Q. In what respect did they try to persuade you to change your testimony?

A. Well, they told me there wasn't any truth in it, and I didn't dare swear to it in court.

Q. Who told you that?

A. Mr. Chandler.

Q. And where was that?

A. In Mr. Allen's office.

Q. Have you told the truth on the stand here?

A. I have.

Mr. Allen: I object to that.

Mr. Frye: Alright, I will withdraw the question. There was an altercation following your statement over in Mr. Allen's office, wasn't there?

Mr. Allen: I object to that as incompetent, irrelevant and immaterial, not proper rebuttal, and has nothing to do with the defense in this case.

The Court: I will sustain the objection.

And that was the end of that. Frye then led his witness on into other things.

Here again, Frye had obtained the thing he was after. Allen knew it; the judge knew it. The effect upon the jury was probably very slight. Prior to this, some of the members of the jury had undoubtedly heard something about the meeting in Allen's office. This exchange had possibly cleared up that mystery to some extent. But as far as being relevant to the guilt or innocence of the defendants, its impact upon the jury was a great big "ho hum." But there is more to it than that.

Frye's purpose was to get this episode implanted in the written record. The record is what an appeals judge sees and "hears." If it comes to an appeal after a conviction in this court, this episode could have a strong bearing on a judge's considerations. Frye was not talking about an altercation in the prosecutor's office. He was dwelling again on his favorite subject, "Chandler Bashing," and merely using the "meeting" as another vehicle to implant it into an appeal court's deliberations.

It was now Allen's turn to cross examine this "hostile" witness. He started out in the almost predictable pattern of such proceedings. He commenced by asking a series of questions of very doubtful significance. After eliciting a few answers from Decker, he would then have him read a few lines from the transcript of the inquest in which Decker was an important witness. The questions involved here were very similar, if not identical with the questions that Allen had just asked. In each of them, Decker's answer had been slightly at variance here from the previous go round. Most of the questions were hardly earth-shaking but there was a slight difference in Decker's response. This effort was hardly significant as an impeachment of the witness because the questions were such unimportant evidence.

Effective or not, it was an interesting exchange.

At one point, Allen had asked Decker a question and the response was immediate.

Allen then asked, "Oh, you remember that after all these months?"

Decker replied, "Yes, naturally, or I wouldn't know now."

Allen seemed to be obsessed with what the actual time was that Decker had been awakened by either the guns going off or the dog barking. At one point they got into an argument as to what time it was when Decker had "gotten out of bed to answer a call of nature." When this was finally established, Allen went on.

Q. But you had gone back to bed again and you were lying there and hadn't gone to sleep, is that right?

A. Not exactly asleep.

Q. You were still conscious, weren't you?

A. Still conscious?

Q. Yes, you hadn't lost consciousness?

A. Well, when you are half asleep, I don't know whether or not you are conscious, half asleep or awake.

Q. How long did you lie there after you went back to bed in that state?

A. I don't know.

Q. Five or ten minutes?

A. I don't know; when you are lying down to go to sleep, you don't know how long you are down there before you go to sleep.

Q. Well, you hadn't been there very long?

A. I don't think so.

On and on it went like this, page after page after page in the record. At one point, Allen was reading a question from the inquest transcript when he was interrupted by the opposition.

Mr. Frye: May I suggest that you also read the next line?

Mr. Allen: We will read it.

Mr. Frye: Please be fair.

Mr. Allen: I'll be fair alright.

Mr. Frye: If we watch you close enough.

At Frye's remark, there was more than one small gasp from the audience. All eyes turned to the judge. He never said a word or indicated in any way that he had noticed this small breech of trial etiquette which would normally have drawn a rebuke from the bench.

Judge Luttrell was known throughout the legal apparatus to be very strict, a man of high moral principles, and above all, very courteous. Later in the hallway during a recess, Court Reporter Ralph McMurry brought the matter up while chatting with Charley Johnson.

McMurry asked, "What did you think of Luttrell's silence at that mild insult thrown at Allen by Frye?"

"Of course I was surprised at first myself," replied Johnson. "But after thinking it over I concluded that even Judge Luttrell, with all his scruples, thought Allen 'had it coming.' I think he felt that Frye's remark topped anything that he could say and let it go at that."

But Allen did not read that "next" line. He went right on with what he was doing. A little later on, Frye, broke in again:

Mr. Frye: Are you going to read those other lines, Mr. Allen?

Mr. Allen: You can read them if you want to after awhile. I am cross examining right now.

With an almost indiscernible sigh of resignation and a slight wave of his hand, the judge said, "Alright, go ahead."

Right or wrong, Allen had been pursuing this line of questioning through twelve pages of the trial transcript. But now he was ready to get down to some serious business. Everything so far had merely been preliminary to what this was all about. It was, of course, all about the impeachment of witness B. F. Decker's testimony.

Q. It is a fact that you are very much interested in the defense of this case, is it not?

A. The defense?

Q. Yes.

A. Not at all.

Q. Isn't it a fact that you have put up money for the defense of this case?

A. I have not given one penny.

Q. Isn't it fact that you have gone around the country ... Isn't it a fact that you went down the river laying this shooting on other people?

A. It is a fact that I haven't been down the river at no place.

Q. Isn't it a fact that in the town of Yreka here, last week, that you made the statement to Frank Dunphy and to Clyde Fairchild that the officers got just what they deserved?

A. No sir.

Q. You didn't make that statement?

A. I did not.

Q. Didn't you, since you have been under subpoena in this case and sworn not to discuss this case, go down in the Purity Store and make a statement there that the officers got just what they deserved? Did you make that statement?

A. I don't think I did, no sir.

Q. You don't think you did?

A. No sir.

Q. You won't say for sure that you didn't, will you? Will you say that you didn't make the statement that the officers got what they deserved? That you didn't make that statement down there in the Purity Store?

A. No sir, I don't. I can't remember it at all.

Q. Didn't you make that statement down in Con Brown's?

A. I don't know where Con Brown's is.

Q. Down at the Con Brown's Pool Hall. Don't you know where that is?

A. No.

Q. You don't know where that is?

A. No.

Q. Do you know where that pool hall is across from the Bank of America, called the Pastime?

A. On this side of the street?

Q. Yes.

A. I have been in there once or twice.

Q. Yes. Didn't you make that same statement there?

A. No, I don't think so. I don't think I ever made it.

Q. You don't think you ever made it. Now, isn't it a fact, Mr. Decker, that you don't know how many shots were fired?

A. No, I don't know.

Q. And isn't it a fact that you didn't notice any difference between those shots?

A. I sure did notice a difference between the shots.

Q. Yes. Now, I am going to ask you, Mr. Decker, if on the morning of August 30th, right down there at the scene of this killing, and after the officers got there, if you didn't make this statement to Ed Mathews? You remember talking to Ed Mathews, don't you?

A. I may have.

Q. And he asked you how many shots were fired, if you could tell; he asked if you could tell the difference between the shots. And you told him that you couldn't tell how many shots were fired, or the difference between the shots. Did you make that statement or not?

A. I did not.

Q. All right. Do you remember talking to Dr. Schlappi down there on the morning at the scene of the killing? Didn't you tell him that you could not tell how many shots were fired; that because of the canyon, there was a certain roar, and that is all you heard?

A. I did not.

Q. You didn't make that statement to Dr. Schlappi?

A. I did not.

Q. I am going to ask you if you didn't make this statement to Joe La Plante on the same morning of the killing down there at the scene of the crime; that you heard a noise; that you did not know how many shots were fired and couldn't tell the difference between them?

A. I may have said I didn't know how many shots were fired. Part of that is right.

Q. Now, didn't you make the statement to Lloyd Fortna that you couldn't tell how many shots, because the echo just sounded like a roar? I mean down here at the scene of the killing the next morning?

A. Sure, I told him I didn't know how many shots; I didn't know.

Q. And that it just sounded like a roar?

A. No sir.

Q. Now, didn't you make the statement to Sheriff Chandler at that time that you didn't know ... at that time on that morning right after the killing, at the scene of the crime...that you didn't know how many shots were fired nor didn't notice any difference in the shots?

A. I did not. None of us were talking about shots of any kind.

Q. You mean to tell me that the officers were there and they weren't asking you, the first man there, about the shots and what you heard?

A. No, we didn't talk. We were getting the people out and they went up on the hill.

Q. Were not people inquiring of you just how this happened and what you saw, Mr. Decker, and what you heard?

A. No, they weren't.

Approximately fifteen years later, then Superior Court Judge James M. Allen gave a speech about this case to the Yreka Rotary Club. He said, "Now take B. F. Decker; there was some witness. He could lie and lie and lie. And when he got through lying, he would lie some more."

With the extensive examination of Decker by both sides now out of the way, Frye called Decker's partner Bob Lanning. He was the first witness presented in the morning on Wednesday, the 16th. Frye had felt that Lanning's testimony would be fairly well uncontested and should not take much time. He was anxious to get on to bigger and better things. But such was not to be. Lanning was on the stand nearly four hours. His testimony matched that of Decker and generated little new information. But Allen's apparent obsession with how many shots had been heard and whether or not they were from big or small guns seemed to prolong the cross examination endlessly. At two o'clock, Fry was ready to go. The overflow audience was considerably bored by it all by this time, but nobody made any movements to leave because they knew what was coming next; the word had been out for two days.

"Call Coke Brite"

The gallery's patience was rewarded at last, when Frye's voice was heard to announce, "Call Coke Brite."

The appearance of one of the accused brothers on the witness stand was of course of great interest to the general public. People who had been attending the trial at any time since it started had seen the two brothers sitting there behind the rail with their backs to the audience. But on this day, many of the people present were there for the first time. Now they were to see and hear from one of the defendants as he faced them from the witness box. After all the publicity and discussions that had run rampant through the press; after hundreds and hundreds of private conversations through the past weeks, it was something of a climax. To see these individuals "in the flesh" and to be in their presence was an emotional experience for many. Some, no doubt, harbored feelings of hate; perhaps some felt sympathetic, but most seemed merely curious. Others were there just wanting to be a participant in this titanic event that had descended upon the community.

Court Reporter Ralph McMurry's youngest son was there. It was a normal school day for the high school but this was not a case of "hooky." The boy's father had made arrangements with the school principal for this one day only.

The public had heard the defendants speak only once before. That was when they uttered the words "not guilty" at the arraignment several days before. The people by now knew all about the background of these defendants; their sparse education and how they lived. They were known to be "mountain men," tough, often resourceful, heavy drinkers and probably mean. It therefore came as quite a surprise when Coke Bright spoke in a clear voice in answer to Frye's questions. He was lacking in some of the grammatical refinements, but he expressed himself in an intelligent, concise and organized manner.

Frye gently took him through the preliminaries of name, age (31), place of residence; the usual opening questions for the record. Slowly, Frye brought the questioning around to that fateful evening of August 29th. He had Coke describe exactly where on the courtroom model of the scene that Coke and John parked the old Ford. He had him describe in detail how they unrolled the "bed" and where they placed it. Coke told about removing the 30/30 rifle from the bed and laying it down at the head on the ground. He told about how "we drank some wine, pulled our shoes off and went to bed."

Frye asked Coke if either of them had a watch. The answer was, "No, sir."

Q. Have you any idea what time it was that you went to bed?

A. Well, I don't have any idea what time it was.

Q. Was the sun shining?

A. No sir; no it was after dark.

Q. It was after dark. Did you sleep?

A. Yes, sir.

Q. After you had gone to sleep, were you disturbed, or did anything happen that awakened you?

A. Yes sir.

Q. What was that?

A. Well, when I woke up, I heard somebody talking.

Q. Could you tell who it was?

A. Well, I couldn't right then. Before the conversation was finished, I could.

Q. What conversation did you hear?

A. Well, the first thing I heard, heard somebody say, "Whose car is that?" And the other man says, "That is Brite's car." The other one says, "Who is Brites?" Another one says, "That is the sons-of-bitches that live up on the hill."

Q. By the time that had been said, did you recognize any voices?

A. Yes sir, I recognized Baker's voice when he said that.

Q. And what did you recognize Baker as having said in that conversation?

A. Well, I recognized the last part of it, when he said, "That is the sons-of-bitches that live up on the hill."

Q. You recognized that as Baker's voice?

A. Yes sir, I did.

Q. What did you do then?

A. I hollered, "Hey, Baker," and jumped up out of bed.

Q. Did you see anyone when you jumped up out of bed?

A. Yes sir, when I got out back of the car. I seen one man go across away from there; the other man stood there.

Q. Did you know that man?

A. No sir.

Q. When you walked up and spoke to this man that you did not know, where had the other man gone?

A. Well, I didn't know where he was at right then. I asked this man what he wanted. And John got up about that time. And then I heard a noise in the brush there and we looked around, and Baker, he stepped out then. We recognized Baker. He stepped out carrying something in front of him. John grabbed it out of his hand then; jerked it out of his hand and hit him with it.

Tussle for a Stick

Q. What was it?

A. It was a stick.

Q. You recognized that man as Baker?

A. Yes sir.

Q. Where was Baker when John grabbed the stick in his hand?

A. Well, he was some place back of the car close to the road; some place in there.

Q. And was the other man standing close by?

A. Yes sir, he was standing there.

Q. Was there a tussle between John and Baker over the stick?

A. Yes sir; John jerked it several times before he got it away from him.

Q. What happened then, Coke?

A. Well, when John struck Baker, he started down the road and this other man went with him. And then we went back to the bed, and sat down, put on our shoes and talked about going home. We decided it was pretty dark and we would just wait there until daylight, so we laid back down.

Q. Do you know what time it was then?

A. No sir, I don't.

This is the core of what trials and juries are really all about. The jury sits there, composed of twelve good men and women. Their task is mainly one of "evaluation" of conflicting versions of the same event. All the clouds of objections, over rulings, claims of incompetence and hearsay are just a jumble in the minds of the individuals impaneled there. But testimony like this is really what it's all about. And they will get little help in arriving at the true version. Baker is the sole survivor of one side of this fracas and he has described it the way he saw it. Coke and his brother John are the only other source of information concerning it. Presumably, John's version will match that of Coke's. Then that is it. That is all there is available. That is the "woof and the warp" of jurying, the very stuff of the jury's job. All the other things concerning it in the trial don't mean a thing. It is an awesome responsibility to be a juror.

Horace J. Frye then took up the matter of the celebrated "owl in the night." After Coke said that they went back to sleep, Frye asked, "Were you awakened by any birds, or anything of that kind around there?"

An Owl in the Night

Coke then vividly described how the hooting of an owl had awakened him and his brother. He told how John had reached over and picked up the pistol at the head of the bed and fired in the general direction of the hoots. He said they heard the bird fly away into the night. Of course, Frye again asked him what time that was and they had to go through the whole discussion again that neither of them had a watch. At any rate, that owl was fast becoming the most famous owl in California and a darling of the press.

The next event to be explored is the very essence of this trial. As with the evening fight, it is a moral drama in the lives and deaths of the people involved in this tragedy. Again, it is the account of the sole survivor, Charley Baker, against the only two other witnesses, the defendants in the box. The physical evidence is of great importance, but the legal and moral values eventually come down to the jury's decision of what really happened that night. No matter how it all comes out, it is ironic that only these three men, Charley

Baker, Coke and John Brite, absolutely know what happened. And obviously, there is a great chasm between the two views.

Mr. Frye goes on:

Q. What awakened you this time?

A. Well, the first thing I knew, somebody was right on top of me, and when I started to raise up in bed, they struck me.

Q. Do you know who it was?

A. No sir, I don't.

Q. Struck you with what?

A. I don't know what it was.

Q. Where did they strike you?

A. Across the nose there, forehead and nose [indicating].

Q. Were you able to see the blow struck?

A. No sir.

Q. How long had you been awake when this blow was struck across your nose and forehead?

A. Well, I just started to raise up. I was just waking up, I suppose.

Q. You hadn't lay awake before?

A. No sir.

Q. Did you hear anyone say anything before that?

A. No sir.

Q. Then, what followed after you had been struck across the nose and forehead?

A. Well, I grabbed my nose that way, my face that way; I tried to raise up and they struck me again on top of the head. Then I kept reaching up that way and I was struck several times on the back of the hand.

Q. You don't know what with?

A. No sir, I don't.

Q. Do you know how many times you were struck over the head?

A. Well, not exactly, no; three or four times though, anyway.

Q. Did you find out afterwards that your head was bleeding?

A. Yes, sir.

Q. Where was the blood coming from?

A. On this side [indicating].

Q. Now, at that time you were raised up on this side; this is the side of the bed near the car [Mr. Frye points at the model], is that right?

A. Yes sir, I tried to raise up then. I kept trying to raise up. I couldn't get up that way, so I rolled over on my stomach and crawled out, crawled out of the bed.

Q. Out at the head?

A. Yes, sir.

Q. Were you able to see what John was doing?

A. No, sir.

Q. Then when you crawled out, what happened?

A. Well, when I started to raise up, somebody hit me at the side of the head and knocked me down.

Q. And where were you then?

A. I was out from the head of the bed on the ground.

Q. You say you were knocked down. Were you standing up, or if not standing, what position were you in?

A. Well, when I started to raise up, someone knocked me down. When I went down, then somebody jumped on top of me before I could get up.

Q. What did you do when they jumped on top of you?

A. They hit me several times on the back of the head.

Q. Were you on your stomach then?

A. Yes, sir.

Q. And out of the bed?

A. Yes sir.

Q. How long did that continue, if you know?

A. Well, they hit me several times. I don't know just what happened. I passed out, I guess; everything turned black.

Q. Do you remember being thrown or knocked into the creek by anyone?

A. The next thing I remember, I was in the creek.

Q. The next thing you remember, you were in the creek?

A. Yes sir.

Q. In what position?

A. I was standing up.

Q. And were any of your clothes wet besides the parts of your legs and feet that were in the water?

A. Yes sir, my arms were wet.

Q. How far up?

A. Well, about my elbows.

Q. And when you came to in the creek, what did you do?

A. Well, I walked out of the creek, and when I got out of the creek, I could see someone standing at the back of the car.

Q. What did you do then?

A. I walked over there. When I got over, I could see it was John.

Q. What was he doing?

A. He was leaning up against the car.

Q. Will you just indicate how he was leaning?

A. He was leaning that way, up against the door of the car. [The witness illustrates by resting his head in his hands.]

Q. With a 30/30?

A. Yes sir.

Q. Was there anything unusual in his actions?

A. Yes sir, he struck at me with the gun.

Q. He struck at you with the gun?

A. I grabbed hold of the gun then.

Q. What else did he do?

A. Well, he jerked back from me then. And about that time, Mr. Decker came over there, and he walked up to John then.

Q. Did you look at the rifle at that time?

A. No sir.

Q. You had no flash light there yourself?

A. No sir.

Q. You couldn't see whether or not the stock had been broken off at that time?

A. No sir.

Q. Do you remember Mr. Decker calling before he came in?

A. I heard somebody call my name, yes.

Q. From which direction did Mr. Decker come?

A. Well, I didn't see Mr. Decker until he come right in there where John was at.

Q. Do you remember very much of the conversation with Mr. Decker?

A. No sir, I don't.

Q. Do you remember any of it?

A. Yes, I remember that he said he didn't know anybody that was there, and then he was going some place. That is all I can remember what he said when he was there.

Q. Do you remember when he left?

A. Yes sir, he left some time then, about the time he said he was going some place.

Q. Then, what did you do?

A. Well, I looked around then. I couldn't see John any place, so I went to the car and John was on the running board.

Q. Sitting on the running board?

A. Yes sir.

Q. What did you do then?

A. Well, John's hat was laying there; I had picked it up and put it on his head. I tried to find my hat; then I went to the head of the bed. I found this .32 pistol laying there and I put it in my pocket, and I went back to the running board. Then I got John up, taken a sack of stuff that we had there and we started up the trail.

Q. You say a sack of stuff. What was in the sack?

A. There was a jug of wine, a half gallon of wine, and a piece of bologna. That is all I remember of now.

Q. You took that and took John, and you took the rifle with you, did you?

A. Yes sir, John had the rifle.

Q. And you started up the hill?

A. Yes sir.

Q. Before you left, did you see any dead or wounded men there?

A. Yes sir, I did.

Q. Where? How many?

A. I seen three.

Q. Will you come down please, and indicate where they were?

A. I couldn't tell you exactly where they were. One I saw here and another here. I could see two men out from the bed here some place [indicating the positions].

Q. Which direction?

A. Back of the car some place.

Q. Well, did you see anyone around that clump of trees there?

A. I don't remember the clump of trees, no, but there was someone close there some place, close to the back of the car.

Q. Did you hear any of those men making any noise; can you remember that?

A. Yes sir, I did.

Q. Do you know which one?

A. Well, I wouldn't say for sure, no; just someone out towards the road and in the back of the car.

Q. Did you know at any time who they were?

A. No sir, I didn't.

Q. Now, during the time that you were in the bed and after these men or man had began beating you over the head, did you hear any voice say anything?

A. Yes sir, I did.

Q. Did you recognize the voice?

A. Yes sir.

Q. Whose voice was it?

A. Baker's.

Q. What did he say?

A. He says, "Pour it on that son-of- a-bitch, he's the one that hit me."

Q. That was when you were in the bed?

A. Yes sir.

Q. Were you able to see Baker?

A. No sir.

Q. Could you see the officers to tell who they were?

A. No sir.

Q. Did you know at any time who they were?

A. No sir.

Q. Did you know they were officers?

A. No sir.

Q. Did you hear them say that they were there to arrest you?

A. No sir.

Q. Or that you were under arrest?

A. No sir.

Q. Or did you hear them tell you to wake up?

A. No sir.

Q. Or, "Hello boys?"

A. No sir.

Q. You heard them say nothing before you were hurt?

A. No sir.

Q. Alright, while you were going up the hill, did John act in any way that was unusual or peculiar?

A. Yes sir, he acted like he couldn't see; he couldn't follow the trail. And when we got up on the steep mountain side, he got off the trail down on the side of the mountain several times.

Q. Did he do or say anything else on your way up there that was unusual?

Mr. Allen: I object to anything he said, because that is hearsay.

Mr. Frye: Well, I don't think it is, Your Honor, showing the condition of the man's mind. It is not proving a fact.

The Court: It may be admissible, as I admitted some testimony here the other day, just on the one question as to the condition of his mind.

[Argued by Mr. Allen.]

The Court: For the limited purpose of showing the condition of his mind, I will admit it, and the jury will only consider it for that limited purpose of showing the condition of the party's mind.

Mr. Frye: Now I will ask you again, Coke, while you were going up the hill, did John do or say anything else that indicated to you that he was not normal or that was unusual in any way?

Mr. Allen: He can answer yes or no, if Your Honor please, but he can't state the conversation. I object to it on the ground that the question must be answered "yes."

The Court: This question calls for an answer, yes or no.

A. Yes, he did.

Mr. Allen: I object to any statement, if Your Honor please, on the ground it is hearsay and self serving.

The Court: The objection will be overruled. It will be admitted for the limited purpose of showing the condition of the man, that is, whether his mind was normal or not normal, and for no other purpose.

A. Well, he said we was going the wrong way several times, that he wanted to go to bed. And then, when we got on up to the corn patch, I asked him if he didn't know where he was at and he asked me…

Mr. Frye [interrupting]: We don't want to know what you said.

A. He wanted to know what I had done to him.

Q. He wanted to know what you had done to him?

A. Yes sir.

Q. Now, you have mentioned a corn patch. Just tell us where that corn patch is.

A. Well, it is about a mile, I guess a mile and a quarter from where the car was at.

Q. And how far is it from your home?

A. Well, it is about maybe 600 yards…800.

Q. How long did you stop at the corn patch?

A. I don't know just how long, it was quite a little bit, though.

Q. After John said, "What did you do to me?," words to that effect, where did you go?

A. We went on up to the house.

Q. And you stayed around the house. Were your clothes bloody?

A. Yes sir.

Q. What did you have on?

A. Shirt, overalls and shoes.

Q. Did you change clothes?

A. Yes sir.

Q. And then, what did you do?

A. Well, I packed some groceries in a pack bag and we started to the mountains.

Heading for the Hills

Q. Why did you do that?

A. Well, we thought the best thing we could do was to get out of the way and go to the mountains.

Q. Well, why did you think it was the best thing you could do?

At this point, Allen interrupted with an objection to the question on the usual grounds that it was incompetent, irrelevant and immaterial and had nothing to do with the issue. A long session of wrangling immediately broke out between the two sides with the judge in the middle. Of course Allen, as well as everyone else involved, knew exactly why Frye had asked the question. It is a long standing principle that fleeing from justice is most always considered an indication of guilt. It was perfectly obvious that the defendants in this case had fled. To overcome this presumption, Frye was trying to demonstrate that his defendants were fleeing not from true justice, but from another kind of "justice."

The arguments were long and heated. It finally came time for the afternoon recess and it was postponed for a spell. After the recess the arguments resumed. Finally the judge ruled:

The Court: I get the idea that the defendant does have the right to explain his flight; it ultimately is passed to the jury to determine. Now that is the question for you to answer now … Why did you think it was the best thing you could do?

A. I knew John had the gun, thought he had killed them men. I thought that was the best thing we could do.

Mr. Frye: Well, did you have any fear of any kind at that time…I will withdraw the question. Was there any idea in your mind at that time that you might suffer from mob violence?

A. Yes, there was.

Q. And is that the reason that you went to the mountains?

A. Yes sir.

Q. Now, after you had been out…how long were you out in the mountains?

A. Sixteen or seventeen days; I guess it was somewhere along there.

Q. And at the end of that period, you gave yourselves up to District Attorney Davis?

Mr. Allen: I object to the question as leading and suggestive; leading and self serving. I think there is ample authority for the fact that a man giving himself up is not evidence. It is self serving.

The Court: I think that would be along the same lines that I have just ruled as to the weight of it going to the jury. I think it is leading, though, and I will sustain the objection on the ground it is too leading.

Mr. Frye: Well, after that period of time, what did you do?

A. We came back home.

Q. And after that, did you ever see Mr. Davis, the District Attorney?

A. Yes sir. We gave up to him.

Q. Explain to the jury what you did on that occasion.

A. Well, our mother came in and got Mr. Davis.

Q. Well, now, never mind that. That might be your conclusion. What did you do, you and yourselves?

A. We gave up to Mr. Davis.

Q. Where?

A. On Horse Creek, down at the end of the trail.

Q. Do you know whether or not Mr. Davis had any guns on his person then?

Mr. Allen: I object to that as incompetent, irrelevant and immaterial.

Mr. Frye: Now, if Your Honor please, I think that goes along the same line of showing that Mr. Davis took these men without any arms, and that happened from that time until they were incarcerated in Folsom Prison. I think it goes to the question of flight, and whether or not flight is for the purpose of evading the law or for the purpose of escaping mob violence.

The Court: No. I think what was done after he gave himself up would be immaterial, and I will sustain the objection to the question and let the record stand as it is. The last answer shows that he gave himself up to the District Attorney.

Mr. Frye: Then you were taken where?

A. Folsom Prison.

Mr. Correia: We object for the same reason, Your Honor.

Mr. Allen: It is incompetent, irrelevant and immaterial where they were taken.

The Court: Yes, I think that is immaterial.

Mr. Frye: The question has been answered.

Mr. Correia: We ask that the answer be stricken.

The Court: It may go out, the last answer.

This last technical exchange was another example of the system's attempt to "unring a bell." The question and the answer were indelibly imprinted in the brain of each of the jurors. There is no way in the world that Luttrell's command that it "go out" is going to change this. The whole exchange is "in the record" and in the event of an appeal, there it is to be read by the appeals court judge. Even though he understands better than the jury the intent of it's "going out," he is also a human being and his brain cells have it logged just like anyone else. He can't unring a bell, either. All of these participants know this; Luttrell, Allen, Frye and Correia. But the system requires them to go through it all just as though it was a tightly choreographed ballet.

Coke's Cross Examination

It was now the prosecution's turn to cross examine the defendant. It should be noted that the rules of the court allow a considerable more latitude in cross examination than in direct examination. Here the questions can be much less relevant, less formally structured and definitely more combative in nature. This also is an area in which Allen was an acknowledged expert and he was ready to go.

In the opinion of some experienced trial technicians, this cross examination turned out to be one of the most surprising events in the whole proceedings. It may have been the most important factor in determining the fate of the Brites. When Allen started off, it didn't sound too ominous. He began with the events leading up to the fight between the Brites and Baker and Seaborn.

Mr. Allen: Mr. Brite, after you got there, you say you took out your bed and rolled it out on the ground?

A. Yes sir.

Q. Sat down and drank some wine?

A. Yes sir.

Q. That was immediately after you got there, is it?

A. Yes sir, a little while after that.

Q. How long did you stay there before you went to bed after drinking the wine; you went to bed, didn't you?

A. No, after we went to bed.

Q. You drank the wine until you did go to bed?

A. Yes sir.

Q. You were drinking out of a quart bottle, weren't you?

A. Yes sir.

Q. You laid it there by the bed when you went to bed, didn't you?

A. No sir, I did not.

Q. Where did you lay it?

A. In the back of the car.

Q. You laid it in the back of the car?

A. Yes sir.

Q. This has been marked as People's Exhibit #24. Does that look like the bottle of wine, Coke?

Note: This was the bottle that had come sailing through the air toward Baker and Seaborn just before the fight. It will be recalled that Baker had found the bottle the next day while he was looking for his hat when the authorities were there.

A. Yes sir, it does.

Q. Just about that much wine in it when you last remember it?

A. I think so, just about that much.

Q. And you laid that in the car when you laid down to go to bed, is that right?

A. Yes sir.

Q. And this gun, you unrolled that and laid it at the head of the bed, is that right?

A. Yes sir.

Q. It was loaded, was it?

A. Yes sir, it was.

Q. Then you took off your shoes, both of you, and got in bed, is that right?

A. Yes sir.

Q. Now of course, you have no way of knowing what time you got to bed?

A. No sir, I do not.

Q. It was dark?

A. Yes sir.

Q. Now, the next thing you remember after that was, I believe, you said you heard some talking there?

A. Yes sir.

Q. Both of you?

A. Yes sir.

Q. You both raised up?

A. Yes.

Q. Stand on your feet, did you? Or just up…did you get right up on your feet?

A. I did.

Q. You did. And John got up, too, on his feet?

A. I suppose he did.

Q. Well, when you got up there, you could see two men there, is that right.

A. I could.

Q. One of the voices, you knew; that was Baker's voice?

A. I did.

Q. You were kind of sore at Baker, anyway, weren't you?

A. I was.

Q. It made you mad just as soon as you heard his voice, didn't it?

A. It did.

Q. So you got up; when you got up, you saw Baker run down the road?

A. I did.

Q. The other fellow stood there, did he?

A. Yes sir, he did.

Note: What follows here is the portion of the testimony that the "Sunday morning quarterbacks" felt was crucial.

Q. You had never seen him before?

A. No sir.

Q. Now, you both walked over and talked to him?

A. Yes sir.

Q. Did he say anything to you when you were talking to him?

A. Not a word, no.

Q. He never answered you at all.

A. No sir.

Q. How long did you talk to him?

A. Not very long.

Q. Just what did you say to him?

A. I asked him what he was doing there.

Q. Did you cuss him?

A. No sir.

Q. Never said an angry word?

A. I never.

Q. John never, either?

A. No sir.

Q. You just asked him what he was doing there?

A. Yes sir.

Q. He didn't answer at all?

A. No sir.

Q. How many times did you ask him that?

A. We asked him that once.

Q. Asked him that once. How many times did John ask him?

A. He asked him once. He asked something about what he was doing there, pulling off, or something in that way.

Q. He never said a word to either one of you?

A. No, he never.

Q. Just walk up here to the model and take that ruler, Coke, and tell me just where that happened, that conversation?

A. It was somewhere out near the edge of the road in here [indicating].

Q. That is where you were talking to him trying to get him to say something to you, when you saw Baker coming out of the brush with something in his hand?

A. Yes sir.

Q. From what direction was he coming?

A. He come out from the right side.

Q. Come down here and tell me just about where he was coming from. You were standing here talking to Fred Seaborn; now, just where did he come from?

A. He came from this side of the road some place [indicating].

Q. You have pointed to the west side. How close was he to you when you first saw him?

A. Well, he was up within three or four feet, anyway; I wouldn't say just how far.

Q. You could tell it was a club, could you?

A. No, you couldn't tell exactly what it was. You could tell he had something in his hand.

Q. That is all now, you can go back again. You could just tell he had something in his hand; you couldn't tell what it was?

A. No sir.

Q. John grabbed it out of his hand, is that right?

A. He did.

Q. He didn't have much trouble taking the club out of his hand, did he?

A. Well, he jerked on it several times.

Q. Just like this was a club in my hand, just tell me how he did?

A. Well, when I seen him, he was jerking back on it that way. He jerked back several times.

Q. He jerked it several times until he jerked it out of his hand?

A. Yes sir.

Q. That is all you saw?

A. Yes sir.

Q. When he got the club, what did you see John do then?

A. He hit Baker with the stick.

Q. Did he hit him hard?

A. Well, I couldn't tell how hard he hit him.

Q. Did you hear it hit?

A. I don't remember hearing it.

Q. Did it knock Baker down?

A. No sir.

Q. Never fazed him at all?

A. Not that I seen.

Q. He seemed just as normal after that as he did before? Never staggered him?

A. He might have staggered him, yes, but it never knocked him down. I don't know just what effect it had on him.

Q. Then, you say after that he went on down the road?

A. Yes sir.

Q. The other man following him.

A. Yes sir.

Q. That is the last you saw of them until later on, is that right?

A. Yes.

Q. Then, according to your testimony, you never hit Seaborn at all; just talked to him?

A. Yes sir.

Q. And that John just grabbed the club out of Baker's hands?

A. Yes sir.

Q. That is all the tussle you had with him?

A. Yes sir.

Q. Now, isn't it a fact, Coke, that you both hit Seaborn?

A. No sir, it is not.

Q. You say you didn't hit him?

A. I didn't hit him.

Q. Or John didn't hit him?

A. Yes sir.

Q. You know that?

A. Yes sir, I know that.

Q. You just talked to him?

A. Yes sir.

Q. The only thing that John did was just grab the club out of his hand, jerked out of his hand?

Mr. Frye: I object to that on the ground it has been answered two or three times.

The Court: Yes, I think so.

Mr. Allen: On cross examination, I have a right to go back.

The Court: Well, I think he answered it twice or three times that he jerked it out of his hand and hit him with it.

Mr. Allen: Now, he didn't strike him any place else, did he?

A. No sir.

Q. Just with the club. Didn't tear his shirt?

A. No sir, not that I seen.

Q. He didn't have hold of his shirt at all? He just had hold of the club, did he?

A. Yes sir, that is all I seen.

Q. Baker didn't go down at all?

A. No sir.

Q. He didn't kick you in the stomach?

A. No sir, he didn't.

Q. Didn't you follow them down or did you go right back?

Q. Went right back to bed from where he was hit with the stick.

A. But you threw that bottle of wine at him, didn't you?

A. No sir, I never.

Q. You never?

A. No sir.

Q. Didn't you take that out of the car?

A. No sir.

Q. The last you saw of that, it was in the car, is that right?

A. It was in the back of the car.

Q. It was in the back of the car. You never threw it at all?

A. No sir.

A Question of Shoes

The above is the end of the portion of the testimony that was considered by some as the most damaging to the defendants' side of the case. This matter will be discussed shortly. But in order to keep things in proper sequence, this cross examination will be continued at this time.

Q. Now, when you went back to bed, you put on your shoes, didn't you?

Allen's last question above concerning the Brites going to bed with their shoes on brought on an exchange that should be of interest to any self respecting sociologist.

Coke's reply: Yes sir.

Q. You had shoes on to travel around in the mountains with; hob nailed shoes?

A. Well, they wasn't hob nailed. They had rubber soles.

Q. High top?

A. No, low top.

To an urban dweller, the above conversation must be unintelligible, most especially so if the listener realized that the conversation was between a sophisticated trial lawyer who was also a state senator and a totally unschooled mountain man. Allen had been raised in some of the remotest areas of Siskiyou County and was perfectly at ease in this vernacular.

Q. When you went back to bed again, you didn't get into bed in the same way you were the first time?

A. We did.

Q. Isn't it a fact you laid there on top of the covers?

A. No sir.

Q. You mean to say that you got in there with those big boots, crawled into bed?

A. Yes.

Q. Do you mean to say that you and John crawled down under this bed with your shoes on?

A. We did.

254

Q. Now Coke, don't you know that both you and John were lying on top of the bed?

A. No sir.

Allen's strategy here was of course to get Coke to admit that they were on top of the covers instead of under them. Failing in that, Allen kept drilling in with it in an effort to plant doubts in the jury's mind that perhaps the brothers were on top of the covers instead of under them. If such was the case, it would destroy the defense's contentions that the Brites were sound asleep "under" the covers. If that idea was implanted, it would be very difficult to swallow the defense's contention that the officers sneaked up on them and started beating up on two helpless people pinned under the covers. It was a little foolish on Allen's part, however, because his own witness, Baker, placed the Brites under the covers.

Allen then went on to something far more important, our old friend the hoot owl. It is difficult to determine what Allen's strategy here was in that he attempted by his questioning to imply that the firing at the owl had a sinister bearing on the case. At one time he seemed to imply that Coke was lying about the owl. Frye also felt he had to get into it at one point. It was all a waste of time as far as any relevancy with the case is concerned but it is at least interesting.

Again, the Hoot Owl

Q. Now, after that, you were awakened by a hoot owl, is that right?

A. That is right, yes sir.

Q. Just where was that hoot owl hooting at?

A. Some place down back of the car over across the road in some trees there.

Q. Over across by Decker's place?

A. No, down in the road in back of the car.

Q. Kind of a southerly direction there?

A. Yes.

Q. Did you see the owl?

A. No sir.

Q. Never saw it at all?

A. No sir.

Q. At no time?

A. No sir.

Q. Well, how far did you see him?

A. I didn't see the owl.

Q. How far away did the hoot seem?

A. Well, just a little ways in the trees here.

Q. You are used to sleeping out in the mountains?

Mr. Frye: We object to that as incompetent, irrelevant and immaterial.

Mr. Allen: I think this is cross examination.

The Court: I will permit it. Overruled.

Mr. Allen: Do you understand the question?

A. Yes sir, I understand the question.

Q. You wouldn't be disturbed by a hoot owl out in the mountains?

A. Well, I might. I woke up that time.

Mr. Frye: We object to that as incompetent, irrelevant and immaterial.

Q. Is this the first time a hoot owl ever woke you up in the mountains?

A. No sir.

Q. You have been awakened before by a hoot owl?

Mr. Frye: We object to that as incompetent, irrelevant and immaterial.

The Court: I think it is answered. I will sustain the objection.

Mr. Allen: Now when the...you didn't get up?

A. No sir.

Q. Just John got up?

A. John just raised up in bed. He never got out of bed.

Q. He raised up in bed?

A. Yes sir.

Q. He reached over and got the .32 automatic, is that right?

A. He did.

Q. He just raised up in bed?

A. Yes sir.

Q. You are sure you never got up and let him crawl out from where he was in there?

A. No sir, he never got out.

Q. Then after that, you both laid down. You said you both got under the covers again?

A. Yes sir.

Allen is still fishing around here in an attempt to trick Coke in to saying that they were never under the covers at all. But now Frye has had about enough of it.

Mr. Frye: We will ask that the answer be stricken out for the purpose of making an objection.

The Court: The answer may go out.

Mr. Frye: We object to the question on the ground that it assumes something not in evidence. It is a misstatement of the testimony.

Mr. Allen: I have a right on cross examination to assume anything and to lead the witness.

The Court: You have a right to lead the witness, but not to assume something.

Mr. Allen: Well, did you get under the covers?

A. Yes sir, we covered up again.

Q. You say you got in bed in the same way you were before?

A. We never got out of bed, no, when John shot at the owl, we never.

At last. Score one for the hoot owl.

Allen then took Coke through the whole fight with the officers up to the point where Coke said that he passed out. Nothing new or startling came out. He then picked it up after the shooting when Decker had arrived in the camp. He went thoroughly through every detail. Then he questioned Coke about the climb up the mountain to the house at which time Allen commenced his standard high speed cross examination windup.

Mr. Allen: After you got up there, how long before you left?

A. Left the house?

Q. Yes.

A. Well, I couldn't say just how long it was.

Q. Can you give us any idea?

A. Well, no, it wasn't so very long, though. I changed clothes; put on some dry clothes.

Q. Was it dark when you left?

A. Yes.

Q. Still dark?

A. Yes.

Q. And you talked to your parents?

A. Yes sir.

Q. Well, now, you hadn't heard anything about a mob then, had you?

A. No sir.

Q. Then why were you afraid of a mob?

A. I knew John had the gun; thought maybe he had killed them men.

Mr. Allen: You knew he had killed them?

A. No sir, I didn't know it.

Q. You didn't know that?

A. No, I didn't know it.

Q. And the reason for fleeing was because you knew you and he had murdered three officers down there and you wanted to get out of the way.

A. No sir, it wasn't.

Q. You knew what they had done to Johnson, and you knew that they would do the same thing to you?

A. That was spoke about.

Q. You talked about Johnson?

A. Yes.

Q. You knew he had killed a peace officer?

A. I heard about him being lynched.

Q. You knew that he had killed a police officer?

A. I didn't know who he had killed.

Q. You thought you had killed three police officers and you were afraid of being mobbed.

A. I didn't know they was police officers, but I was afraid of being mobbed, yes sir.

Q. You say you were down right on the bed here when they were beating you?

A. Yes sir.

Q. You can't see any blood on the pillow or bed there, can you [indicating the bed cloths on the floor that had been introduced in evidence]?

A. No sir, I can't.

Q. You can't see any blood on the canvas here, can you?

A. No sir.

Q. You never did see any blood on it, did you?

A. Not that I know of, no.

Q. You have been convicted of a felony before; haven't you been, and served time in the Florence Penitentiary?

A. I have.

Mr. Allen: That is all of the cross examination.

Mr. Frye had one last thing he wanted to touch on before excusing the witness. He therefore asked for a short session of re-direct examination, which was granted. He asked his first question to which Allen immediately objected. This finally got Allen in trouble with the judge who promptly put him in his place.

Mr. Frye: Coke, when you were convicted of a felony in Arizona, in what year was that?

Mr. Allen: The witness has already answered that.

Mr. Frye: If you want to make objection, make it.

Mr. Allen: I don't see any use of the heat of counsel whenever I make an objection, make it.

The Court: Well, the difficulty arises by your talking to counsel instead of making your objection to the court. I would like to have each counsel, when an objection is made, make your objection to the court. In the heat of a trial, it often occurs, counsel in the trial will address each other instead of making the objection to the court. That starts the difficulty, so try and avoid that and we will get along better.

Now, the state of the record is that the answer was not given and the Court will overrule the objection. Let the question be answered. Read the question, Mr. Reporter.

The Reporter: Coke, when you were convicted of a felony in Arizona, in what year was that?

A. In 1925.

Q. How old were you then?

A. Well, let's see; I was 26, I guess.

Q. How old are you now?

A. 31.

Q. You were 20 years old then, weren't you?

A. 20.

Mr. Frye: That is all, your honor.

With that poignant observation, Coke Bright was finished with his legal efforts to save his life. In the courtroom for a fleeting moment, one could have heard a pin drop.

It had been a long day. As the courtroom slowly emptied, the court reporter's son went out and down the hall to his father's office. He was troubled by something.

In the privacy of the office, he asked his father, "Daddy, Coke Brite was lying when he told about the first fight with Mr. Baker and Mr. Seaborn, wasn't he?"

His father replied, "I'm having trouble with that testimony myself. I'll tell you what. The Johnson's are coming to our house for dinner this evening; why don't we ask Charley about that and get it from a real expert?"

As the boy nodded in agreement, the father went on to say, "It's been a hard day for me. I could use some rest before our guests arrive. Come on, let's you and I walk on home together."

By the time the two of them left the courthouse, there wasn't a soul left in the corridors. All was quiet.

About six o'clock the Johnsons arrived at the McMurry home. It was only a short two and a half blocks and they had walked. The boy was eager to hear what Charley had to say about the court matter, but his father kept him in check. The McMurrys did not drink to any extent, but when the Johnsons visited, Ralph McMurry always had his little ritual drink with Charley. When he appeared with their "high balls," McMurry opened up the subject of the case.

"The young one here is disturbed with Coke Brite's testimony regarding the first fight with Baker and Seaborn," he said. "He wants to know what you think about it."

"Well," said Charley, "That testimony has been on my mind ever since he laid it out there. What seems to be your problem, Son?"

The boy had always liked the comical Charley Johnson, who always seemed to enjoy horsing around with the kids. Charley had also cut his hair many times down through the years. He felt complimented that he was being accepted into this "grown up" circle of discussion.

The boy said, "Well, it seemed to me that it was so obvious that he was lying, it ruined his chances to get anyone to believe all the rest of what he has said. It's hard for me to believe that Mr. Frye would have handled him that way."

"Son, you have hit the nail right on the head," replied Charley. "That is exactly what I meant when I said a moment ago that testimony has been on my mind.

"As a matter of fact, I have been totally shocked about it because I cannot understand Frye's thinking in letting his client go down that road. None of us up here in Siskiyou knew Frye before. But as we got to know him, we learned that he was a very nice fellow, that he knew the law inside and out, and that he was a very superior legal tactician. Now he comes along in the latter stages of the trial and literally commits what could turn out to be a colossal blunder. That blunder is as you have stated, Son. He may have allowed his client to destroy his credibility.

"The fact is that Seaborn and Baker had one whale of a fight with John and Coke. It was just a country brawl but it was a smasher. Both Seaborn and Baker had been worked over by that famous "little stick" that Coke described. When the two victims arrived at Judge Rainey's house to swear out a warrant, both their shirts were all bloody; Seaborn had a knot on his skull half the size of a goose egg and one of his eyes was swollen nearly shut. All of this was apparent to Judge and Mrs. Rainey as well as their house guest. Captain Seaborn told the whole story of the fight to the Raineys. And Captain Seaborn was not the type of a person you doubt. He was a high ranking naval officer and held the position of Chief of Harbor at Vallejo. He was a man of impeccable character, a man whose word was acceptable anywhere.

"In addition to this, Charley Baker, testified in depth as to what happened at the fight both in the inquest and in this very same trial. I think that anyone who is knowledgeable in these matters feels that Charley Baker is one of the most believable witnesses that has ever testified in any trial. In spite of some of his obvious shortcomings, I do not think that Charley has enough imagination to lie, even if he wanted to.

"Now, the defendant in this case, who appears to be a very good witness himself, describes this fight in effect as follows:

"'We heard these voices with one of them calling us sons-of-bitches. I hollered, "Hey Baker." We went down there and walked up to one man and asked him, "What are you pulling?" He never said a word. Baker comes out of the brush with a stick; he never said a word; John took the stick away from him and tapped him with it. They went down the path and we went to bed.'

"That isn't at all like it was. Can you imagine? A practically 'silent' fight? Fights just are not conducted that way. You know there is plenty of cussing and rough brawling going on in any worthwhile Siskiyou County mayhem like that. The way Coke paints it, it sounds like four old ladies declining an invitation to tea. No, we can't buy Coke's version of that fight. The pitiful thing about it is that the fight has little to do with the case; it was only a 'leading in' event and certainly not worth lying about.

"Now that in essence is what Coke testified today. His manner on the stand is such that he has obviously been very well coached by his attorney; and this is as it should be. But everyone knows that Coke is telling an out and out lie in the process; and therein lies the trouble."

Charley was really getting warmed up. The boy was on the edge of his seat. But Ralph McMurry had to break in. "Charley, you have my son and me spellbound as usual, but the ladies are calling us for dinner. We can recess the case while we eat and go right at it afterward."

As always, the dinner, cooked on the big old wood stove, was absolutely delicious.

Back in the living room while the ladies were finishing up the dishes, Charley resumed his explanation.

"Mr. Frye has a very tough case to defend. He has on his hands a triple murder of police officers. The community is aroused. All of the evidence conclusively indicates who did it. He has only one defense. That is what has already been dubbed the 'Decker Theory.' This theory more or less states that the arresting officers, by approaching the defendants' camp in the dead of a dark night, did not adequately identify themselves to the two sleeping men when they entered their camp in order to arrest them. The defendants, having had the earlier fight the same evening, when awakened reasoned that they were being attacked by their previous assailants plus reinforcements. They came up fighting and fought to the death under this assumption.

"The physical evidence conclusively shows that even though the brothers were out-manned and out-gunned, they were able to thoroughly slay all of their adversaries but one. The evidence probably also shows that after the heated battle was over, they methodically made the rounds and finished off each of the victims at point blank. With this kind of evidence, there is no way to offset it on balance. The only thing that Frye could use was what is commonly known as the "blackout" tactic. This tactic in this case holds that during all the time that the actual killing and coupe de graces were taking place, everything in the defendant's consciousness went black. They didn't remember anything that happened from the time their assailants were attacking them in their bed until they woke up afterwards and became aware of the havoc that had taken place. While this scenario is almost incredible, it could be a possibility. If it can be sold, it gets the defendants away from having to be totally accountable for what had obviously taken place. All the professionals understand what Frye is doing here. From his point of view, maybe the jurors, or at least one of them, might buy it. But generally speaking, everyone really knows it is all a load of bull. This is about all Frye has and that is what he is attempting. But even in failing to convince the jury, there is still a faint possibility that this type of defense will, on appeal, get them a reversal at best, or at the worst, a commutation to life instead of hanging.

"But in order to pull off such a defense as the 'blackout,' the defense must tell no other lies. The defense must be squeaky clean all the rest of the way through. Hopefully, it goes like this. The jury hears this wild tale about 'everything' going blank. It sounds far fetched, but after all, no body has proved the defendants didn't go blank. In everything else, it appears that the defendants have been very frank and have told the truth throughout.

"Frye, up to this point, has done a craftsman's job of using this approach in the defense maneuvers. But all of a sudden he lets his defendant under cross examination testify with that cockamamie lying story of the earlier fight that is patently and obviously untruthful. It negates his whole approach from the very beginning and I consider it a first class blunder of blunders for which there is no repair available at this point.

"Now, please don't misunderstand me. I am not favoring the Brites in this analysis. We are just discussing the technical aspects of how one lawyer handled a case; just that, and nothing more.

"Let me make one final observation. It is my opinion that from the very beginning, no matter what kind of a defense tactic Frye adopted, there has never been a chance that this jury would not bring in a guilty verdict. And when that happens, the Brites will be sentenced to the noose. But it is obvious that Frye is also looking to an appeal. And if and when it goes up, I have always felt that a commutation would be the result. Now, in view of this episode that we have discussed this evening, I believe that a commutation is just a little bit less likely than it was before today's testimony took place."

There was dead silence. The boy was looking up at Charley in awe. Then Charley said, "What do you think of all that, young man?"

"Well," the boy said, "that is pretty much what I thought when I asked Daddy about it. But I sure didn't know what I was thinking was that deep or that complicated."

They all chuckled over this.

And here came the ladies with pie and ice cream.

John's Turn in the Box

The next day it was John Brite's day in the box. The gallery was smaller on this day because the public well knew that his testimony would be a carbon copy of Coke's. As Frye started him through the process, it immediately became apparent that the public was correct.

John spoke in a soft voice and seemed calm in spite of the obvious predicament in which he now found himself. The lawyers and even the judge had to repeatedly request that he speak louder. While he didn't seem as articulate as his brother, he was able to get his answers across in an authoritative and understanding manner.

But of course, it all was a replay of everything that had just been covered by Coke. As with Coke, Frye started him out with the early evening fight with Baker and Seaborn. It was exactly the same except that under Allen's cross examination John allowed that "Seaborn may also have been hit with the stick."

The scene at the killing was just the same. He said that he was sound asleep under the covers when he felt these people start pounding on his head with "something hard." He said out loud, "For God's sake, Coke, can't you help me?" But the beating continued until he passed out. The next thing that he remembered, he and his brother were in the corn patch on the way home. He heard no gun shots, didn't hear the dog barking, and didn't even remember when Decker had come into the camp.

In spite of the fact the story was identical to the other, it consumed an equal amount of time. The lawyers went through the same arguments, objections, and even some of the insinuations. But it was all the same and anticlimactic.

At the end of it, the defense rested.

In rebuttal, Allen called nine short time witnesses, some of whom had previously testified. These witnesses added little to the picture except to clear up some items that the prosecution wanted to elaborate a little further. Only two of them brought any flash of interest into the proceedings. But these two exchanges did finally throw some light upon the reason for Allen's apparent obsession with the sound of the gun shots upon which he had earlier spent so much time. Based upon what he asked these two witnesses, it appeared that Allen felt the opposition was going to try and claim that everyone there at the scene that had a gun was shooting it in the battle. His contention seemed to be that only the rifle was used, the big gun. The only rifle on the premises of course was the 30/30 that belonged to the Brites. The two officers had only pistols. Even though testimony had fairly well established that the officer's pistols had not been fired, Allen wanted to nail this down just in case.

Allen first recalled Deputy Sheriff Eddie Mathews.

Mr. Allen: I will ask you if you had a conversation with Mr. Decker relative to this alleged killing at the scene of the alleged crime on the morning of August 30th, 1936?

A. I did.

Q. In the presence of yourself and Decker and Fortna and the sheriff and others?

A. I did.

Q. And I will ask you if at that time Mr. Decker made this statement to you in substance or effect: That he didn't know how many shots were fired, he didn't distinguish any difference between the shots, it sounded like a roar?

A. He did.

Mr. Allen: Cross examine.

Mr. Frye: Just what did he say, Mr. Mathews?

A. I asked Mr. Decker how many shots were fired, and Mr. Decker said, "I don't know how many shots were fired, you can't tell here in the canyon." He said, "It echoes," and he said, "You couldn't tell how many shots were fired." And then I asked him if there was any difference in the reports, that is, whether there was more than one gun, and he said that he could not tell.

Q. How did you happen to ask him that last question?

A. Well, there was a circumstance there that might have led me to believe that there was another gun.

Q. What was that circumstance?

A. I thought that there had been a .32 automatic shot there.

Q. What made you think that?

A. The holes in Martin Lange's head.

Q. They were smaller were they?

A. They were smaller and looked to me like they might be a smaller caliber.

Q. Well, did it?

A. Yes sir.

Q. You are sure that Mr. Decker said that?

Possible Frame Up?

A. I am.

Q. You are sure that is not a frame up among the deputies in the Sheriff's Office?

Mr. Allen: I object to that on the ground that the tone of the counsel is insulting to the witness.

Mr. Frye: I beg your pardon, Mr. Mathews, and yours, Mr. Allen.

The Court: Yes, there is quite a bit of excitement put into the question.

Mr. Frye: Yes, I am sorry. Mr. Mathews, are you sure that that is not a frame up between Mr. Chandler and the other members of the Sheriff's Office?

A. I am absolutely positive that there is no frame-up from any angle in the Sheriff's Office, and this case included.

Mr. Frye: I ask that be stricken out as not responsive, Your Honor.

The Court: Yes, that may go out. You are referred now to this particular incident.

Mr. Frye: Now, will you answer my question?

A. I am absolutely sure.

Q. You say there were no frame ups at all?

A. Nothing that I know of.

Q. There was a frame up about what the sheriff said before you started up the hill, wasn't there?

Mr. Correia: We object to this as not proper cross examination, Your Honor.

The Court: Yes, I think so. I will sustain the objection.

Mr. Allen: Call Dr. Schlappi.

Q. You told us you were down to the scene of the alleged killing at that time?

A. Yes sir.

Q. I will ask you if at that time you heard a conversation with Mr. Decker relative to the alleged shooting down there in substance or effect as follows: That he didn't know how many shots were fired or distinguish any difference between the shots, because it just sounded like a roar on account of the echo in the canyon?

A. Yes sir.

Mr. Allen: Cross examine.

Mr. Frye: Where did that conversation take place, Doctor? You weren't all grouped together, were you, at that particular time?

A. No, we were in bunches of twos and threes.

Q. Who else was standing right in that immediate vicinity, Doctor, if you remember?

A. I believe he was telling it to Sheriff Chandler and one of the deputies.

Q. Which deputy?

A. I think it was Mathews, if I am not mistaken. I wouldn't be sure. I know he was talking to the sheriff.

Q. Do you remember the exact words that he used?

A. No, not the exact words, but the text was that he had gone to bed and heard this shooting. He was asked as to the number of shots. He said he didn't know, but it sounded like a heavy gun. He says the echo came back off the side of the hill, the hill being on this side of the road.

Q. Did he say anything else in that connection at that time?

A. About the shooting?

Q. Yes.

A. Well, he said that he had heard the shooting, and then Baker had come running to the house, that is all.

Q. I mean about the sound of the guns.

A. He said it sounded like a roar; it sounded like a heavy gun, the echo came back from the hill.

Mr. Frye: That is all, your honor.

Mr. Allen: The prosecution rests.

The Court: You may proceed with the argument. Now, does counsel want the argument reported or not?

The judge here is asking whether or not the counsels want the arguments taken down by the court reporter and put into the record. The law is that neither side's argument will be reported unless either side requests otherwise. Each request can be only for the opposite side's argument to be reported.

Mr. Allen: We don't care to have counsel's argument reported.

The Court: It is the privilege of counsel on either side to have it if you so desire.

Mr. Frye: Well, the only thought that I have in mind, Your Honor, is whether or not there might be prejudicial misconduct on the part of the prosecution.

The Court: Very well, you should like to have it reported then?

Mr. Frye: I think so, Your Honor.

The Court [To Mr. Allen]: You may proceed with the argument.

The Final Argument

In fiction and in the movies, final arguments invariably consist of exciting speeches by the lawyers from start to finish. The lawyer comes to a quick finish with a flourishing summation after which the case is then placed in the jury's hands. In fact, the format is often as it is in real life courtroom dramas. But this case does not fit that description.

What follows here is actually a somewhat disjointed Final Argument, not well organized, and one in which one side is continually being interrupted by the opposition.

Because of these interruptions and arguments in this particular case, it is very difficult to sort out what was Final Argument and what was merely lawyer's wrangling that took place within the Final Argument.

In order to minimize this problem, the formal prepared text of the argument is shown in italics with the wrangling inserted in regular type.

Allen and Correia had divided the Final Argument between them. Correia went first:

Mr. Correia: *May it please the court and you members of the jury. The evidence shows here that after these officers informed these defendants they were under arrest, these defendants commenced cursing and moving around in bed. The evidence further shows that at the head of that bed was a 30/30 rifle fully loaded. It shows that there was a .32 automatic fully loaded. It shows further that these defendants, after they went to bed the second time after they had this altercation earlier in that evening, put on their shoes.*

You know that is a significant factor. People don't go to bed with their shoes on, unless they are expecting trouble. The defendants, when they went to bed that second time, were fully dressed, which shows they were prepared for any emergency, and they gave ample demonstration when they killed Fred Seaborn, Joseph Clark and Martin Lange.

The evidence shows that these officers, pursuant to a right, which as a matter of law they have, and I believe this court will instruct you, that an officer in making an arrest, if he has reasonable cause to believe that he is going to be resisted in performing his duty, can use whatever force he deems reasonable, and whatever force a man reasonably might apply, under those circumstances in performing that duty in arresting these men.

Mr. Frye: I think counsel is misstating the law, Your Honor.

The Court: Lady and gentlemen of the jury, the instructions will be read to you and you are to take your instructions from the court. Of course, the jury will understand that counsels have a right to call attention to what they feel the court will instruct, but for the law of the case, you will be governed by the instructions given by the court, and you will take the law of the case solely from the Court and not from the attorneys.

Mr. Correia: If I misstated that in any way, you will get the instructions from the court and apply it to the facts.

There is a cardinal principle of law when a prosecuting attorney puts a witness on the stand, he has to be able to vouch for his honesty and for the evidence which he is going to adduce by means of that witness. And do you, lady and gentlemen of the jury, think it possible for any prosecuting attorney, or for that matter, any other attorney to vouch for the honesty of Benjamin Franklin Decker? I imagine Benjamin Franklin would have turned over in his grave to have thought anyone like Decker should bear his name. He was a witness that had a ready explanation for every inconsistency in his testimony. He made statements several times before he came on the stand here, and each time he made some remark or other that was inconsistent with what he told you here, and each time when those remarks were called to his attention, he had a ready and facile explanation for it. He even went to the extent of telling you that when he was testifying before the grand jury and told them that the Brite boys admitted using the rifle, which was here in evidence, he was talking at the time about a rifle used for hunting deer.

Mr. Frye: There is no such testimony as that, Your Honor.

The Court: The jury will be the exclusive judges of what the testimony is. If counsel, in making the argument, should misquote the testimony, the jury will take the testimony given by the witnesses in determining what it is. The evidence, you have already heard, lady and gentlemen of the jury, and if it is misstated by counsel in any way, you are the sole judges of the evidence and you recall just what the testimony was that Decker did give here.

Mr. Frye: It was on cross examination when that question was asked him on impeachment.

Mr. Correia: And there are numerous other respects in which the character of that witness is borne out.

Mr. Correia, continuing: *But we have Decker's statement that when he went down there, both of the boys admitted to him that they shot that rifle that evening.*

Mr. Frye: That is a mistake in the testimony, Your Honor. We submit that it is not proper for counsel to misstate the testimony.

The Court: Well, as the court has stated to the jury, if counsel does misquote the testimony inadvertently or otherwise, it will be for the jury to determine for themselves what the testimony is and what the facts are. So far as the facts are concerned, you are to be governed by the testimony of the witness alone.

The above bit of friction had come upon Correia's completion of his portion of the Final Argument on behalf of the People.

Mr. Frye then presented his Final Arguments for the defendants. Inasmuch as Allen had not requested recordation, it is not available here.

[Mr. Allen now commences the Closing Argument on behalf of the People.]

Mr. Allen: *Defendants said they threw no bottle of wine. It is really not important, but it goes to corroborate other statements here. A bottle of wine was in the car. Mr. Frye floundered around trying to explain about the wine.* [The prosecutor is here referring to what Frye had said in his Closing Argument just previously which was "unreported."] *The wine was taken out of the car and was found down here, and there was an imprint in the bank where the bottle struck the bank. That is what they threw and that is what Charley Baker said they threw.*

Mr. Frye: Counsel is not stating the testimony correctly. Mr. Baker said he didn't know what they threw.

Mr. Allen: Mr. Baker said they threw something in that direction. A bottle of wine was in the car and a bottle of wine was found down there, so use your own judgment of what they threw.

Now I want to get this corroboration right. This was read into the record. I am reading here from the record, starting on page 24:

Q. Did you see any firearms there while you were there?

A. I did.

Q. Just one size, or did you see more than one size gun?

A. I did not, no. All of the different guns I saw, was the revolver that the officers had and the 30/30 it was, I think.

Of course, he explains that. He said he didn't know but what Seaborn was an officer.

[Reading again] *Q. You stated that you heard what you thought was a small gun?*

A. Yes, I know I did, and Mr. Lanning did too: we both talked about that.

He is seeking corroboration there.

[Reading again] *The shooting was only 100 yards away from us. We were both up. He was up, too.*

Q. A 30/30 is not a small gun.

Mr. Frye: That is not in the record, Your Honor.

Mr. Allen: That is in the record.

Mr. Frye: I object to this on the ground that it is not in the record.

Mr. Allen: I submit that it is in the record and I will stand on the record.

Mr. Frye: The first part that counsel quoted is in the record.

Mr. Allen: This part that I am quoting now is in the record. I will stake my reputation on it.

The Court: That is the same proposition that came up this morning; one counsel says it was in the record and the other says that it wasn't. The only way is to get the record.

Mr. Allen: (Reading) *Q. A 30/30 is not a small gun.*

A. No. They used a 30/30.

Q. Who do you mean by "they?"

A. Why, the Brite boys. They acknowledged they used that.

Mr. Allen: *Now, that is just what he told the Grand Jury. They acknowledged they used that. And he told that to Homer Burton. He tried to twist it around. That is a corroboration of what he did tell Homer Burton.*

Mr. Frye: *We submit that counsel is misquoting Mr. Decker's testimony.*

The Court: It is for the jury to determine what the testimony is, lady and gentlemen of the jury. If counsel could in the argument misquote the testimony inadvertently or otherwise, disregard the argument in that regard and be guided so far as the facts are concerned by the testimony as given by the witness.

Mr. Allen: I know whether I am telling you what is in the record or not; and if I am telling you anything that is not record, hold it against me.

The Trial Concludes

With that disclaimer, Allen's disclaimer finally whimpered to an end.

That was it. The trial was over. All that remained now was for the judge to read his instructions to the jury. After that it would be in the hands of twelve stalwart citizens of Siskiyou County to decide the fate of the Brite brothers.

But it was late Friday afternoon. The judge still had some work to do before his instructions were ready for the jury. The instructions also had to be finished up by the court reporter so that they could be handed to the jury after the judge recited them. Court was adjourned until 10:00 a.m. the next day.

When Ralph McMurry returned to his office, Charley Johnson was inside waiting. Johnson appeared to be in a high state of agitation. "Can you believe it," Johnson nearly shouted. "It can't be. No, I don't believe it."

"I'm dumbfounded," replied McMurry.

"How many pages of testimony do you have there, Ralph?"

"I think almost 800 pages counting today," answered the reporter.

"800 pages of testimony," said Charley, "with a twenty minute final argument by the prosecution. I can't believe it."

"I knew there was something unusual coming down when Judge Luttrell went right ahead and asked Allen to proceed after Frye had finished his argument," said McMurry. "I knew that the judge had a short meeting with both of them in chambers just prior to convening this afternoon. I see now that he had apparently questioned them as to how much time they were going to need for arguments. It never occurred to me that the subject of the meeting could be argument time. I had always assumed that Allen's final argument would take between a half and a full day which is usual for a case of this caliber and length."

"But how come?" asked Johnson. "I don't know how many cases I have tried against Allen and some with him. Never, never would he have made such a short and incomplete argument in any case, let alone this one, with all its political and social ramifications. How do you figure it, Ralph?"

"Well, I see only a small clue that might point to an explanation," replied the court reporter. "Let's assume that Allen decided that he had a very certain 'open and shut' case here. He felt that no jury 'anywhere' could fail to bring in a guilty verdict. But even failing in that assumption, he probably convinced himself that this was a case that no 'Siskiyou County' jury would ever bring in anything but a guilty verdict."

"I agree that was undoubtedly Allen's state of mind," remarked Charley, "but if that is the case, why not just yield, and announce that he will let the case be judged on the testimony given?"

McMurry replied, "He had two things that still needed reinforcing before he could let himself turn loose of it. The first was because of the Decker Theory. He had to implant into the minds of the jury the matter of intent to kill rather than an intention to merely 'defend' themselves. This is why he had Correia get into that lecture about how well the Brites had prepared for a murderous battle by keeping their shoes on and carefully laying out the guns before they went to bed.

"The second item that was bothering Allen was that in his mind, even though he had a preordained verdict on the way, it may turn out to be a split decision. Maybe it would be a first degree verdict for one of them and something less for the other. In an effort to head off any consideration that the officers had shot any of their pistols, Allen had made great effort to establish that only the rifle was used. To dodge this bullet, Allen went into that reading of Decker's testimony concerning the fact that he had said 'they' used the rifle; not just John, and not just Coke, but 'they' used the rifle."

Charley thought about all this for a moment. "By golly Ralph, I think you have it. That is about the only way that Allen could have ever decided to do what he did."

"Well, right or wrong, not stretching out the argument for three quarters of a day saved me one whale of amount of work," replied McMurry. "So OK, what's your prediction, Charley?"

"Well, after Frye's big goof, and Allen's possible one today, I guess that consideration is about a tie. I say 'murder one' for the two of them. What's your prediction?"

Smiling, Ralph said, "Charley, you know I never predict".

Judgment Day

The next morning, Saturday at 10:15, December 19th, the trial was called to order.

The Court: We took a few minutes longer than expected to get these instructions numbered up and put together.

As far as Court Reporter Ralph McMurry was concerned, this was the understatement of the year. He had been working far into the night in order to get the instructions "numbered up" and typed. He had returned to the courthouse at eight this morning in order to obtain the last of them from the judge to be incorporated into the list for reading in court. "These instructions" to which the judge had referred were, of course, the Instructions to the Jury which he was about to read aloud.

The general public to this day is hardly aware of the importance of these instructions. In modern movies and TV dramas, the Instructions to the Jury contain little excitement and are seldom included or even referred to in these productions. But notwithstanding, they are a vital part of the case, and very often the outcome hinges upon which of the instructions are presented and whether or not the jury ultimately abides by them. Additionally, if the verdict is later appealed, many an upper court decision hinges upon whether or not the proper instructions were included or omitted as well as whether or not improper instructions were employed.

The procedures involving these instructions during a case are as follows: Both the prosecution and the defense have the right at the end of the trial to submit a list of instructions to the judge. In the meantime, the judge will have been making notes or actually assembling pertinent instructions that he intends to issue. These instructions are not made up or created by the lawyers or the judge. They consist of selections made by the judge and the two contending lawyers from the vast store of legal records of prior cases in which certain laws were previously applied.

The source records for this are prior cases or merely legally applicable statutes that have been passed and are on the books; most frequently, they are combinations thereof.

After the testimony in any case, the opposing lawyers hand in their suggested lists to the judge for his consideration as to whether or not he will use them. He makes his selection and tunes his own list up by adding some, but never all of them, to his list. Then on the last day of the trial the whole thing is dumped upon the court reporter for typing. In this case, the judge's final list consisted of forty-two separate instructions which required thirty-two pages of double spaced typing. Needless to say, Ralph McMurry was already tired this day even before the formal proceedings got under way.

The list given the judge by the prosecution contained thirty-eight suggested instructions.

The box score for these was as follows:

> Used by judge: 9
> Used by judge, but modified: 1
> Refused because already on judge's list: 9
> Rejected: 19

The defense submitted sixteen suggestions. The box score for these was as follows:

> Used by judge: 5
> Refused because already on judge's list: 6
> Rejected: 5

Examples of some of the instructions accepted by the judge that had been submitted by the prosecution are:

1. The court instructs the jury that if mental unconsciousness of the defendants at the time of the alleged offense, from any cause, is relied upon as a defense, the burden is upon the defendants to establish such mental unconsciousness by affirmative proof.

2. The flight of a person immediately after the commission of a crime, or after he is accused of a crime that has been committed, is not sufficient in itself to establish his guilt, but is a fact which, if proved, the jury may consider in deciding his guilt or innocence. The weight to which such circumstance is entitled is a matter for the jury to determine.

3. The court instructs that a police officer making an arrest has the right to use all the force which from the surrounding circumstances seem to him as a reasonable man, is necessary. Where the offense charged is a felony, he has a right if apparently necessary to a reasonable man, to kill the person whom he is seeking to arrest.

Examples of two instructions submitted by the defense and accepted by the judge speak right to the heart of Frye's defense:

1. The court instructs the jury that a person cannot be convicted of a crime committed by him without his being conscious thereof. Accordingly, in this case, if you find and believe from the evidence that the defendant, John Brite, alone, fired all of the shots resulting in the death of the deceased, and if you further find that the other defendant, Coke Brite, did not in any way aid or abet in the slaying of the said deceased, or any of them, and if you further find that at the time of the said affray the said defendant, John Brite, was not conscious of his acts by reason of having been struck by a billy or other weapon in the hands of the deceased, or any of them, under those circumstances, you must acquit both of the defendants.

2. The court instructs the jury that even though the defendants, at the time and place here in question, were subject to arrest by the officers and those acting in concert with them, the defendants nevertheless had a right to protect themselves from any unwarranted attack, if any, made upon them by the officers. The law is that every person has a right to resist an unlawful attack upon his person, whether that attack is made by a private citizen or an officer of the law, and the degree of force one may use in resisting such an attack, whether by a private citizen or by a police officer, is governed by the

force and danger of the attack. One unlawfully attacked in such manner as to reasonably appear to endanger his life or limb, may resist even to the extent of taking the life of his assailant if that to him appears reasonably necessary. Accordingly, if you find and believe from the evidence in this case that the officers and those acting in concert with them, did make an unlawful attack upon the defendants and that the attack was such as to make it appear to a reasonable person placed in the position of the defendants, that they were in immediate and imminent danger of losing their lives or receiving great bodily harm, or, if you have a reasonable doubt whether or not such a condition then confronted the defendants, you should give the defendants the benefit of the doubt, and return a verdict of not guilty.

Upon completion of the reading of the instructions, the clerk of the court was instructed to file them with the jury. The judge then asked Deputy Sheriff Mathews to come forward.

The Court: Now, the jury may retire in charge of the officers.

It was 11:20 a.m. The jury filed out to the deliberation room. The courtroom slowly emptied.

A group gathered for a short time in the court reporter's office but there was really nothing much more to discuss. In short order, McMurry found himself alone in the room. He was completely exhausted. He leaned back in this swivel chair and gazed up at the ceiling. He promptly fell asleep for several hours. About 5:30 he went home after leaving instructions with the court clerk as to where he would be.

The Verdict

About 7:45, the phone rang. The jury was coming in. At 8:12 the court was convened.

The Sheriff: Your Honor, the jury has reached a verdict.

The Court: Bring the jury in, Mr. Sheriff.

[The jury here comes into the court.]

The Court: Call the list of jurors, Mr. Clerk.

[The clerk calls the list of jurors.]

The Clerk: The jurors are all present, Your Honor.

The Court: Lady and gentlemen of the jury, have you agreed upon a verdict?

The Foreman: We have, Your Honor [whereupon the Court receives the verdict of the jury].

The judge had given extensive instructions to the jury as to how to fill out the verdict form sheet. The foreman had laboriously written it out in scrawled handwriting with a pencil:

"We find both defendants murdered Martin Lange, Joseph Clark and Fred Seaborn and are guilty of murder in the first degree."

The Court: The court will fix Tuesday, December 22nd, 1936 at 10:00 o'clock in the forenoon, as the time for pronouncing judgment in each of the three separate counts in the indictment [whereupon the Court thanks and discharges the jury].

The Court: I am going to ask the audience, as the sheriff passes through with the prisoners, not to express or manifest any approval or disapproval of the verdict.

The Sentence

On the 22nd it was short and quick. Judge Luttrell sentenced each of the brothers to be "hanged by the neck until you are dead."

This came as no surprise to anyone present, including the defendants or their counsel.

Mr. Frye notified the judge that he was filing an appeal.

The judge remanded the prisoners to the sheriff and ordered that they be delivered to the warden at Folsom Prison pending the outcome of the appeal.

The murders had been committed three months and twenty-two days before the sentencing. The defendants had been in custody three months and one day before the verdict had been rendered.

There had been some talk about a lynching; there had possibly been some preparatory action toward a lynching. But there was no lynching. This time, Siskiyou County had done its duty. The speed and dispatch with which this duty had been performed would be unheard of in the legal environment of fifty years later.

The subject of lynching in any subsequent case in Siskiyou County has never arisen again.

7

It's Not Over Yet:
The Aftermath

Sheriff Chandler with two of his deputies delivered the Brite brothers to Warden Larkin at Folsom Prison on Christmas Eve, 1936. The warden, in a rather macabre statement, reported that the "boys seemed cheerful" as they were placed on Death Row; they were the only occupants thereof.

Immediately after the trial the indomitable Mrs. Brite stirred up a new controversy. Because of it, she suffered a considerable amount of criticism from the general public.

During the manhunt the county Board of Supervisors had announced a $1,000 reward for capture of the Brite brothers. Henry Pallage had filed for $500 of it. His claim was based on the grounds that he had been instrumental in setting up the "capture" and it was only through a mixup in arrangements beyond his control that he was not the one to bring them in.

Anyone that was conversant with the legalities of the claim knew that in no way was Pallage eligible. For one thing, he was on the sheriff's payroll at the time that he was rendering these services.

The public was not aware at first that Mrs. Brite had filed a claim for the whole $1000. When Pallage's claim became known, Mrs. Brite got busy.

In the February 10th, 1937 issue of the *Yreka Journal*, the following article appeared on the front page:

MRS. BRITE SAYS PALLAGE
REWARD CLAIM IS FALSE

Through her attorneys today, Mrs. A. J. Brite, mother of John and Coke Brite, convicted slayers of Martin Lange, Joe Clark and Captain Seaborn, branded the claim of $500 reward, filed by Henry Pallage, Oak Knoll fire guard and Deputy Sheriff, as false. Through her attorneys she stated that Pallage was employed by the Sheriff's Office during the manhunt for the two Brite boys.

He received for his compensation during that period $4 per day. According to a version of law given her by her counsel, Pallage was ineligible for the reward in that he was employed and paid as a Deputy Sheriff. Secondly, he did not influence her in urging her boys to give up.

She further stated that Pallage did appear at the Brite home on Horse Creek during the manhunt and attempted to talk her into having the boys surrender to the sheriff. She stated that if she had followed his advice the boys would have been lodged in Yreka in the county jail and that the possibility of bodily harm in this event was uppermost in her mind.

She also stated that the surrender to the district attorney was only made on the stipulation that the boys be immediately taken

After the trial was over and the sentencing done, John and Coke Brite were booked into Folsom Prison on Christmas Eve, 1936. They had been given death sentences but their mother still refused to give up hope.

out of the county and to safe keeping at some distant point.

Mrs. Brite has filed a claim for $1,000 with the county and action on the reward by the Supervisors has twice been laid over. Attorneys for Mrs. Brite state that action of a probable suit may be taken shortly after the next meeting of the Board of Supervisors unless some definite action is taken by that body.

With the matter fully out in the open now, the County Board of Supervisors asked the district attorney for a ruling on the matter. Inasmuch as District Attorney Davis was the man with whom Mrs. Brite had negotiated the surrender, he knew that a ruling either way he went would result in a howl of controversy. He therefore, in turn, asked the California Attorney General for a ruling.

Attorney General Webb's ruling was that Ms. Brite "is entitled to the $1,000 reward for surrendering her sons." But even he apparently felt some of the heat from both factions in the Siskiyou community. He thereupon passed the buck back to Davis by adding the words, "providing it is approved by District Attorney Davis." Webb then went on to say that the "reward money may properly be considered by the county as necessary expenses of the case."

Davis, of course, lost no time in conveying his recommendation to the Board of Supervisors that the money be paid.

At the end of the *Yreka Journal*'s coverage of the matter, the following was reported:

Several citizens of Yreka expressed themselves as amazed at the decision of Webb. It is understood that a representative body will be present at the next meeting of the Supervisors to forestall action on the Brite reward.

As usual, it was reported that former District Attorney Johnson got off his expectable laconic quip concerning the matter:

"I believe," he said, "that Horace J. Frye will be very pleased to hear that the Brite family is coming into some money in order to pay certain bills."

Court Reporter Ralph McMurry's youngest son, a high school sophomore, had been hearing a lot of talk on both sides of the reward controversy. He had been diligently reading all that both the *Yreka Journal* and the *Siskiyou News* had been printing on the matter. He finally asked his father about it.

The father was somewhat bemused that the boy should ask. Instead of an immediate answer, he responded with a question, "I have noticed that you have been taking quite an interest in this particular matter. I have seen you reading everything you could concerning it; you probably know as much about it as anyone in the whole community. Why do you ask?"

"Well, it just seemed to me like that Mrs. Brite is really pushy," the boy said. "Sure, I know that she is really the one that was responsible for the Brites giving themselves up. But after all she's also guilty of hiding them from the law. It looks like now she is going to get the money and that seems screwy to me. Is that fair?"

"No, it is not fair," replied the father. "I also agree with you that it is 'screwy."

"Well, then how can that be legal for her to get that money?"

"That's a very good question," said the court reporter. "I'm not sure at all it is completely legal, but it may be. You must realize that when laws are created it is a process in which the 'creators' try to anticipate a situation and make a law that governs it. Then in real life when something happens that seems to be like the situation upon which the lawmakers acted when they made the law, it never seems to exactly fit. That is why the application of laws often causes a controversy and frequently results in an erroneous outcome. That may be the case here. I know this is pretty heavy stuff for you, but I'll try to keep it simple.

"Obviously it costs money to conduct the whole law enforcement effort of each level of government. In other words, the government, the county in this case, must spend money to enforce the laws. You know the Attorney General advised the Board of Supervisors that they could consider this money as a 'necessary expense of the case.'"

The boy didn't seem too confused yet, so the father continued.

"Attorney General Webb knows how controversial this case is. So he dropped that little piece of advice about considering it normal county costs into his recommendation so that the Board of Supervisors could legally allow it. The point here is that it is pretty far fetched to consider that type of expenditure a proper and legal use of government money. He is probably stretching a point in ruling it legal, but it would also be very hard to make a case that it is not."

Now the boy was perplexed.

"Save Them Boys"

"Why does the Attorney General care one way or the other about the whole thing?" asked the boy. "It seems to me that if there was any doubt about its legality, he wouldn't have mentioned it."

"Now we are getting to the core of the whole matter," replied the father. "And that gets Mrs. Brite back into this discussion where she should be. Mrs. Brite isn't going to get that money. The lawyers are going to get that money. The Brites obviously have no money; no money at all. I would venture to say that Horace J. Frye so far has not received one cent for his services in this case. I feel that Mr. Frye took this case because of the notoriety of it even though he never expected to collect anything. There is nothing wrong with that. In fact, the kind of thing that he did enables a lot of poor people to obtain superior legal help that they would never otherwise receive."

Mr. McMurry hesitated a moment to gauge whether or not he was holding the boys interest. He was.

"So that brings us back around to Attorney General Webb. He is a lawyer; Mr. Frye is a lawyer. Lawyers look after each other. The little matter of the reward money being given to Mrs. Brite so that it can be paid over to the defense counsel is probably legal. Therefore Webb encourages it by adding that last sentence in his ruling. Here again, I want to emphasize that this amount won't even make a dent in what Horace Frye's expenses were in the case, not even counting what he will still be spending during the appeal."

The boy had a pensive look on his face and the father waited for him to speak.

"I see what you mean when you said that isn't fair," the boy said. "Mrs. Brite doesn't get the money but she takes all the flack. That isn't the way I looked at it when I said it wasn't fair. I was against her on it but not any more."

The father smiled when he heard this.

"I'm glad you agree with me on it," he said. "We have been talking here quite awhile but we are now finally around to the point that I wanted to discuss with you when you opened up the matter. I want to talk some about Mrs. Brite."

With a surprised look, the boy said, "She sure comes on strong. A lot of the kids' parents are really mad at her."

"I know that," replied the father. "That is what I want to talk to you about. The thing that her two sons did was a terrible thing. This latest thing about the reward is very minor. I've noticed the public attitude toward her ever since the case broke. From the beginning, the people equated these horrible murders with her because she was the only visible character in the drama.

"As you say, she comes on strong. That's her nature; but it runs deeper. Let's take a look at these Brites in order to see what makes her go.

"As you know, the country is now in the throes of the worst depression that we have ever experienced. Many people are down to their bottom dollar and have practically no means of existence. Of course others who have an education and a job are getting by. But even with them, and this includes us, times are tough.

"As a result of the economic conditions, sometimes whole families have hit the bottom, lost all their worldly goods, and in desperation, 'hit the road.' They have moved on; searching, seeking some place where they can get work and get their lives put back together again. You are familiar with the term 'Okie,' I'm sure. The Okies are the kind of people that I have described that came from Oklahoma to California. Well, the Brites are just the same as the Okies only they didn't come from Oklahoma. They came from somewhere else, but they are typical nonetheless.

"Now here we have this Brite family. They drift to Arizona, then to Oregon. Finally they land here in Siskiyou County, living up on a very steep mountainside above Horse Creek in an old miner's cabin. They try mining up there; you can imagine how successful that was. Two big sons and the Ma and Pa; those two sons are kind of wild; the father never seems to say much. But they are getting by, somehow. Well, something up there on that hillside is running things so that they can exist. And you guessed it; it is that scraggly old woman, Ma Brite."

"You know, Son, Sheriff Chandler saw it right away, right from the beginning on the morning after the murders when he went up there to the Brite's cabin. He told me that after talking a few minutes with her that she was the 'chief honcho' in that camp and that she was the key to any effort on his part to catch up with those two boys.

"Then when all the publicity started she suddenly became highly visible to literally the whole world. She knew very well what a terrible crime her sons had committed. But that didn't slow her down one bit. She was the head of that family in every sense of the word. Not her husband, Archie; she was it, and she well knew that if those boys of hers were going to survive this awful thing they did, she had to be the one to do it for them. She just buckled up and pitched in so she could 'save them boys.' She was here, there and everywhere in all those weeks that followed. And all of it was fueled by the fact that no matter what, she was out to 'save them boys.'

"Now the wheels of justice have turned and those two boys appear to be doomed. But does that stop her? No, not one bit. She will persist in what she is trying to do. And she will not quit until she either wins or loses. It is a powerful driving force that makes her go.

"What is this all-consuming driving force that propels her? I'll tell you what it is. It's her sense of family. A legal and fair court of the land has brand-ed those boys as murderers, but something far more powerful than that is keeping her going in their behalf. Those boys, good or bad, are 'family.' Be-cause they are family, it has never occurred to her to abandon, slow down or give up on 'them boys.'

"Yes, Son, I admire that woman. Some might call her 'white trash' or other mean names, but by golly I respect her without reservation in spite of what has happened in her family. We can all learn a lesson from her."

The boy had been rapturously listening to his father. He remained very quiet for a considerable spell before speaking.

"I understand what you are telling me. You are right, this is heavy stuff. I'll never be able to convince any of the gang at school to look at it this way."

"I know you won't; the reason you won't is because their parents have not thought it out and consequently openly criticize her. But the reason that I am telling you all this is that some day you will be the head of your own family. When that time comes, you will do well to remember that little old hillbilly lady that lived up there on the mountainside above 'hard scrabble creek.' She knew what 'family' was all about."

The Reward Money; the Appeal

Four months later in May, 1937 the matter of the reward money was still kicking around the courthouse without the Supervisors having taken action on it. Then Frye filed a "petition for a writ of mandamus" in the Third District Court of Appeals seeking to force the Siskiyou County Board of Supervisors to pay the claim. At that point the record is lost as to whether or not it was ever paid.

Frye had filed the appeal of the Brite case with the California Supreme Court in May. On November 9th, 1937 the court's decision was issued. The State Supreme Court Decision was very colorfully written by Justice Sewell. In his description of the events of the evening of the crime, he went so far as to reintroduce one of our old friends in the case:

"They went back to bed with their shoes on and were next awakened out of their sleep by the hooting of an owl from a nearby tree. John took a .32 automatic pistol from under the head of the bed and shot in the direction of the tree from which the hoots emanated. The ancient solitary bird's reign having been thus molested, it flew from its secret bower and the defendants again fell asleep."

They affirmed the judgement and sentence of the lower court and denied a rehearing of the case.

The *Yreka Journal* printed this article following the judgement:

MRS. BRITE TAKES VIGIL AT FOLSOM

Would Camp on Highway to Be Near Boys

Mrs. Margaret Brite is here looking for work. She said she would camp on the highway near Folsom Prison, "before she would leave her boys," John and Coke Brite, who were sentenced to hang for slaying three men last year on Horse Creek."

Robert Houston, one of the attorneys for John and Coke, said he would ask Governor Merriam to commute the death sentence to life imprisonment..."

The action of the State Supreme Court now required that the Brites be resentenced. Judge C. J. Luttrell had anticipated this and he was ready. Under date of November 15th, six days later, the local superior court filed a thirty-seven page Warrant of Execution that set the date for the hanging of the Brite Brothers for January 21, 1938.

On December 3rd the Associated Press came out with the following story that was featured the next day in the *Yreka Journal* under one inch high headlines:

BRITE ATTORNEYS ORGANIZE CITIZENS DEFENSE COMMITTEE FOR SAVING KILLERS

A Brite brothers' defense committee is being formed by their attorneys to raise funds to keep up the fight to save John and Coke Brite from execution.

From a local point of view, hardly anyone in Siskiyou County ever heard of this defense committee, either then or later. It was generally attributed to a move on the part of the lawyers to get some publicity in anticipation of what they were getting ready to do. And they had not been idle.

It landed in Yreka on December 22nd in the form of another AP wire service story featured in the Yreka papers. The article in the *Journal* follows:

BRITES MAY ESCAPE NOOSE

WOULD BLACKEN ARRESTING OFFICER'S RECORD

AFFIDAVIT CLAIMS JOE CLARK INTOXICATED AT TIME OF ARREST

Two Trial Witnesses State They Question Credibility of One Trial Witness in Case and Now Doubt Justice of Death Sentence

Affidavit Asserts That Deputy Sheriff Clark Was Drunk on the Night of the Killing

Governor Merriam automatically referred to the Advisory Pardon Board today the application of John and Coke Brite for commutation of the death sentences to life imprisonment. This is in accordance with an amendment relating to prisoners with prior convictions passed by the last Legislature.

The pardon board meets Thursday. If the Board makes favorable recommendation, the applications then go to the State Supreme Court. If a majority of the justices recommend clemency, the Governor is empowered to grant it or he can refuse to do so.

Petitions from several hundred residents, chiefly from Northern California, accompanied the application. They requested a commutation, based on the plea of extenuating circumstances in connection with the killing of the two arresting officers and a civilian near Horse Creek.

Affidavits of two jurors, E. E. Deyamire and Charles Hoffman, state they question the credibility of one trial witness and they now doubt the justice of a death sentence. Both recommended a commutation to life sentences.

An affidavit by David Lawe asserts that on the night of the killings, a few hours before Deputy Sheriff Clark went to Horse

Creek to arrest the Brites, Clark was drunk. Lawe stated that he went in search of Clark to get him to stop a threatened street fight, but found the deputy not in a condition to perform his duty.

An affidavit by George Barandun said he and Clark had some drinks together at Yreka and shortly before Clark was to leave "to arrest a couple of punks" he was "slightly intoxicated." Barandun asserted he had tried to dissuade Clark from "making an arrest in his condition but Joseph Clark insisted that he was going to go."

Barandun said he had remained silent regarding the information in the affidavit because he was a friend of Clark and did not think the Brites would be convicted on the existing evidence.

Attorney Horace F. Fry said he held evidence disproving premeditation on the part of the Brites. He said a physician's affidavit declares that Coke Brite suffered a skull fracture at Horse Creek on August 30th and this indicated provocation. He said he based his appeal also on affidavits from two jurors, who now felt doubts as to the Brites having premeditated the killings.

After Frye's application for clemency had been received by the governor, it was routinely referred to the Advisory Pardon Board. The board then set a hearing for February 10, 1938 in Sacramento. This scheduling now became a target date toward which many various players and factions took aim.

The New Year's Day issue of the *Yreka Journal* led off with the following:

STATE INVESTIGATING BRITE CASE

THOROUGH & IMPARTIAL STUDY TO BE UNDERTAKEN

Chief Criminologist Has Agents in Yreka Checking on Brite Case

Every Angle Is Being Studied -- Petition To Be Checked

Harvey Hickok, Harold Gillett and William Slattery have been appointed by C. S. Morell, State Chief Criminologist, to make an impartial investigation of the Brite case.

Hickok states, "We have just arrived in Yreka and have as yet made no contacts. I fully believe that we will have some definite information for the press within the next 48 hours."

Siskiyou County's fighting District Attorney, James Davis, stated, "I have not been contacted by Hickok, and had no information that such an investigation would be made. I will devote the entire facilities of my office to these men."

On January 5th, the *Journal* followed up with another article:

INVESTIGATORS TO VIEW SCENE OF KILLING

WITNESSES and CITIZENS OF HORSE CREEK NOW TO BE INTERVIEWED

Investigators from Office of State Criminologist State Some Time Yet Required To Complete Analysis

Harvey Hickok and Harold Gillett, special investigators from the Office of C. S. Morrell, State Chief Criminologist, will leave today or early tomorrow morning to visit the scene of the Brite murders on Horse Creek. Hickok states that they will interview a number of the witnesses and others along Horse Creek who may be able to throw some light on the case.

Since arriving in Yreka last Friday, a great many local citizens and witnesses have been interviewed by Hickok and Gillett who are attempting to make an entirely impartial investigation of circumstances prior to and after the murders of officers Joe Clark, Martin Lange and Captain Fred Seaborn.

District Attorney James Davis, Prosecuting Attorneys James M. Allen and Joe Correia have all given their version of the case as well as assistant defense attorney Everett Barr.

Superior Judge Luttrell has not yet been contacted.

Hickok states that their investigations to date have been completed by their shorthand reporter, William Slattery, and reports will be in form for presentation on their return to Sacramento.

By the time that the state criminology investigators returned to Sacramento, The Brite brothers' date with the gallows was fast approaching; at this point it was but days away. Consequently, the Advisory Board people quickly requested a postponement from the Governor. He responded by granting a reprieve from the January 21st date to April 15th. Thus the Brite brothers, as the *Yreka Journal* put it, "had the immediate shadow of the gallows removed so that a study of the information compiled by the state criminologists may be studied to give the Prison Board and Governor Merriam a clear conception of the case."

In the meantime, Horace J. Frye, along with another individual had also been busy. It seemed that the Brite family had at one time lived in Cimarron County, Oklahoma, which is contiguous with Union County, New Mexico. Frye presented to the Advisory Board and the Governor a petition urging clemency for the Brites signed by sixty-five residents of Union County, New Mexico.

It did not require a detective to figure out who the "other individual" was. The peripatetic Ma Brite, of course, had achieved this small miracle.

Both Sheriff Chandler and Senator Allen were in attendance at the hearing on the 10th. But it was none other than District Attorney James Davis who dominated the proceedings. Davis presented an hour and a half argument, closing with the statement that "there is ample mitigation to warrant commutation."

At the end of the hearing, the Advisory Board stated that it would be a considerable time, possibly a matter of some months, before their recommendation would be submitted to the governor. After that, probably more time would be consumed before a resolution of the case would be achieved.

So the Yrekans came home to wait it out. But Davis came home ready for a fight that he knew would be awaiting him as a result of his presentation at the board hearing. But he had figured this in advance. He was well armed.

The *Siskiyou News* in its issue of February 14th featured an article as follows:

DAVIS GIVES REASON FOR BRITE PLEA

FORMAL STATEMENT TO BE ISSUED EXPLAINING PLEA FOR COMMUTATION

District Attorney James Davis, who returned the end of the week from Sacramento where he appeared before the Advisory

Pardon Board to recommend commutation of the death sentences of John and Coke Brite, triple slayers, to life imprisonment, today said he did so because he felt the true story of the killing had not yet been told.

"Charles Baker has told four different stories regarding the killing of these men," he said. "And I am convinced the officers were baited by Baker into the melee which cost their lives."

Davis said that shortly after the shooting Baker told him an account of the killings which tended to show that the Brites thought they were acting in self defense. "That was the time I made the statement that the evidence pointed to only manslaughter charges," he said.

"I was trying to get this story out of Baker at the coroner's Inquest when the hooting of the crowd interrupted and made it virtually impossible to bring out the story as formerly told by Baker."

Davis said today he was preparing a formal statement which would be given to the press within the next few days to explain his stand in the matter."

Locally, Davis has been severely criticized for intervening in the case at this time. Senator James M. Allen, who also spoke at the Sacramento hearing, told the board that "if Davis possessed any information favorable to the defendants, he should have made it known long before this." Allen contended that the Brites anticipated the coming of the officers and shot them down. He pointed out that the bullet wounds and severe beatings administered to the victims clearly showed the savagery of the Brites....

Davis' Long-winded Side of the Story

Three days later Davis was ready with his detailed explanation of his position. It was carried in the newspapers far and wide generally as follows:

DAVIS EXPLAINS ATTEMPT TO SAVE BRITE BROTHERS

STATEMENT ISSUED BY DISTRICT ATTORNEY REGARDING PLEA MADE FOR SISKIYOU COUNTY TRIPLE SLAYERS

The public is entitled to know the views I hold in the case of the Brite brothers who are now condemned to die after conviction of first degree murder in Siskiyou County. The public is entitled to know why I, as District Attorney of Siskiyou County, recommended a commutation of sentence for these brothers from death to life imprisonment.

I make this statement in the light of unjust criticism directed at me by certain elements, particularly in the town of Yreka. I would not take the time to make this statement merely to offset this criticism mainly arising out of the local element who thought they would put me out of office between the time of the slaying and the delivery of these brothers to Folsom Penitentiary by Dr. Harris and myself on September 16th, 1936. This type of criticism I deem malicious and actuated by political motives. I hold only contempt for this because those behind this political intrigue, those behind the threats made against my life, those behind the vicious statements made against me in 1936 over this case, are not even worthy of consideration.

This same element, mostly localized in the town of Yreka, I know did not leave a stone unturned to get me out of the way politically. But be it remembered that this clique does not speak for Siskiyou County. By now the people of Siskiyou County know me well enough to realize that any stand I take must be based upon some thorough reasoning. It is out of regard for those people and particularly out of regard for those who were induced by misrepresentation and falsification to take a position against me in 1936, that I want to clarify my position. I want it clearly understood that I have absolutely no apologies to make.

At the outset, the public must know that the state's witness, Baker, told four official stories about the case. I questioned him in the presence of the witness, Decker, in another room of the Barton store at Horse Creek on the day of the killing. The sum total of his statement in the presence of Mr. Decker, when questioned by me, was that the attack of the officers in which they broke some of the weapons used, was launched as these men lay asleep in their beds. It is true that he testified that officer Lange had said substantially, "Hello boys. We are officers and you are under arrest." But he offered no evidence at that time that showed either of the Brite brothers heard the officers warning or heard anyone speak at all because they remained under the covers and did not answer. Officer Clark stepped ahead of the others and threw back the bed covers. Officer Lange went up beside the bed and hit John Brite over the head with his billy. Then Officer Clark hit Coke Brite first on the side of the head and later, as Baker expressed it in the Barton store, he "beefed him between the eyes" with a billy.

Later on, and this is the crux of the whole case, Baker testified before the coroner's jury in Yreka.

Davis Rehashes the Coroner's Jury Testimony

Remember, I had questioned him in Barton's [Horse Creek] store on August 30th. On September 2nd before the coroner's jury, some three days later, he practically corroborated what he had told me in the Barton Store as shown in the following questions and answers of record, Page. 26, Line 30:

Q. All right. Now, I will ask you: You said what, "There they are?"

A. "There they are."

Q. What did Captain Seaborn say?

A. He didn't say anything.

Q. Who spoke next?

A. Mr. Lange.

Q. All right.

A. "Hello boys!"

Q. He says, "Hello boys!?"

A. "Hello boys!"

Q. Did you see any stir under the blankets when he said "Hello boys?"

A. Yes, they kind of stirred under the blanket. He said, "We are officers."

These questions and answers definitely show the position of the Brite brothers in bed and all that happened in response to what the officer had said. Now I quote from the coroner's transcript, Page 28 commencing at Line 14 to Line 15 on Page 31:

Q. Then, you came up there and spoke and you said, "Here they are" to the officers, did you?

A. Yes, sir.

Q. When you said "Here they are" to the officers, Officer Lange spoke next?

A. Yes sir.

Q. And he said "Hello boys!" did he?

A. Yes sir.

Q. When he said "Hello boys!" what did he do then?

A. He stepped right up, right up there hasty like.

Q. He stepped up beside the bed?

A. Yes sir.

Q. And these two men were on their backs covered up?

A. Yes sir.

Q. And the blankets were over their heads covered up?

A. Yes sir.

Q. Then Officer Lange stepped to that side, did he?

A. Yes sir.

Q. After he stepped to that position and said "Hello boys!" did he say anything else?

A. He said, "We are officers." Mr. Clark stepped right where I was at.

Q. Then Officer Clark stepped right up alongside of you?

A. Right between me and Mr. Lange. Mr. Lange stepped up hasty like when he said "We are officers," and Mr. Clark taken his place.

Here, Davis continues his questioning for a considerable amount of time that only involved which was the right hand and which was the left hand of the bed relative to where each was then standing. After this is settled, he goes on:

Q. Now, Officer Lange said, "We are officers?"

A. Yes sir.

Q. Did he then make the statement, "You are under arrest?"

A. "You are under arrest."

Q. Still these boys were under the covers?

A. Yes sir.

Q. Then what did Officer Lange do?

No answer.

Q. Now, where did Mr. Clark stay, in front of you?

A. Yes sir, right in front of me. Officer Lange walked up there when he says, "Hello boys!," he just made another step and Clark stepped right in here between me and Lange. And he says, "We are officers; you are under arrest." Mr. Clark reached over and pulled the blanket out.

Q. Did he reach over with his right hand or his left hand?

A. I don't know. He had the search light in one hand. He pulled the blanket back. He jerked the blanket right off their faces.

Q. He jerked the blanket right off of their faces?

A. Yes sir.

Q. Did they try to grab for the cover in any way? Did they grab those covers in any way?

A. Well, I won't say that they did; don't know.

Q. Well, just after that, the next thing that happened? Who went into action next?

A. Mr. Lange reached over and hit John with the billy.

Q. That is your story. Mr. Lange reached over and hit which one, John or Coke?

A. Coke. John raised his head up. He was cursing. He told Mr. Clark, "There was no son of a bitch of an officer could arrest us."

Q. All right. Now, after Officer Lange struck this blow, struck the man who was lying in the bed, what did Officer Clark do?

A. Coke then raised up like and Clark reached over.

Q. Officer Clark then struck Coke?

A. Coke.

Q. What did he hit him with?

A. Hit him with a billy, or black jack, or something of the kind.

Q. You were how many feet of where those officers were doing this?

A. Well, I was anywhere from two to three feet.

Q. Anywhere from two to three feet. Where was Mr. Seaborn?

A. Seaborn was standing right behind me, looking over my shoulder.

Q. You saw Officer Lange strike?

A. Yes sir.

Q. Did you see Officer Lange strike a second blow?

A. Yes sir.

Q. And a third blow?

A. He had a handcuff then.

Q. He then tried to get the handcuff on him, is that right?

A. Yes sir.

Q. What was Officer Clark doing all of that time?

A. He was trying to make Coke behave.

Q. What method was he using to make Coke behave?

A. Hitting him with the billy two or three times.

Q. Hitting him with the billy?

A. Yes sir.

Q. What were you doing, standing there?

A. I was standing there looking on.

The Thin Line of the Law

[Davis' statement continues]

You will note that John Brite uttered his first statement after he had been struck, and not before.

This fixes assault before resistance. There can be no resisting of arrest unless the party sought to be arrested is aware of what is being done. The Grand Jury and trial versions fix resistance before assault. This represents the thin line of law between murder and self-defense.

The public will note from this piece of transcript not one iota of evidence exists showing premeditation. As a lawyer, as a woodsman and as a matter of constitutional right, I will say that any man living would have reacted just exactly the same way the Brite brothers reacted. Their reaction was normal and nothing else.

It therefore follows that I acted after the coroner's inquest entirely upon the truth of Baker's statement in the Barton store and of his recorded statement before the coroner's jury. I had absolutely no fear of any two men, however many had been killed, who reacted normally under such circumstances because my reaction under the same circumstances would have been exactly the same. That is why I offered to meet these men in the woods unarmed and to act as their escort in surrendering to the law. I had told Baker in the Barton [Horse Creek] store in the presence of Mr. Decker that this evidence tended to exonerate rather than to convict the Brite brothers.

From September 2nd to November 4th, the date of the Grand Jury session in this case, I never saw or talked to Baker. In the meantime, between September 2nd and September 16th, when Dr. Harris and I delivered the Brite brothers to Folsom penitentiary, a recall petition was launched against me, my life was threatened, and I was told that I was set for political annihilation.

Lo and behold, when Mr. Baker appeared before the Grand Jury on November 4th, the missing elements that existed in the first two stories were all there so that the Grand Jury couldn't do anything except act upon his testimony and return an indictment. Now the question is, would Baker suddenly remember in that period of sixty days certain evidence necessary to convict the Brite brothers of murder or would someone remind him what was necessary and arrange for its telling? Right here I want the public to understand that Senator Allen never took this case as Special Prosecutor until after the indictment. He and Mr. Correia presented the kind of a case Mr. Baker offered. They had to go with what Mr. Baker offered after the time he testified at the Grand Jury session. As prosecutors, they had to present the case as he offered it and the defense had the right to impeach him with the coroner's transcript. The jury that tried him under the law was guided by the evidence offered and the evidence offered showed murder had been committed, hence they could only return a verdict accordingly.

When Mr. Allen took the case it was understood specifically that he have complete charge and control! He never asked me a single thing about it because it was unnecessary. The defense could not call me however many subpoenas they might have had, because facts learned by a district attorney in the performance of his duty are not admissible over the objection of the state, although practically all of the time of the trial I was present in my office and could have been called at any time by either party. I was not necessary to the defense, however, because the coroner's transcript was a record which the defense could use, and did use without avail.

Now suppose that Baker had told me in the Barton store or at the Coroner's inquest the same story that he told the Grand Jury and that he told to the trial jurors. Had he told me these stories in those two places, or either of them picturing the men as vicious murderers, I would have been guided by them in my subsequent actions. In the face of these last two stories, who in Siskiyou County can be led to believe that I would have been d_____ fool enough to meet such men in the forest, unarmed, take with me my closest friend and father of three half orphan children, and ride all through the night to Folsom Penitentiary knowing that these men could kill us both, take our car, what money we had, and be on their way to some foreign country. Nothing could be more ridiculous.

On the contrary, I believed and acted upon the first two stories and judged these men by what they had done as told by Baker in the first two stories, not the third version because it had not yet been told. I figured those boys to be harmless. I met these men as agreed with their mother, wholly unarmed, without hand cuffs, and with no method of protection whatever in hauling them to Folsom. All through the night these men rode practically all of the way in the back seat of the car. I never entertained one bit of fear nor did these brothers ever threaten us in the least. They rode as any normal person would ride, in utter friendliness; all this in the face of having slain three men.

The mutilation of the bodies of the slain men did not influence me because the mutilation could have only taken place after the fight in which these brothers had been beaten. Only medical experts could testify as to their probable state of mind which clearly indicated abnormality after such beating.

It is the duty of a district attorney to be guided by this analysis of the truth or falsity of evidence as he finds it. His business is to seek out the truth, subject always to human error and be guided by that truth as he sees it wherever it may point. As the attorney for the people, the constitutional rights of citizens must be regarded by him with care and discretion. He must view the situation in the light of substantial justice. Whoever might be killed, whatever might be the roar of the mob, if a district attorney cannot withstand the onslaught of apparent injustice, although he may stand alone in his convictions, that district attorney is not worthy of his job. He takes the oath of office to uphold the constitution of this country, of this state and all laws made pursuant thereto. Any other stand places him in a position of betrayal of his trust.

In view of my belief in the first two stories told by Baker and the circumstances therein shown, I recommended the commutation of the sentence for these men because I believe that they are entitled to it. I also am absolutely opposed to any more bloodshed because of the feudal hatred of Mr. Baker. I feel that Baker baited not only his best friend Mr. Seaborn, who later himself unconsciously assisted in further baiting two old time officers of Siskiyou County, officers whom I consider were led into that unusual position possibly not through any fault of their own. I draw this conclusion because I know that Officers Lange and Clark would not have used that method of arrest. Seaborn and Baker drove ahead to the Baker house where Seaborn changed from a light shirt to a dark shirt so he would not be recognized and his car was driven into the garage. The officers followed them in their own car, arriving later at Baker's home. They then parked their car at the Baker home, took flashlights, and stalked the Brite brothers' bed a quarter of a mile away. Their approach was so amateurish as to be pitiable when they could have driven their car to the foot of the bed, turned the lights on the bed, covered the Brites with their guns and asked them to surrender without ever laying a hand on either man. If they were asleep, their attention could have been called by shouting at them or by blowing the horn. I know Joe Clark and Martin Lange well enough to know that in arresting dangerous men, they would have taken the safe course. Because the method used is so amateurish and because Seaborn had changed his shirt and parked his car in the Baker garage, I know the plan of arrest was formulated by Mr. Seaborn who already must have made an unusual sales talk to get these officers to serve him in the middle of the night after a trivial fight. Upon these facts I have always been well satisfied that the officers, and even Mr. Seaborn in the beginning, were not in any way to blame, nor were the Brite brothers in their situation to blame. To me, it is purely and simply an officer-baiting case.

The following testimony shows Baker as interested in saving his own skin:

Q. And after Seaborn got into the fracas, you still stood there, didn't you?

A. Well, I had walked around there where they was scrapping where that little tree stood there, the first tree by the ditch…

Q. Yes.

A. ...when Coke made a grab for the gun and pulled the gun out.

Q. Did you see him do this?

A. I seen him do it.

Q. You saw him when he pulled the gun out?

A. Yes sir.

Q. He was three or four feet from you, was he?

A. Yes, he was about eight feet.

Q. He was about eight feet?

A. Yes. I saw him when he reached for the gun and when he pulled the gun out.

Q. And what did you do?

A. I hollered to the boys, "He's gone for a gun!"

Q. You didn't do a thing, Mr. Baker, to stop that man with that gun?

A. Well, I couldn't. He was too far away.

Q. Eight feet?

A. Yes sir. Yes sir.

Q. All right. And after you said, "Boys he has got a gun, you made your flight?"

A. Yes sir.

Q. Which way did you go, up the creek?

A. I went up the creek.

Q. Along the creek or in the creek?

A. Along the bank right by the side of them trees up to the walk-log there.

Q. How far had you run before you heard the first shot?

A. Well, I hadn't went a step."

In conclusion, why should I indulge any presumptions against fellow officers, especially when the Lange family has always been friendly to me, knowing that Henry and I left Yreka for the war together; especially when Fred Seaborn's brother and brother's son were fraternity brothers of mine in Delta Chi at the University of California; especially in the face of the fact that I have known Officer Clark and the Clark family since I was about ten years of age. Officer Clark and his wife used to send food home to me when I was a starving boy in Sawyer's Bar. Everyone who has ever known me cannot deny my loyalty to friends in any walk of life. But I, as District Attorney, must suppress life-long ties of friendship in the administration of the duties of my office where I am led to believe evidence to the contrary. If Baker had told me what he later told the Grand Jury and what he told the trial court, instead of the story he told me at the Barton store, and instead of the story at the coroner's inquest, I would have been guided in my conduct by my belief in the truth of such versions. On the contrary, I was guided entirely by my analysis of what happened as he told it in the Barton Store, and before the coroner's jury. The Grand Jury version came sixty days after on November 4, 1936.

Then again, who fired the first unaccounted for shot of small caliber? It is easy to fire at one man and hit another in the dark especially where men are fighting in close embrace.

All in all, in view of these conflicts, no harm can be done by commutation of sentence from death to life imprisonment, and maybe some day Baker will be able to tell us how he managed to remember the vital testimony showing premeditation and re-sisting of arrest when he failed to remember it on the day of the killing and at the coroner's inquest three days later. I want no more men to die over Mr. Baker.

JAMES DAVIS
District Attorney For Siskiyou County

Submitted to the press of Siskiyou County with the express understanding that this article shall be published verbatim including punctuation and underlining.

The publication of Davis' "explanation" hit the Yreka community like a bombshell. The impact on the rest of the county was there, but to a lesser degree. Davis, of course, already had a substantial core of detractors in the communities and this long scholarly article just inflamed them all the more.

The lesser quantity of citizens that seemed more apt to side with Davis on the issue felt the explanation bolstered their position. It gave them additional strength in order to go along with their approval of him in what he had done in the case as well as what he appeared to stand for in the press release.

There seemed also to be a third but tiny faction who had been with him all along that accepted it word for word in a sort of "I told you so" attitude and were gratified that Davis had brought it all out in the open.

Then there was also that very small group of legal scholars. They had long continued to wonder where on earth Davis had gotten his ideas from the very first time that it appeared he was thinking of something other than a first degree indictment. As discussed here early on, the consensus was that he had gotten these ideas through talking to Decker on the morning after the killing. But this conclusion now required that Baker be added as an additional influence.

Back to the "Decker Theory"

The whole long document is simply a resurrection of the famous so-called Decker Theory. It should be remembered that the theory was to the effect that in the dead of night the officers entered the Brite's camp and failed to adequately identify themselves. The Brites, thinking they were being attacked by the same people with whom they had the previous altercation, came out of their bed fighting in self defense.

There was a very unfortunate thing here that was immediately apparent to a serious reader of the article. It was that Davis' presentation may have contained a glaring misconception.

In referring to Baker's testimony at the inquest, Davis states that Baker "practically corroborated what he had told me in the Barton Store." Davis then recites the pertinent inquest testimony to illustrate this. After quoting this testimony, Davis says, "You will note that John Brite uttered his first statement after he had been struck, and not before."

The testimony that Davis quoted may not show that at all. It could show just the opposite. In paraphrase, the quoted portion of Baker's testimony is as follows:

Baker: Officer Lange walked up there when he says, "Hello boys." He just made another step and Clark stepped in. He says, "We are officers; you are under arrest." Mr. Clark reached over and jerked the blanket away from their faces.

Davis: After that, who went into action?

Baker: Mr. Lange reached over and hit John with the billy.

Davis: That is your story; Mr. Lange reached over and hit which one, John or Coke?

Baker: Coke. John raised his head up. He was cursing. He told Mr. Clark, "There was no son of a bitch of an officer could arrest us."

Baker, continuing: Then Officer Clark struck Coke.

A few lines farther down, Baker answered in the affirmative when Davis asked him if he saw Lange strike a second and a third blow. But it does not show who was getting hit by these.

That series of testimony is a poor choice to conclude that "John Brite uttered his first statement after he had been struck, and not before." It in fact may prove precisely the opposite.

A serious reader of Davis' article may have noticed that there is a slight cloud over the interpretation of what Baker meant in that exchange with Davis where Baker said, "Mr. Lange reached over and hit John with the billy." This was in point of time prior to any statement by John.

But Davis himself, as the testimony reads, straightened this up when he came back with, "That is your story; Mr. Lange reached over and hit which one, John or Coke?"

Baker responded, "Coke. John raised his head up. He was cursing...," etc.

No, that doesn't help Davis' hypothesis.

But there could be a further explanation of that particular exchange. Suppose that there was a reporter's or transcriber's error in the record. Suppose the record inadvertently omitted one word, "not." It is a well known fact that Baker had a hearing impairment; suppose also that when Davis said to him, "That is your story; Mr. Lange reached over and hit which one, John or Coke?"

Possibly Baker only heard the last word, "Coke" and not "John or."

Then the question would therefore have sounded to Baker as, "That is your story. Mr. Lange reached over and hit which one, Coke?"

Baker's reply then could have been, "Not Coke. John raised his head up. He was cursing. He told Mr. Clark, 'There was no son of a bitch of an officer could arrest us.' Then Officer Clark struck Coke."

Or possibly when Davis asked the question, Baker heard it all and his reply was "Coke? John raised his head up. He was cursing ..." If the reporter recognized the word "Coke" in the context of a question but failed to insert the question mark, this would also result in throwing this cloud over the exchange.

All this is merely hypothetical and could have no standing in the case. The law is that the record stands. But even if it were accepted by some, it does not get Davis off the hook for using a portion of testimony to prove his point when in fact it may do just the opposite.

The testimony that Davis chose to quote in his article of explanation was of course given at the coroner's inquest, three days after the killings. It should be kept in mind that those quotations came from Davis' cross examination of Baker.

A half hour before that, with Davis right there in the room, Baker had given his testimony in response to coroner Felix Kunz's questioning. It should be recalled that Kunz asked him only nine questions during which Baker just took off on that very accurate step by step description of what had happened with out any further questioning being required.

The point here is that Davis, in his article, based his whole explanation for his position on the variance of Baker's story at Barton's store and at the inquest from the one that he subsequently told much later to the Grand Jury as well as in the trial. Davis used only "his" questioning at the inquest in his explanation; he failed to mention anything whatsoever of what Baker had said under Kunz's examination.

In all fairness to Baker, it should be pointed out that the testimony he gave only minutes before Davis questioned him was probably more accurate and very much in line with what he gave in the trial. It was felt by not a few serious followers of such matters that because this testimony was given by Baker without the restraints of the formal question and answer format, it was probably the most accurate given by him in the entire case. But the way Davis presents it, much of the public did not even know that the Kunz/Baker questioning took place. If in fact these answers for Kunz are in line with what he gave at the trial, Davis has no case here at all in the claim that Baker changed his story.

The pertinent portion of Baker's testimony in response to Kunz reads as follows (Baker is speaking with no prompting or questioning required):

> "Mr. Lange, he made probably a step right in front of them. He says, 'Hello boys!' He says, "This is the law; this is the Sheriff. You are under arrest." Mr. Coke's voice… they had their heads covered up, blanket pulled right over their heads… Mr. Coke's

voice rang out, 'The hell we are!' He says, 'No damn sheriff can arrest us!' Mr. Clark at that time reached over and pulled the blanket from over their heads. They both commenced cursing and blackguarding and abusing the sheriff. Mr. Lange struck John over the head; I call it a billy, and he kind of quieted down for a second. Coke started to raise up and Mr. Clark struck him over the head with the billy. He quieted a little bit. Mr. Clark struck him again and Mr. Lange tapped John again. He stepped right over Coke and calmly knelt and kind of squatted down about in this position. He says, 'Hold still; don't move, I am putting the handcuffs on you.' That was John. He had his hand cuffs right by John's left wrist. John kept moving his hand and he kept telling him to be still and not move a muscle.'"

It would seem that the above testimony would more definitely indicate that the Brite Brothers knew very well that they were being arrested by officers rather than being attacked by their previous assailants who were now reinforced.

Ralph McMurry's youngest son had been very thoroughly following these developments in the newspapers. When he discussed it with his father, he asked him how on earth Davis could take this position.

The father replied, "Not too many months ago I had a long talk with Sheriff Chandler about our friend Davis. I remember vividly what I told Chan and the same thing still applies. It went something like this:

"Davis is not dumb, he is not stupid. The only thing wrong with him on this issue is that he is 'wrong.' Dead wrong. Thoroughly wrong.

"But having that point settled, Davis is to be admired because he is standing on principle. He may be successful in the end in saving the lives of the Brite brothers. Be that as it may. But he is sticking to his moral principles and with this development he can't help but realize that he is driving the last nails in the coffin of his career as a district attorney. But he believes in what he is doing and he intends to stick with it regardless of the consequences.

"To do that, it takes a man of solid character, and that is exactly what Jimmy Davis is. Instead of the scorn that he is reaping, he should be receiving admiration from his peers."

On February 21st the Associated Press released an article that brought a new question of poignant interest. It read as follows:

When a newspaper man today called Governor Merriam's attention to the fact that John and Coke Brite, Siskiyou County triple slayers, were scheduled to hang on Friday, April 15th, which is Good Friday, the Governor stated that a new date would be set for the execution of the two brothers.

Since it is customary to hold legal hangings on Friday, it was assumed here that the date would be changed to Friday, April 22, provided the Advisory Pardon Board does not recommend commutation of their sentence to life.

The March 9th issue of the *Yreka Journal* carried big news with one inch high headlines as follows:

BRITE BROTHERS TO HANG

CHANCE TO ESCAPE NOOSE ONE IN TEN THOUSAND

FINDINGS ARE PRESENTED

Final Reprieve for Siskiyou Killers May be Granted by Governor Merriam to Avoid Good Friday

Ten Thousand to One Chance That Brite Brothers Can Now Escape Noose

Final Loophole Closed in Decision of Advisory Board

Today Governor Merriam said that he probably will forward to the State Supreme Court the application of John and Coke Brite for commutation of the death sentence although the Advisory Pardon Board recommended against clemency.

Merriam said that the Advisory Board, headed by Lieutenant Governor George J. Hatfield, was unanimous in its vote against commutation. "However," he stated, "they asked that the Brites be given every opportunity to present their case and have the fullest hearing. I am inclined to think I will forward the application to the State Supreme Court for a recommendation."

The Governor has granted the Brites a reprieve until April
15th, but since this is Good Friday, Governor Merriam indicated
a further reprieve was in prospect.

Ma Brite Back in Action

Before the end of the month, Mrs. Brite was back in the news.

The brothers had felony convictions for burglary in Arizona. This constituted a problem for them in consideration of the commutation decision. It
was not a complete block to a favorable decision, but it was a factor nonetheless.

The postponement of the execution until final resolution of the appeal
was now assured. Consequently Mrs. Brite undertook a project to see if she
could get the potential damage from the "priors" decreased or eliminated.

The facts of the Arizona case for which the boys had served time involved the burglarizing of a curio store. The Brite Brothers had pled guilty of
stealing two blankets and some miscellaneous curios and given them to their
girl friends.

Mrs. Brite set out on a hitchhiking trip to Winslow, Arizona in a search
for the boys' two former "sweethearts." She was staying overnight with relatives, friends, and various local relief agencies along the way.

In an interview, Mrs. Brite said that the blankets and curios were in fact
taken by the girls. Her sons, in a spirit of chivalry, in order to protect the girls
assumed the blame and pled guilty to the charges. She says now that the lives
of her sons hang in the balance, she will plead with the young women, if she
can find them, to tell the true story of the burglary.

"The two girls can furnish this evidence," Mrs. Brite said, "which might
save my boys. But I will not tell their names. Blankets stolen from the curio
store between Winslow and Flagstaff in 1924 were given to my sons by the
two girls and my sons gave the blankets to officers. They protected the girls,
but denied any knowledge of the theft. They then pleaded guilty and were
sentenced to a year in the reform school."

Mrs. Brite went on to say, "This previous charge influenced the court
when my sons were sentenced for the Horse Creek slaying. If I can find the
two girls the court may listen to my plea for the boys. I have broadcast by
radio from Sacramento asking the girls to help me and now I want to find
them."

She closed the interview by stating that for nearly two years she lived at
Folsom, walking two miles daily to be near her sons. She remarked that she

had already walked twenty-seven miles when she couldn't get rides on the hitchhiking trip she was then on.

It is not known if she ever found the girls; the assumption was that she did not. The matter of the previous convictions was never again raised. But that is not quite the end of this episode.

On April 4th, it was learned that Mrs. Brite was stranded in Arizona and had made application to the Flagstaff, Arizona welfare department for aid in getting her back to California. The Arizona welfare people had contacted the Siskiyou County Welfare Department. The last report on it from the Chairman of the Siskiyou Board of Supervisors was that they were "considering taking it under consideration."

A short time later, Mrs. Brite's request for help to get home was denied by the Siskiyou County Board of Supervisors on the grounds that she "could not qualify under the state requirements for aid." But Mrs. Brite, of course, did manage to return.

More Delays, More Hope for Ma

On Friday, April 8th Governor Merriam postponed the hanging until May 20th. He had not yet received the recommendation from the Supreme Court, but hoped to have it before that date.

On May 16th, the governor still had not received the Supreme Court recommendation and therefore granted another reprieve until July 22nd.

On July 2nd, Governor Merriam finally got his answer from the Supreme Court. The *United Press* wire from Sacramento carried it as follows:

> The State Supreme Court today recommended commutation of the death sentences of John and Coke Brite, condemned Siskiyou County triple slayers, who are at Folsom Prison under sentence to hang later this month.
>
> In view of the fact that several reprieves have been granted by Governor Merriam, it was predicted here that the recommendation of the court would be followed by him and sentences of the two brothers commuted to life.

But the prediction of the UP was not correct, at least not yet.

Instead of as predicted, Merriam sent the Supreme Court recommendation back to the Prison Advisory Board. He asked them to review it once again because there had been new evidence introduced since they last had it. He also asked the board to advise him if they could not have a recommendation in his hands before July 22nd. This, of course, was an indication that the governor was ready to grant another reprieve if necessary.

The board came right back with the news that it would be impossible to meet the July 22nd deadline. Merriam thereupon granted a new reprieve setting the execution date for December 9th [1938].

With this news, former district attorney Johnson got off one of his wry quips.

He said, "One of these days our governor is going to run out of people to whom he can pass the buck on the Brite brothers' decision. I think I have figured his strategy. He is hoping to be defeated for reelection, then he won't need to make a decision."

It turned out that there was more truth than poetry in Johnson's analysis of the governor's motivation. By the time December 1938 rolled around, the elections were over in California and Merriam was now a "lame duck" governor.

Associated Press wire, December 2:

Sacramento. In order to give the new State Parole Advisory Board a chance to review the case after January 1st, Governor Merriam granted Coke and John Brite a fifth reprieve from death.

The Governor set the execution ahead to March 10th [1939].

Execution clemency was recommended by the State Supreme Court but the present board was opposed to such an action. The Governor hopes that the new board would be able to harmonize its view with the Supreme Court.

The new board members are Earl Warren, Attorney General-elect, and Ellis Patterson, the new Lieutenant Governor.

Perhaps the old saying that "time heals" is also applicable to newspaper coverage. By the time the next development in the case arrived, the *Siskiyou News* ceased featuring its coverage under those flashy one inch high headlines.

The *Journal*, however, continued to persevere.

The March 1, 1938 edition appeared in its usual headline treatment as follows:

BRITES GIVEN SIXTH REPRIEVE

GOVERNOR OLSON GRANTS STAY OF EXECUTION
TO HORSE CREEK KILLERS

Sacramento, Feb. 28 (AP) John and Coke Brite won an extension of the scheduled execution day from March 10th to May 12 under a reprieve issued by Culbert L. Olson today.

The governor said that a lengthy study of the records is needed in view of an apparent conflict. The State Supreme Court recommended clemency but he said the Advisory Pardon Board recommended against it. Olson said the Governor's Office had received a letter from Chief Justice H. Waste of the Supreme Court, as of June 22, 1938, saying that the majority of the justices recommended commutation to life imprisonment. The Advisory Pardon Board held a meeting on September 29th, 1938, at which time it recommended the application be denied.

Bert Green, the Keeper of the State Archives, has revealed that he found the missing files in the case in a desk in the governor's office.

Governor Merriam granted five reprieves to the Brite Brothers.

It is interesting to note that the corresponding article that appeared in the *Siskiyou News* the next day referred to Olson's reprieve as the "seventh" reprieve. The actual count at this point is six; the *News* was in error. In fairness to the *News*, it should be pointed out that most everyone had lost count after all this time; a "one reprieve error" at this point seemed entirely acceptable.

When the news broke concerning this last episode, Charley Johnson's latest remark was being quoted up and down Miner Street:

"I knew something like this was going to happen," he said. "Those two governors should never have shaken hands at the inauguration. Now Olson has caught the same disease that Merriam had; its called 'reprieve disease.'"

The Long Wait is Finally Over

On May 9th, 1939 the Brite brothers had then been incarcerated at Folsom prison for two years, four months and sixteen days. In that period of time they had six times faced a date with the gallows that was but days away before a reprieve had been issued. On this day, on May 9th, they thought they had only three days to live.

Even the *Yreka Journal* by this time had reduced its treatment of the Brite Case to very much smaller headlines. Here is its report in the issue of May 10th:

BRITE BROTHERS ARE GIVEN LIFE TERMS

Sacramento, May 9th. Governor Olson today commuted to life imprisonment the death sentences of John H. and Coke T. Brite. The defendants, who are in Folsom Prison, were to have been hanged May 12th.

The Brites were granted five reprieves by Governor Frank Merriam, and one by Governor Olson.

Governor Olson said he acted upon the recommendation of Chief Justice William Waste and a majority of justices of the State Supreme Court, and on the recommendation of James Davis, Siskiyou District Attorney at the time of the Brite's trial.

The Governor announced that he had received hundreds of letters from Siskiyou citizens requesting commutation. "Many of these letters," the Governor said, "contained clues and information which strongly indicate the possibility that the two applicants acted in self defense. Many other letters indicate that among Northern California citizenry there is considerable doubt that the applicants received a fair trial in a detached judicial atmosphere."

The Governor also said that two of the trial jurors wrote, stating that after calm reflection, they now consider the death penalty to be extreme and recommended commutation.

The Governor said, "While I am not prepared to state unequivocally these two men acted entirely in self defense, I do believe there is sufficient doubt of their guilt of murder in the first degree to warrant commutation to life imprisonment, in the hope that additional evidence may be revealed which will offer a more illuminating picture of the incidents of that fatal night."

Critics Hit at [Governor] Olson in Brite Case

The next day the *Siskiyou News* came out with the same story from Sacramento that had appeared in the *Journal*. But it also contained additional local comment. It read in part as follows:

COMMUTATION OF BROTHERS DEATH SENTENCES RESENTED HERE

Although the action was expected in some quarters because of the number of reprieves given to the condemned men, the commutation of the death sentences of John H. and Coke T. Brite to life imprisonment terms Monday by Governor Olson caused considerable unfavorable comment and criticism of the state's chief executive.

In Yreka there was some bitter resentment over the final decision in regard to the fate of the two brothers convicted of the killing of three members of an officers' posse that sought to arrest them in a Siskiyou County mountain camp. Others merely shook their heads and appeared perplexed over the ends of justice.

Election Battles

It had been almost three years since the crime was committed. With no more flaming headlines to proclaim, the papers had little if anything to report. The general public went on with their lives with little further interest in the case.

During the year 1938, all of the action in the case had been in Sacramento involving the potential commutation matters. But 1938 was also an election year in which two of the major "players" in this drama had battles of their own to fight.

In the general election in November, the offices of both district attorney and sheriff were in the contest.

Charley Johnson was born in Knight's Landing, California in 1872. As a young man, he came to Siskiyou County before the turn of the century. He worked in Montague as a barber while studying on his own to become a lawyer. Upon passing the Bar Examination he practiced in Yreka until he was elected District Attorney in 1922. He served in that capacity for three consecutive terms until Davis defeated him in 1934.

Now, in the 1938 election, it was Johnson trying to upset Davis. The campaign became very antagonistic with one local paper supporting Johnson and the other for Davis. Six days before the November 8th election, Davis released a bitter tirade through one of the papers vehemently criticizing Johnson's administration through three terms. Johnson immediately fired back three days later with a blast that was equally vitriolic.

The general feeling in the community was that Davis had no chance at all in view of his positions in the Brite case. It was felt that it would be a landslide victory for Johnson.

Johnson was the winner, but it was by no means a landslide when the final count showed him with 56% of the votes. The local coffee shop and bar room analysts were very surprised. It made everyone pause momentarily because it seemed to prove that there must be a considerable number of people out there who had silently been on Davis' side of the issues involved in the Brite drama.

With his new victory, Johnson served two more terms as district attorney, making it a total of twenty years. This is the longest tenure in that office that anyone has served before or since.

After retiring as district attorney, Johnson resumed his practice in Yreka. In 1949 he unexpectedly died at home; he was seventy-one years old.

Davis stayed in Yreka through 1939 in private practice. He then moved to San Francisco and entered into practice there. In 1942 he had a case that was left over from his previous law practice in Yreka. In February he returned to Yreka in connection with the case. He had been under treatment for an ailment in San Francisco for three weeks and his doctor had advised against making the trip. While in Siskiyou he was staying with his old friend Louie Sbarbaro in Weed. After the hearing, in the evening at the Sbarbaro home, he collapsed and died. He was fifty-two years old.

So the little part Indian boy, born in the mountains of Siskiyou at Sawyer's Bar, was now gone from the scene. He had attended school in remote Sawyers Bar and later in Etna, but somehow made it out of the woods to graduate from the University of California at Berkeley. He had been District Attorney in two counties, Del Norte and Siskiyou. He was a man of principle; sometimes right and often wrong; but a man of principle nonetheless.

And the Sheriff?

In the contest for sheriff, Chandler knew he was in deep trouble. It seemed that the general public did not realize that it was only the bad luck of the timing when Mrs. Brite had made her moves to surrender the boys. It will be recalled that according to the scenario that she had signed at the request of Henry Pallage, it could have been Chandler just as well as Davis, had events worked out a little differently when she came to Yreka to make the arrangements.

But she ended up with Davis instead of the sheriff, and the public never really forgave Chandler for his bad luck in the episode. So when election time rolled around, Chandler felt cornered. He knew the election would be difficult. Only three and a half years ago he had uprooted his family in Dunsmuir and moved them to Yreka; he felt he must give it one last gasp.

His opponent was Ben Richardson, a well known and popular rancher from the Ager area east of Yreka. It wasn't close. Richardson took 69% of the votes.

As soon as his term was over, Chandler left Yreka and his family followed him later after the school term was completed.

The Other Players

Judge C. J. Luttrell, another product from the mountains of Siskiyou County, was elected Superior Court Judge in 1922. He served in that position for seventeen years, from 1922 through 1938. From a very humble beginning, he became highly respected by the public and his peers in the legal structure of Northern California. He took tremendous pride in his record as a judge, having never been "reversed" in a civil action by a higher court. He was highly articulate and thoroughly versed in the law. He died in 1960.

James M. Allen was also of humble beginnings, born and raised in the backwoods in much the same area from where both Davis and Luttrell had come. He served as Siskiyou County District Attorney from 1915 through 1923. He was elected State Senator in the district that then covered Siskiyou and Del Norte Counties in 1927. When Luttrell decided to retire at the end of his term in 1938, Allen was elected Superior Court Judge.

In 1960, Judge Allen appointed Ralph McMurry's youngest son to be foreman of the Siskiyou County Grand Jury for the year. In August of that year, Judge and Mrs. Allen were returning in their car from Sacramento to Yreka. The judge was a noted fast driver on the highways. In the dark of the night between Gazelle and Yreka, the Allen car plowed straight into the back of a very large truck and both the Allens were instantly killed. Thus ended a brilliant career of forty-one years public service.

With the vacancy created by the loss of Judge Allen in midterm, Governor Pat Brown appointed Everett Barr to succeed him as Superior Court Judge. With this development, the "young" lawyer who was hired as assistant to Horace J. Frye and was scared to death when Frye was sick and didn't show up the first day of the trial, was now the top man in the judicial structure of the county. He too served with distinction for ten years until he died in 1970.

Joseph P. Correia, the other "young" lawyer that was retained by the county as Assistant Prosecutor remained in Yreka and became one of the leading attorneys. He retired from practicing in 1985 and died in 1987. Court Reporter Ralph McMurry was appointed by Judge Luttrell in 1921 and came into office with him at that time. He served 34 years until he had a stroke in 1955. He died in 1957; he was 72 years old.

Deputy Sheriff Eddie Mathews at this time in 1988 [when the book was originally written] is very much alive and well. He has proven to be most articulate about the various portions of the story in which he was involved. He has a steel trap mind and appears to enjoy talking about the cases. He has been of invaluable help in the research effort involved here. [Ed Mathews passed away in 1998.]

In the summer of 1934, Court Reporter Ralph McMurry's youngest son got his first job. He was at the time twelve years old, between the seventh and eighth grades in elementary school. The W. A. Bray family of Hilt were friends of the McMurry's and the two fathers got together and arranged for the boy to hire on to the Bray's hay crew as derrick horse driver on their huge cattle ranch. The family home was the old Cole's Station, a former stage coach stop on the Oregon Trail. The boy spent two summers doing this and it was an exciting experience and very educational.

Two years later in 1936, Mrs. Ruby Bray turned up on the Brite brothers' trial jury. She was the one to whom the proper Victorian Judge Luttrell was referring when he would say, "lady and gentlemen of the jury." She was the only woman on the jury. At that time, Ralph McMurry invited Mrs. Bray to come home each noontime during the trial to the McMurry's for lunch. Needless to say, the three children still at home were sternly instructed that there were to be no comments or questions concerning the trial in the presence of Mrs. Bray. This rule was faithfully obeyed by all.

Forty years later in 1974, the "boy" was giving a lecture for the Siskiyou County Historical Society. The subject was the three famous murder cases in Siskiyou County in the 1930s. In the question session after the speech, Bill Bray, Jr. got up and introduced his mother, "a member of the jury in the Brite brothers' case." The speaker was astounded because he hadn't seen her since the lunches at the McMurry home during the trial.

Ruby Bray also made valuable contributions in furnishing insights into the trial phase of this case. [Ruby passed away in 1990.]

There is one other individual to be mentioned. This particular person was not actually a participant in the case, but he thought he was at the time. Court Reporter Ralph McMurry's youngest son is still living in Yreka [at the time of his writing this book, 1988]. His father always wanted him to become a lawyer. But after graduation from college and hoping to go on to law school, World War II got in the way. After the war he had a long career as a businessman. He eventually became a writer (of sorts), including the penning of this book. [Alan McMurry passed away in 2003.]

After the commutation of the sentences in 1939, the Brite brothers with the consideration of execution removed, just sat it out down through the years. In eight years, they were eligible to apply for parole. They applied in 1947 for the first time. It was "Denied. Further parole consideration postponed one calendar year."

Free!

They applied each year thereafter with the same result until 1950, when the decision was "Submitted for consideration and decision." When the Parole Board met again in 1950, the decision was, "Granted parole effective September 17, 1951; not to go to Siskiyou County." This development was reported with no particular fanfare or emphasis in the local papers in Siskiyou County. About the only thing really noticeable was that a rumor made the rounds. It went to the affect that the "authorities" had evidence that the Brite brothers intended to come to Yreka and kill Judge Allen. The story further specified that "around the clock guards were posted at Allen's home and office."

At that time and some years later when Allen was questioned about it, he stated that it was just a rumor, he had heard nothing of it, and as far as he knew, it never happened.

Some few years later the word around Yreka was that in some manner, the Brites had violated parole and had been sent back to prison. The story goes on that John Brite was murdered while in prison and Coke was later paroled again. After some years, Coke stopped reporting to his parole officer and was never heard from since.

In an attempt to uncover the true facts of the matter in preparation for this writing in 1987, the California Department of Corrections was queried. While it cannot be certainly concluded that the department was unwilling to help, it was found that such information was extremely difficult if not impossible to come by. After checking by telephone with the Department and being referred to another office six successive times until the last one referred the caller to the original starting point, current [1987] State Senator John Doolittle was called upon for help.

After more than three months delay which appeared to be in Doolittle's Roseville office, his efforts finally brought forth a response from the Department of Corrections, California State Prison at Folsom.

Unfortunately the Department's response muddies the waters more than it helps.

The next records available in Yreka show that only Coke applied for parole in 1963 and again in 1964; both were denied. After that we have only the letter from the Department of Corrections that says that John in 1972 "was presumed dead." As for Coke, the letter says that "on April 29, 1973, he died while on parole."

Disregarding the aforementioned rumor and using only the local records and the Department's letter, one can only conclude that John must be the one that just stopped reporting to his parole officer with the department losing all track of him. Then some twenty or more years later they found out that he was dead. This is the only conclusion that can be made because there is no record which shows that he was ever back in prison after first going on parole as was the case with Coke.

Another conclusion that can be drawn by using part of the rumor and all of the records we now have seems a bit more plausible. Suppose the rumor is true to the extent that John was actually murdered while in prison. Surely if that was the case it is in the prison's record on him. But public agencies do not always wish to release all of the information. A murder of a convict might have been interpreted by the Department as detrimental to them and therefore expunged it from the record. We do not need to accuse the Department of this here. All of this lies in the distant past, but it must be admitted

Brite Brothers Timeline

Aug. 29, 1936 - John and Coke's confrontation with Baker and Seaborn

Aug. 30, 1936 - Shooting up Horse Creek (early morning)

Aug. 30 (afternoon) - Sept. 18, 1936 - Manhunt for Brite Brothers

Sept. 18, 1936 - John and Coke turn themselves in to D.A. James Davis

Sept. 19, 1936 - John and Coke delivered to Folsom Prison

Nov. 9, 1936 - John and Coke arraigned

Nov. 10, 1936 - Change of Venue hearing (unsuccessful) in Yreka

Dec. 7, 1936 - Trial begins in Yreka

Dec. 19, 1936 - Brite brothers convicted of first degree murder

Dec. 22, 1936 - Brite brothers sentenced to hang

Dec. 24, 1936 - Brite brothers booked into Death Row at Folsom Prison

May 19, 1937 - Appeal filed

Nov. 9, 1937 - Appeal denied, sentence reaffirmed

Jan. 21, 1938 - Date of execution

Feb. 10, 1938 - Execution postponed, appeal for clemency to Advisory
Pardon Board

April 15, 1938 - New execution date pending clemency appeal results

May 20, 1938 - Clemency not recommended, new execution date set due to
April 15 being Good Friday

July 22, 1938 - New execution date pending Supreme Court recommendation

Dec. 9, 1938 - New execution date pending Supreme Court recommendation

March 10, 1939 - New execution date pending Supreme Court recommendation

May 12, 1939 - New execution date pending Supreme Court recommendation

May 9, 1939 - Sentences commuted to life in prison by Governor Olson

Sept. 17, 1951 - Brite brothers paroled

Unknown dates - brothers returned to prison periodically for lesser crimes. Coke
died while on parole in 1973. Circumstances of John's death unknown.

that such an analysis is possible. If the above is applicable, it all fits together in a much more plausible manner as follows:

Bear in mind that the Brite brothers were very close and always did things together. When they were on parole the first time, they did something to have their parole revoked. They both came back to prison sometime between 1951 when they went out and 1963 when only Coke applied for parole again. Sometime between those two dates, John was murdered in prison. Later Coke applied for parole again. Sometime after 1964, the year of his last parole denial, Coke went on parole again and ultimately died in 1973. In the meantime the prison record of John's murder was either expunged or changed to merely "presumed dead" in 1972.

The above two scenarios seem to be the only reconstructions that can be made with the existing records and information we have on the matter. Take your pick.

Remember Robert Barr?

There is one more major player in this series of dramas to account for: Robert Miller Barr. Recall that in September, 1936, while in the midst of the search for John and Coke Brite, Robert Barr was arrested in San Pedro, California on burglary changes. Fingerprints revealed him to be the suspect wanted in connection with the slaying of Police Chief Jack Daw in Dunsmuir the previous summer, the crime which resulted in the lynching of his partner, Clyde Johnson. Barr was returned to Siskiyou County and in October was sentenced to life imprisonment for his part in the murder although his gun had never been fired. He was sent to San Quentin. In 1940 he was transferred to Folsom. He served forty-two years and was discharged from Folsom Prison in 1978.

So all the players are now accounted for in one way or another. To the younger people of today, it all was all so long ago that the lessons learned might not seem applicable today. But to those of us that experienced it, most certainly we learned something that is enduring and still applies, and surely something of value came out of it.

8

Fifty Years Later

Now [1988] that the great mystery has been cleared up as to who this writer really is, I feel that it is safe to conclude this work by adopting the "first person" style of speaking.

In Chapter Three I related how I had asked my father, the court reporter, if it was the "right thing" that had been done when Clyde Johnson was lynched in Yreka. I related what my father's answer was.

I was but thirteen years old at the time. I suppose that when we are that age, we tend to prefer action to speeches. I told how my father's answer bothered me to some extent. I related how some years later I asked one of my college philosophy professors the same question. As you recall, his answer was very learned and carefully phrased. But in effect, it really just threw the ball back into my court with the implication that I must work it out by myself within my own standards.

It took a few more years but I have now answered it. But I didn't work it out entirely by myself. My answer is the one my father gave me in 1935.

I will repeat it here. The question was, "Did the lynchers do the right thing?"

"No," he replied, "no man has the right to try, convict and execute another man under any circumstances outside the law. If a man objects to the inequities of the law, his quarrel is with the law, not the case or the defendant. There are remedies available to him to get redress for this. Any course outside this principle will lead to chaos in the end and then we lose all of the protection that the laws give us."

Another consideration in support of my position is that there is the very grave danger that in the commission of a lynching, an innocent man may be killed. This question is especially relevant here because that may have occurred in the 1895 lynching described in the first chapter.

I am referring here eighteen year old Garland Stemler, who was hanged in the courthouse square along with the other three murderers. It will be recalled that he was arrested and charged with "assisting" Moreno, an older man, in a murder. He hadn't even had a preliminary hearing before he was lynched. He had been saved for the last by the lynchers. There had been some discussion inside the jail about omitting the eighteen year old lad from the proceedings. But in the end, the extremists in the group won out and Stemler was taken to the rail along with the others. Just before he was yanked off his feet by the noose, he had shouted, "Tell my brother to tell my mother I am innocent."

Surely Garland Stemler's demise must have given more than one man present a guilty feeling afterward. There was so little known about his case; it should have been extremely difficult for those men to justify what they were about to do. But do it they did; they may have killed an innocent boy. This for me is a spine chilling thought.

The question of whether or not a lynching achieves the objective of the lynchers should be viewed here. In order to take a look at that, one must sort out what the objective is.

It seems that in general, lynchers are trying to get a message across to other potential murderers. The message is that a date with the noose is what they will be risking. I feel that was what the 1895 lynching was about.

On the other hand, in my opinion the 1935 lynching was an attempt to get a message across to the judicial system. The citizenry had "had it" with the long delays involved before the resolution of all murder cases in general.

It seems to me highly doubtful that any potential murderer has ever been deterred from committing the crime out of fear of being lynched. In the first place, most murders are not conceived as an out and out premeditated murder. Most of them happen as a result of something going wrong during the commission of a crime and the villain ultimately committing the murder to escape. Of course he knows that this is a potential risk as evidenced by his arming himself in case just such a situation arises. It appears to me that he full well knows the legal consequences of his acts and is apparently willing to take the risk. The fact that he may suffer a potential lynching in addition to all the other illegal trouble he would be in is probably of only passive consideration.

It should be recalled that the Brite brothers did mention lynching when they were talking to Decker after the crime. But at that time they were talking about it in connection with their potential flight. It never even had crossed their minds prior to the commission of the crime. They also mentioned it to their parents who in turn discussed it with both Chandler and Davis. But again, the subject of lynching was linked in context with the subject of fleeing or giving up.

Then there are the other kinds of murder. These are the "crimes of passion." The driving force in them is "hate." For a person to premeditate murder as a result of hate, he must be driven by an unreasoning passion. That murderer will never sit down and calmly consider the risk of being lynched no matter how many signals of its possibility may have been sent by lynchers.

Of course there is no record available to anyone as to whether or not a potential crime has ever been abandoned through fear of a lynching. But as explained above, my gut feeling is that it has never occurred.

We still have the question of whether or not lynching is an effective way to get a message to the judicial system. The answer to that one is a resounding "no." Or put another way, even though the story of the cases in this book show that the message did in fact get through to higher levels of government, it had no effect whatsoever.

Let's take a look at the record. After the Johnson lynching followed by the Brite case, we have many references to a potential lynching by high officers in the statewide legal and judiciary infrastructure. Even California Attorney General Webb dwelt upon it. Yes, the message that the public demands faster action in the processing of the apparently eternal prolongation of the system came through loud and clear. But there is no evidence whatsoever that the message produced any changes. In fact, the system has become longer and less efficient ever since. I do not know what the norm is for the amount of time between county superior court verdict and final resolution of a murder case, but I suspect it is between six and eight years. That can hardly be called progress in achieving the thing that the lynchers had in mind.

To sum up this situation it therefore must be concluded that a lynching is a futile gesture if its purpose is to get a message to either the high government officials or the potential murderers themselves. A lynching is a useless gesture with no gain whatsoever for society. In fact it is the exact opposite in that it degrades society and its institutions. It is my sincere hope that we will never have one again.

But will we?

A fair question but I doubt it. In the first place, the jails we now have are much more highly secure. They are so constructed that a lynch mob could be held off indefinitely. The technological nature of the jails is such that even a carefully calculated and secret lynch operation similar to what was conducted in the Johnson case could be successfully resisted.

Then there is society in general. Very much the same emotional motivations persist in mankind today as they always have. But as time has gone by, our society is more sophisticated. It is possible to get into some heavy philosophy and sociology on this subject. But at the risk of oversimplification, it seems that society today would simply not fail to recognize the moral implications of taking a life outside the guidelines of its established institutions. To do so would be a rejection of many of the basic moral values we have fought so hard to obtain and preserve.

The thing that I am getting at here has often been crudely referred to as "guns or ballots." As late as 1986, the state of California put on a resounding demonstration of the use of ballots as opposed to the guns.

The public complaints had been building for many years in exasperation with the judicial system's inability to resolve California murder cases. The exact same complaint that we heard in this book from 1895 onward. Here is what happened:

Under the California law, members of the State Supreme Court are appointed for life by the Governor, exactly the same as in the national government. But every four years at election time, the members of the court appear on the regular ballot where each voter can indicate that he wants to retain him or reject him. In the entire history of the system until 1986 there has been only one case of a justice being rejected by vote.

Leading up to the election of that year, there was a well organized movement led mostly by the conservative wing in state politics. The movement put out huge amounts of preelection literature including TV adds urging the voters to reject the sitting Chief Justice along with three other members of the court.

The issue was the constant overturning by the state Supreme Court of murder convictions on appeal.

On Election Day, 1936, the voters, by using ballots instead of a rope and noose, gave our 1935 Siskiyou County lynchers exactly what they wanted. The Chief Justice and two of the most liberal members of the court were summarily rejected. This was fifty-one years after the last lynching. Hardly a speedy process, but it came about, and that is what counts.

In all fairness, it must be pointed out that the vote of 1986 did nothing about the length of time it takes for a capital case to be finally resolved in California, but it helped.

There is one other subject that I feel should be included in these comments. This involves the procedures, or rules of the court.

In the preparation work for writing of book, you can imagine how familiar I became with the three volume, 814 page trial transcript of the Brite brothers case. This huge document, of course, was produced by my father.

In his position as court reporter he produced many; some longer and some shorter. In some of these, in the later years, I myself was involved to a very limited extent. But never before was the depth of my involvement in details as it has been now in this one.

Of the 814 pages of the Brite brothers transcript, 766 of those pages consist of the actual testimony. The remainder consists of the prosecution's final argument, the written instructions to the jury, certificates of the court reporter, the judge and other more or less "housekeeping" matters.

Within the 766 pages of testimony, there are 187 incidents where one side or the other makes an objection and argument then ensues. These episodes involving both sides as well as the judge, take up approximately eighty two pages of the transcript. That represents more than ten percent of the whole thing.

Most of these situations are quite simple. Whichever of the lawyers is conducting an examination of a witness, asks a question. The opposing lawyer interrupts and registers an objection to the asking of the question because it is something like "incompetent, irrelevant and immaterial or constitutes hearsay." Then the judge makes his ruling. If he agrees with the objection, he responds by saying, "That will 'go out." Then he turns to the jury and advises them that they are to pay no attention to what was asked (and often enough answered) and advises them that they cannot consider it in their deliberations.

This procedure is alright providing it is a trial of one day or at most, two days. But how on earth can a jury member keep all these things stored away in his brain if it is a much longer case?

In this case the judge, in effect is saying the following to the jury:

"There are eighty-two pages of testimony in this case where 187 separate arguments took place. In each of them I ruled that the particular testimony involved was to be either considered by you in your deliberations or you were to disregard it. Please remember all of it and act accordingly."

This case lasted approximately one week. What if it lasted one month as some do?

That is imposing a mandate on the jury that is impossible for them to obey. The end result of this is that the jury does not even try to observe this admonition because they can't. Juries do the best they can, but few of them have a memory that can handle this one. In the end, all that arguing, eighty-two pages of it, might just as well have never happened as far as having any effect upon the jury.

There is also the added consideration that in the episodes where the objection is made a little late, the jury's memory bell has been rung, and remember, you cannot "unring" a bell.

My only reason in bringing up this matter is to get a lick in for the idea that the judicial system should do something about this. I have some ideas as to method, but it would be inappropriate to launch into them at this time.

I want to mention another consideration that I feel needs improvement in the system. This falls into the area of the Rules of Evidence.

Whenever an inexperienced witness starts to tell about something, he usually is immediately admonished to not mention what he thought or what he said. He is told to testify only to what he saw, or in certain situations, what was said to him but not what he replied.

Bear in mind that at the risk of over simplification, the entire trial process is an effort to find out "what happened." Witnesses are almost always inexperienced and know nothing of the rules that apply when they are testifying. They are often nervous and embarrassed.

Each of us has a certain way of expressing ourselves. Generally if you ask anyone to describe some particular incident, he will start right off telling it as he remembers it. That includes what he thought, said and heard the others say. What difference does it make in the evidence gathering process if we hold still a few seconds and allow the witness to tell it in his normal fashion of expressing himself. My point is that if we use this tolerance, we will get a more accurate recitation.

A case in point: In the Brite case when Decker was being asked to tell his story about when he heard the gun shots, the court got on him because he started to tell what he thought.

He was asleep and he heard these shots going off. He immediately awakened and went to the window.

He said, "I thought some deer hunter was down there taking a shot at my pet deer that have been coming into the garden lately."

In my opinion, the fact that he told what he thought added some color and clarity to what he was asked to tell. But he was admonished sternly by the court to omit anything he thought.

My point here is that the system should listen to the witness tell his story in all the nuances to which he is accustomed. A more accurate picture of the event is the result and that is the thing the trial is attempting to bring out.

9

Searching for Gold in the North State: The Siskiyou County Origin Story

In 1895, the year of the first lynching talked about in this book, Yreka, Siskiyou County, California was a young town by national standards, but by the standards of the West, it was old. California itself had never amounted to very much until that fateful day in 1848 when John Marshall discovered those little glimmers of the "muck called gold" in the mill-race at Coloma. That was the catalyst that started the great westward migration dubbed the California Gold Rush. This brought the Forty-niners west by the hundreds of thousands. As the miners spread out in their relentless search for the yellow metal, northern California fast became one of the major destinations.

The area of the first discovery, the "Mother Lode," soon became over-crowded and frustrating for the later arrivals. It seemed that all the good spots were already occupied with established claims. These men fanned out in ever widening circles. Some headed up through the valley that filled the space between the two great mountain ranges running north and south in California, the Sierras and the Coast Range. Others boarded steamers and traveled up the coast, dropping off at coves or the mouths of some large rivers that were pouring into the sea from the mountains to the east.

The going was tough for those who chose to leave the ships and travel on foot up one of the rivers, "panning" all the way. There were tributary streams to cross, Indians to fight, claim jumpers to contend with; not an easy trip to say the least.

Three groups of miners traveled inland from the coast, up the Klamath River to the mouth of the Shasta, a journey fraught with hardship, disappointment and even death for some along the trail. At the mouth of the Shasta they turned to the south, following the rugged canyon. As the Shasta coursed eastward, they abandoned it at the mouth of Yreka Creek in order to continue southward. After three miles on this creek, they stopped at a generally recognized camping place located at what was eventually to become

Yreka. Disgruntled, from this point on they continued south to return to Sacramento or San Francisco in order to give up the chase. In so doing, they had passed up three of the biggest gold strikes in the entire Gold Rush; Scott Bar, Yreka and Greenhorn.

The first gold discovery in what was to become Siskiyou County was made on the North Fork of the Salmon River by a group that had come overland from the port of Trinidad on the coast. As was always the case, in no time at all the most promising claims had been staked and overrun with miners who had no place to mine. Some of these hiked over the mountain ranges traveling north until they encountered the Klamath River. It was these men that made the big strike at Scott Bar.

It was late in the summer when the miners had arrived at Scott Bar. By the time they had developed their diggings and proven the strike to be of huge proportions, fall had arrived. They began to worry about how they could subsist in this out of the way location that was practically unknown by anyone else and getting colder every day. They knew nothing about what kind of weather could be expected in the winter. They didn't even know how far north they were. Consequently they decided they had to leave. There were less than ten men in the group. They swore each other to total secrecy concerning the gold strike and headed out.

Most of them "wintered" in the bars and honkytonks of Sacramento and San Francisco. As the long months went by in this atmosphere, it became very difficult to remain true to the secrecy oath they had sworn. More than one of these men slipped in his resolve.

In the following spring, 1851, literally hundreds and hundreds of miners arrived at Scott Bar. In a matter of days, the remaining claims had been staked and as per the usual pattern, there was no room left for the late comers. This is what set the stage for the one of the biggest strikes of the entire Gold Rush.

In leaving, some of the unlucky ones went back down the Klamath River to the coast to catch a steamer and give up in disgust. The rest came up the Klamath. Some turned north at the Shasta River, to go back to where they had originated in Oregon. The larger remainder turned south at the Shasta River and eventually arrived in the campgrounds on the "Yreka Flats" where there were other travelers coming and going.

All this moving about; trying here, trying there; finding the proven locations overrun by their comrades or discovering the rumors to be untrue; this was the typical lot of the great majority of the 49ers. A hard life it was. No women, no mail, constant dirt and dust; and always it was the other fellow who found the pot of gold at the other end of the rainbow.

The camping place at the Yreka Flats was a typical gathering place for those who had struck out. Here the men would sit around their campfires and discuss but two subjects: where to try next, or whether to give it up and go home. In this atmosphere, liaisons were made and little groups were formed to do one or the other of the two available options.

In late March of 1851 there were many groups around the fires on the Yreka Flats. Most of these men had arrived too late at Scott Bar and had subsequently drifted to the Flats. At that time, this place was almost the end of the line. There was very little mining activity to the north in Oregon and only a few small diggings in the steep mountains to the west and south of the Flats. Silas Day with the Garfield brothers was there having pushed on from Scott Bar. They intended to go back to Oregon. Dr. Hearn's party had also become dissatisfied with Scott Bar and intended to try for gold at Greenhorn, the closest active diggings, about a mile southwest of the Flats. There was one other large party there that morning that had come in from Oregon. Abraham Thompson and his partner, a man named Bell, were also there. They had all participated in the discussions around the fire the night before as to what their options were. Thompson and Bell decided that they would give it up and return home. But before doing so, they would give it one last chance by trying a half day prospect at Greenhorn to the southwest before heading out.

As the men formed up to leave in the morning, Abraham Thompson was a half hour ahead of everyone else. While the rest of the group was preparing their gear to move out, Thompson said that he was going to go on and take a look at the higher ground immediately west of the camping areas.

He said, "You fellows go on to Greenhorn and I'll meet you over there later this afternoon."

The others all laughed at this idea because "anybody knew that you don't find gold on the flats. The gold is in the mountains or along the streams."

Thompson smiled and waved goodbye. This unknown man with his one mule pulled out, not knowing he was about to make history.

"The Flats" was really a misnomer. Yreka Creek flowed at this point south to north until it eventually emptied into the Shasta River. There was some level ground on each side of the creek, but in both directions, east and west, the land very rapidly began to rise into some rather large mountains, most especially so to the west. It was often joked among the miners that the "Flats" really weren't flat at all; they just seemed to be flat after the rugged mountainous terrain in which they most usually found themselves.

Thompson proceeded almost due west of the camp, going up a gentle rise that became a little steeper as he walked. He had traveled less than a half mile when he encountered a small gulch that had some water running in it. He decided to give it a try.

He washed three pans and immediately got a good prospect of "coarse" gold, and coarse gold is what miners are after. He had no idea of the magnitude of what he found. He only knew he found something that could be the first indication of something much bigger. Then he happened to glance at the mule that was busily munching on new sprouts of green grass, pulling it up by the roots. Thompson was astounded at what he saw. There, clinging to the roots of the grass as the mule pulled them up was the moist earth in which the grass had been growing. Laced throughout the dirt were veins of "fine" gold in excessive quantities.

Abraham Thompson had found the first of millions upon millions of dollars in gold that was to later be extracted from this little corner of the earth.

Thompson and the mule took off at a fast pace for Greenhorn in order to tell the others.

By the time that Thompson got himself to Greenhorn and found his buddies, who all returned with him, it was getting late. The next morning they conducted a "miners meeting." The first order of business was to pick a name for the location. It was obvious that the little stream was nothing more than a trickle and that any extensive mining at this location would need be of the "dry diggings" type. The name that was adopted was therefore Thompson's Dry Diggings.

The next order of business was to stake out the claims. None of them really knew much about what to do in regards to this matter. They staked them out at thirty feet, awarding Thompson two claims in accordance with custom for the discoverer. They didn't know that the law provided for fifty foot claims.

With these formalities out of the way, they all began mining in earnest.

In a month or so, the water in the gulch gave out. From then on, each miner had to dig what "ore" he could carry in his pack sack or load on his mule if he had one, and head down hill to the creek in order to pan it.

Word of the discovery soon reached Sacramento where it was published in the *Placer Times* on the 18th of April, 1851, and the rush was on. Within six weeks, 2000 miners were camped on the west bank of what is now Yreka Creek.

As the crowd began to arrive and camp on the creek, they soon learned that in order to guard their claim they must sleep at the diggings. The whole bunch eventually moved up to where the gold was and there they lived. They threw up brush shanties or slept under the stars; a rugged way to live, but by golly, they were right in the middle of a good strike and meant to make the most of it.

Soon the packers came and set up stores. Gamblers came and brought their cards and wheels of fortune. Sam Lockhart set up a saloon.

As new arrivals and additional packers arrived, more useful things became available. Various tools and pieces of old wagons materialized from which wheelbarrows could be fashioned. And wheelbarrows were an absolute must in view of the type of mining operation that had to be conducted here. The miners would dig up the ore and load it into their wheelbarrows for transport down to the creek for panning; a tedious procedure.

Early on, all began to realize that the place to live was down by the creek instead of up on the hillside. The "town" slowly began to move in that direction and before long, it was there and not at Thompson's Dry Diggings. Another name was chosen then for the settlement, Shasta Butte City, in honor of the great 14,000 foot tall perpetually snow-covered mountain looming over them to the south.

D. H. Lowery, together with his wife, the first woman in the new town, set up a boarding tent. For $1.50, bacon, coffee, rice and biscuits were available. That first summer, four other wives came plus Josephine Rollins, a single woman.

Rough streets were laid out and a huge public corral was erected in the center of town. Construction of some solid buildings of logs and shakes was commenced. Many others were still just brush shanties, tents or combinations thereof.

A vigilante committee was formed and Abraham Thompson was designated constable. Such committees were how such "instant" Gold Rush towns, where there was no governmental law enforcement, tried to maintain law and order.

In September, the first white child, a boy, was born to Mr. and Mrs. James Hill. He was named William Shasta Hill and thereafter nicknamed Shasta Beauty.

So a new town was now underway and growing fast. But there was a problem with the name. Another gold town a hundred miles to the southwest had sprung up with the name of Shasta. It was confusing to the postal service and the other higher levels of government. Therefore in the spring, when Siskiyou County was designated and named, the legal papers began referring not to "Shasta Butte City" but to "Yreka." This was a corruption of the Indian word, Ieka, meaning "white," in reference to snowy Mt. Shasta.

So by 1852 Yreka was an established western town in every sense of the word; rough hewn in nature, but a town, nonetheless. The towns of the Gold Rush were a long way from being the typical American community. In order to understand the nature of these settlements during the periods of their early formation, one must consider who their citizens were and the circumstances that had brought them here.

The first consideration that must be addressed is that all of the inhabitants with few exceptions were young. The long trip coming west in the wagon trains or on horseback was no place for the old, the halt or the lame. It was a rugged and dangerous undertaking that could only be attempted by the young and courageous.

It must be admitted by the descendants of these raucous would-be miners that they definitely were not typical of the established leaders or solidly entrenched makers and shakers in those communities that had spawned them. What successful businessman, lawyer, doctor, even government employee, or a solidly entrenched family man, would consider such a wild and dangerous undertaking? It meant giving up everything, joining a wagon train on a two or 3,000 mile journey full of hardship and danger to chase an elusive prize in a faraway place they knew little about.

No, the 49ers were not the respected pick of the community, but on the other hand they were something special. They had to have guts; they had the nerve to take a chance. They furthermore had to be the "doers" and often the leaders, to finally decide on this exciting and hopefully rewarding venture. There is a phrase of recent origin that fits them to a tee:

"When the going gets tough; the tough get going."

That's what we had here. These men were tough, and they got going. Time and necessity would eventually turn them into the makers and shakers. And that is what we had in all these mining settlements that had sprung into existence by 1852, Yreka included.

Fire was an ever present threat to the gold towns during the early beginnings. During 1852 there were two large fires in Yreka. The first one eliminated the center of town by burning out the entire central square block. The second fire later in the year went over the same ground and extended it somewhat in each direction. Business partners Churchill and Parker had a fine wood building on Miner Street that was destroyed in the first fire. They rebuilt it just in time to lose it again in the second round. They vowed that "enough was enough" and proceeded to replace it again, but this time with brick and stone.

Up to this point, there had been no trouble with Indians. There were several tribes of Indians in what was to become Siskiyou County, but very little friction of any magnitude had been encountered.

The Shasta Indians lived in the immediate vicinity of Yreka but they had proved to be very docile and caused no trouble whatsoever. The Modocs occupied most of eastern Siskiyou County and their relations with the white man eventually led to trouble. The Modocs seemed to be more agile and proud than the other tribes and were perfectly willing to participate in a fight if one came along. And very shortly one did. Ironically, the fuse that set off the trouble was a lynching.

The trouble started with the fact that someone stole a miner's horse.

The Pit Indians* occupied the area to the south of the Modocs that lapped over the boundary between what were to be Siskiyou and Shasta Counties.

All Indians, it appeared, liked to gamble. Various stick games were traditionally played at the intertribal visits with the other Indians in the area. Heavy wagers were always made during these affairs; often enough the wagered stake was someone's wife.

At one of these conclaves a fine horse that everyone figured had likely been stolen from a white man became the stake in one of the stick games. It was won by a Pit. As the party continued, the horse was again offered in the betting and this time it was won by a Modoc.

Some weeks later the Modoc was riding his fine new horse along a trail several miles south of Yreka when he rounded a bend and came face to face with a half dozen white men. One of them was none other than the former owner of the horse. The exact facts of what happened next are not known except that the white man came riding his stolen horse back to Yreka. Several days later, the Indian was found hanging by a rope in a tree beside the trail.

When the news of what had happened to the Indian finally worked its way back to the Modoc tribe in eastern Siskiyou, the chiefs called a tribal

---

* The Pit Tribe (in 2020) consists of eleven bands of indigenous residents of present day California. The Achomawi are the band just south of Modoc territory.

meeting. The result was that the Modocs declared formal war on all the white men. This was a natural thing for the tribe to do under the circumstances. But there was one hitch in this and that was the fact that the Indians didn't understand that if a war was declared, the other side should be notified. This little technicality resulted in a terrible tragedy.

Many of the people that came to Yreka seeking gold came by wagon train from the east. The routes for these caravans after traveling west for weeks and even months eventually turned northwest and finally passed through the Modoc territory. After that they were on the last leg of the journey across Little Shasta Valley and into Yreka.

The route through the Modoc territory came out at the top of a high bluff that overlooked a large lake, then and now one of the greatest migratory bird sanctuaries in North America. The lake later became known as Tule Lake. As the wagon trains descended down the bluff to the shore, the people knew that they had only the last lap to reach their goal. Most of the trains stopped at the lake for a night or two.

These trains had been coming through without incident heretofore. But after the declaration of war, the Modocs had been sending scouts out in order to anticipate the arrival of the next train. When the wagons arrived at the top of the bluff, the Modocs were ready at the bottom. There were two survivors; the rest, men, women and children, all perished. The two survivors ultimately made it to Yreka to report the tragedy. Some of the victims were relatives of people already there.

That was the beginning of widespread and almost continuous friction between the Modocs and the white men that continued for twenty years. It was far from being the only cause of the friction, but it culminated in the end with a real war that historians have generally overlooked. As a matter of fact, the casualties in it actually exceeded those of the Spanish American War. It is a long tragic story that is not generically related to the story at hand except for its macabre relationship with the subject of lynching.

1852, Yreka's second year in existence, was not working out as a banner year. As the rebuilding after the second big fire was drawing to a close in December, the weather turned extremely severe. Torrents of rain brought on a situation of tremendous floods and mud flows. The roads became impassable and the snow in the mountains blockaded the trails. Supplies were exhausted as the pack trains were unable to get in. Current stocks of salt, flour, bacon, beans, rice and other foods dwindled and became unavailable. There was plenty of fresh meat available from cattle in the area. This supply, in a final emergency, could be augmented by eating horses and mules. There was also game that could be hunted which helped fill the breach. Salt, being so necessary with a fresh meat diet, was the scarcest commodity. Prices for salt went as high as $1 per ounce.

But their was no mass exodus; the "tough got going" and the community weathered it.

The next year things were better. At least, that is until the middle of summer when another fire got started. This one burned out the entire center of the downtown area with the exception of Churchill and Parker's new building.

Before the year was over, all of the town had been rebuilt with brick and stone.

From here on out, the town was prosperous and growing. For nearly all of the Gold Rush towns, the word "growing" meant growing in character, stability, public services, and such. It did not mean growing in population. The Gold Rush towns, insofar as population count, all "grew" backwards. Yreka was no exception. The nature of events determined this in a more or less universal pattern.

First came the miners. Some on horseback and many on foot. As was always the case, in the first rush, only the earliest arrivals were able to stake out the good claims. Always there was a surplus of miners for the amount of "good shows." Initially, in the good claims that showed "color" right from the start, employment was available for those who had lost out. But the quantity of jobs was generally far short of the number of men seeking them. After a few months the miners that had arrived too late began to drift on to other diggings or return home. This caused a very sharp reduction in the actual population count in all of the "boom" communities.

Then towns around the highly successful diggings began to increase in population again, but seldom in the great numbers that had so quickly been lost. This phenomenon was created by the fact that the "diggin's" were slowly being developed into genuine operating "gold mines" with a need for workers. Water supplies needed development, shafts in many cases were dug to extremely deep depths, and heavy equipment was brought in, one piece at a time, via mules or wagons. Site buildings at the mines had to be erected. Transverse tunnels were dug to connect the vertical shafts for both access and air venting. If a particular diggings was "hard rock," the rock had to be drilled and "blown." If a mine produced ore that was "veined" rock, huge stamp or ball mill machinery had to be imported and erected.

In short, these wild roughhewn towns that were established on location with the successful diggings had to be converted into industrial communities with all the required characteristics. All this in addition to the fact that the infrastructure of the town itself had to be created and further developed. Finally the homes themselves were erected to house the citizens.

All this was a slow process but it furnished employment on an ever expanding basis.

In Yreka's case, this scenario initially generated a population of approximately 2,000 in the first six weeks. When the rush continued to throw off news of additional successful strikes, the figure probably reached 5,000 by the end of the first year. From that time on it undoubtedly took a sharp dip as the disappointed miners left; probably down to 2,000 again.

The next three years brought it back up to the 5,000 level as the town itself was developed along with the industrialization of the mines. The situation at this point is most beautifully illustrated by Harry Wells in his wonderful 218 page *History of Siskiyou County*, written in 1881:

> The season of greatest prosperity in Yreka was from 1855 to 1857. The population was then about 5,000, and at the presidential election in 1856 there were cast 1,128 votes in this precinct. According to the last census the population is but 1,059.
>
> Yreka today has three churches, a fine school building, courthouse, jail, hotel, eighteen stores, two markets, three shoe shops, six blacksmith shops, stage repair shops, bank, jeweler, Masonic Hall, Red Men Hall, Odd Fellows Hall, weekly and semiweekly papers, telegraph office, express office, two breweries, tailor, several dressmakers, photograph gallery, livery stable, gas works, foundry, saddlery shop, two engine houses, three physicians, six attorneys, several saloons, and many other things that go to make up a town.

As described by Wells, the town had shrunk to a population of 1,059 by 1881, possibly its lowest count ever. This decrease was due to the maturing of the physical development of the mining industry in the years from 1855 to 1881.

After 1881 there were two new economic factors that began to appear that caused a long but slow growth. This was the coming of age of agriculture and lumbering in the county. Government operations were a third minor factor due to the fact that Yreka was the county seat.

As the mining industry had been making its booming expansion through 1857 and thereafter leveled off, agriculture had been making a slow growth which continued upward. The logging and lumber industries started later but made the same steady growth along with agriculture and the level activity of mining. The population slowly increased to about 2,500 by 1930 and continued on to approximately 6,500 at the present time. [Note: In 1988, at time of writing. In 2017 the population was 7,600].

Looking back upon the little bustling town of Yreka in 1857 as described by Harry Wells calls for an ending that says "everyone lived happily ever after." Unfortunately, such is not the case. Yreka still had one more devastating disaster to overcome before drifting on down through the rest of the years to follow. It struck on the Fourth of July, 1871.

Let the incomparable Harry Wells describe it as he wrote in 1881:

> When the citizens of Yreka arose on the anniversary of our independence, they little dreamed of the spectacle the shades of night would rest upon. Joyous and happy they commenced the day; weary and sad were they at its close. There was no special celebration in Yreka, and quite a number of the people were absent in Scott Valley and elsewhere. They returned to find their property in ruins. Small boys and firecrackers formed the surface patriotism and made the noise inseparable from a proper observance of the day. To these little explosives is attributable the almost entire destruction of the town.
>
> About the middle of the afternoon, a bunch of crackers ignited on the back porch of a Chinese wash-house on the north side of Miner street, just west of Second, set fire to that tinderbox, and in an instant the whole structure was wrapped in flames.
>
> The alarm was instantly sounded, but during the short interval that elapsed before the fire department appeared on the scene, the flames spread with frightful rapidity. Opposite the place where it originated, stood the old Yreka House, a heavy frame structure with hewn timbers, one of the earliest buildings in the town. It was formerly a hotel but at this time was used as a stable, and the upper part was full of hay. The flames stretched their scorching arms across the street, and seized upon this building, the hay blazing up with indescribable fierceness. The Colton Theater, just west of the washhouse was also soon blazing, and by the time the engines were ready for action the fire was burning from Second to Fourth streets. Chief Engineer Raynes directed the movements of the firemen with energy and

good judgment, but the headway the flames had made and the extremely dry condition of the buildings rendered all efforts to check the progress of the destroyer seemingly futile. Great sheets of flame leaped into the air, their fiery tongues hissing and crackling. Long arms of scorching red reached out in all directions; seized the buildings in their warm embrace, and in an instant laid them in ruins in their pathway. Firemen, citizens and women worked with desperate energy, tearing down fences and buildings in the path of the flames, carrying water, spreading wet blankets, and removing goods and furniture. Many Chinamen worked at the engine brakes. All the water in Scheid's City Waterworks was turned into the cisterns to supply the great demand made upon them by the engines. By means of wet blankets at Engine House N. 1, the fire was prevented from crossing the street at that point, so that the north side of Miner Street, above Third, was saved. Checked in this direction the fire spread rapidly towards the east and south, and consumed everything between Miner an d Butte streets, Fourth street and the creek, including the Colton Theater, Union House, old Yreka House, Metropolitan Hotel, Catholic church, Odd Fellows Hall, the first house built in the town, and stores, barns, shops and residences. This was the work of but one hour and in that hour many that were in good circumstances were reduced almost to poverty, while many others lost the little that they possessed as well as the means of procuring more.

For two days the engines were kept at work extinguishing the many smoldering fires that threatened to break out anew and destroy what had been spared.

Only 30% of the total loss was covered by insurance. But once again "the tough got going."

On the July 6th, a town meeting was called at the courthouse to assess the damage and institute steps to be taken. Funds were pledged by the fortunate to relieve the losses of the unfortunate. Food and clothing were offered for those who had literally been wiped out. Money came pouring in from surrounding towns. Former citizens of Yreka who had moved to San Francisco organized a drive there and sent over $5000, a princely sum for those days.

This fire had been a terrible loss, touching almost everyone in the community in one way or another. But the good burgers of Yreka had seen worse times than these. Like the Phoenix, the town literally rose from its own ashes and reconstituted itself and went forward into the future.

Down through the years everything was replaced and the town seemed to be finally settling into the quiet prosperous rural western community envisioned by the civic leaders. All was well in Yreka.

That is, until one o'clock in the morning of August 26th, 1895…

Made in the USA
Monee, IL
12 March 2020